COUNTRY MUSIC
CHANGED MY LIFE

COUNTRY MUSIC CHANGED MY LIFE

Tales of Tough Times and Triumph from Country's Legends

KEN BURKE

CHICAGO
REVIEW
PRESS

An A Cappella Book

Library of Congress Cataloging-in-Publication Data
Burke, Ken K.
     Country music changed my life : tales of tough times and triumph from
country's legends / Ken Burke.— 1st ed.
          p. cm.
     ISBN 1-55652-538-9
     1. Country musicians—United States—Biography. 2. Country musi-
cians—United States—Interviews. I. Title.
     ML385.B945 2004
     781.642'092'273—dc22   2003027690

Photo credits—Introduction: page xv, courtesy Ken Burke; chapter one: page 2, courtesy
Brenda Lee Archives; pages 11 and 16, courtesy Hank Adam Locklin; page 18, courtesy
Platinum Express Records; page 28, courtesy Brokaw Agency; chapter two: page 41, cour-
tesy Real Music; page 46, courtesy Johnny Legend Worldwide Enterprises; page 49, cour-
tesy Don Bradley collection; page 55, courtesy Deke Dickerson; page 61, courtesy Brandy
Reed, RPM Media; page 67, courtesy Jake Austen; pages 72 and 80, photos by Tommie
Wix, author's collection; page 82, courtesy Rhino Records; chapter three: page 92, cour-
tesy Joe Stampley; page 104, courtesy Freddy Weller; page 112, courtesy Bar None Music,
Inc.; page 117, courtesy Sony Music; page 122, courtesy RMG Records; page 129, photo
by Henk Van Raay, from the Kenneth Lovelace collection; chapter four: page 144, cour-
tesy Michael Bloom Media and Wanda Jackson Enterprises; page 150, courtesy Don
Bradley collection; page 152, courtesy Brokaw Agency; page 157, courtesy Tillman Franks
Enterprises; chapter five: page 161, courtesy Gordon Stoker; pages 170 and 174, courtesy
Barbara Pittman; page 180, courtesy Michael Bloom Media and Wanda Jackson
Enterprises; page 183, courtesy Bobby Wayne collection; chapter six: page 201, courtesy
MCA Nashville; page 209, courtesy Dr. Demento; page 213, courtesy Sand Spur Records;
page 220, courtesy Richard Davis Management; chapter seven: page 230, courtesy
Richard Davis Management; pages 244 and 249, courtesy Brokaw Agency; pages 256 and
263, courtesy D. D. Bray Management; pages 267 and 279, courtesy Richard Davis
Management; chapter eight: page 291, courtesy Epic/Legacy; pages 299 and 308, courtesy
Don Bradley collection

Jacket and interior design: Rattray Design

© 2004 by Ken Burke
First edition
Published by A Cappella Books
An Imprint of Chicago Review Press, Incorporated
814 North Franklin Street
Chicago, Illinois 60610
ISBN 1-55652-538-9
Printed in the United States of America
5 4 3 2 1

For Lorraine and Emily—who change my life for the better every day.

CONTENTS

ACKNOWLEDGMENTS

When you're on a deadline, that's when you know who your friends really are.

My thanks to *Roctober* chief Jake Austen for recommending me for this project, and to my editor, Yuval Taylor, especially for his patience with a writer attempting his first book.

Some very nice people shared their contacts with me, and I am in their debt. They include Jim Bagley at *Goldmine*, Don Bradley, Sonny Burgess, Tillman Franks, Gary Pig Gold, Dan Griffin, Roy Harper at *Outer Shell*, Linda Gail Lewis, Phoebe Lewis, Martha Moore at So Much Moore Publicity, Brandy Reed at RPM Media, Jeff Remz at *Country Standard Time*, Dom Salemi at *Brutarian Quarterly*, the first northwest rockabilly, Bobby Wayne, and my dear friend Tommie Wix.

I am particularly grateful for the many talented artists who took the time to speak to me at length. Their candor and generosity of spirit I will always hold dear in my thoughts.

Two people should be singled out here for services rendered above and beyond the call of duty. Sandy Brokaw of the Brokaw Agency came through for me in a way that no other major publicist did. Richard Davis, personal manager to Little Jimmy Dickens and Ferlin Husky, made valid suggestions, put me in touch with many of my favorite classic artists, and told me a pretty funny story about country great Faron Young. Since there is no place else to put it, I'll tell it here.

Davis and Bobby Wayne were backstage after a show when Young, a notorious ladies' man, mentioned that he had made a date with famed transsexual Christine Jorgensen. Wayne and Davis laughed at the notion, but Young assured them it was true.

The next day when they saw him, Young acted depressed and wouldn't say what had transpired. Davis, sensing something had gone disastrously wrong, asked sympathetically, "Faron, why did you try and date someone who had a sex change in the first place?"

"Aw," Young moaned in frustration, "I thought it would change my luck."

Well, the efforts of Sandy Brokaw and Richard Davis changed my luck on this project, and their contributions represent the heart and soul of this volume.

And last, my wife, Lorraine, did her best to make sure what I wrote was in English. She, along with our daughter Emily, contributed to my well-being by allowing me to prattle on endlessly about the subjects of this book. I love you both.

Thank you, one and all.

Let's do it again sometime.

INTRODUCTION

Country music changed my life.

No, not in the cataclysmic way that some of this book's subjects have been changed. More like the gradual change that occurs when water steadily drips on a rock. One way or another, country music has insinuated itself so completely into my world that I cannot imagine life without it.

I was raised in the downriver area of southeastern Michigan, where country music was part of the soundtrack of my youth. My sister's record collection included singles by the Everly Brothers, Ricky Nelson, Brenda Lee, and Elvis Presley, who infused country with the catchy big beat of early rock 'n' roll. My favorite radio station—WKNR, Keener 13—regularly mixed hits by the Statler Brothers, Johnny Cash, and Roger Miller with soul, pop, garage rock, novelty, and British Invasion records. They put those diverse styles on the same playlist and let them fight it out between your ears like some sort of sonic pinball machine. It was cool. When not reviewing a specific project for print, this is still the way I play music at home.

My dad's life could've been the blueprint for the song "Detroit City." One of ten kids, he hitchhiked from his boyhood home in Kentucky to the Detroit area factories. He worked ungodly amounts of overtime making sure my sister and I had the things he never had growing up. Naturally, when you give your kids things you never had, they become people you don't understand, but that came later.

Dad liked country music, although he was not a fanatic about it. The first and only record he ever bought was a forty-five of Johnny Horton's "North to Alaska." Years before he lost his teeth, he would often whistle a pleasant, bluesy rendition of "Your Cheatin' Heart," and when Loretta Lynn sang about going barefoot during the summer because she wouldn't get new shoes until fall, he chuckled knowingly. Charley Pride's "Kiss an Angel Good Morning" was probably his favorite song of all time: he'd sing "love 'er like the *devil* when you get back home" with appreciative gusto.

That said, the details or circumstances surrounding music and musicians were unimportant to him, as they were to most people from his generation, I suppose. He told me that once, as a boy, he saw Bill Monroe and His Bluegrass Boys perform in a large pitched tent. When I asked how the show was, he seemed confused by the reference. "Show? We were there to dance."

Outward appearances suggested that our dad had assimilated quite well to suburban life. Good-looking and generally well liked, he spoke with little trace of his native accent and socialized easily with both blue- and white-collar workers. Yet I often sensed that he never really felt comfortable up north. Every now and then, when too much overtime or life in the downriver area weighed heavy on him, he'd think

My dad, a true country boy.

of Kentucky and mutter, "You know, they're making a hundred dollars a day down in the mines." But he knew he could never really go home again. "Boy, don't ever work in a factory," he told me. "The money's too good for you to leave, but not enough to make you rich."

His wife, our mother, died at the tender age of thirty-seven. I was twelve. My sister and I lost our father that same day. Always a bit of a binge drinker during his time off, our mother's death furnished him with the excuse to become a full-time alcoholic. Beer by beer, he drank himself out of house, health, job, friends, and family.

Country music was a part of those awful first years when I realized my dad was never going to stop drinking and there wasn't anything I could do about it. We had a Columbia Records compilation that included Ray Price's classic "For the Good Times." While my dad drank and grieved, he played that song so many times that I still cannot bear to hear it today. The end of his life twelve years after my mother's was the bitter afterthought one usually hears only in old Porter Wagoner records like "Skid Row Joe."

However, all that didn't transform me into a fan of country music. During my early life, I generally regarded country with a big ol' dose of smart-ass irony. My friends and I would laugh at Porter Wagoner and Dolly Parton's commercial for Breeze, wherein Parton's ample bosom would do a happy hop as she announced her intention to collect all the towels included with the powdered detergent. We'd deliberately tune in the fringe TV station WTOL in Toledo so we could yell at "Whisperin'" Bill Anderson, "Hey, Bill, speak up! I can't *hear* you, man." And *Hee Haw*? Well, *Hee Haw* was beneath our contempt. We watched it anyway for the scantily clad girls, and while doing so, we were exposed to the peerless talents of Buck Owens and Roy Clark. (Insidious, weren't they?)

But there was one person and one person only who was responsible for persuading me to love country music: Jerry Lee Lewis.

During the late 1960s and early '70s, a '50s rock 'n' roll revival cropped up. My teenage buddies and I started buying oldies reissues, digging the goofy sounds of novelty doo-wop, greasy rockabilly, and raving R&B. It was fun, something we talked about at the high school lunch tables. On my own, I read about Lewis's wildness in *Rolling Stone*, listened to his seminal piano-pounding sides, and marveled. Seeing him manhandle the keyboards with such joy and verve on the *Tom Jones Show* made me a fan instantly.

Soon I was raiding the $1.99 racks at Shopper's Fair for the seemingly endless supply of cutouts issued by Sun International. After I grew accustomed to the Sun sound, with its bluesy echo and hard-core southern articulation, I was hooked. Indeed, everything else seemed hopelessly over-produced by comparison. Jerry Lee led to Carl Perkins, Johnny Cash, Billy Lee Riley, Charlie Rich, and a reevalua-tion of Elvis Presley.

Initially, I only liked Lewis's rock material—the faster the better—but a collection of his country comeback hits, *The Best of Jerry Lee Lewis*, grabbed me with its naked soul and riveting personal expression. If there was one song that hipped me to the cathartic emotional possibilities of country, it was "She Even Woke Me Up to Say Good-bye."

In a textured performance that balanced deep sorrow and fruitless denial, Jerry Lee sang about his woman leaving him. What were the reasons? Was it his drinking? (After all, his mind was "aching.") Was she clinically depressed? Whatever the cause, he wouldn't dream of casting aspersions, and instead assures us, "It's not her heart, Lord, it's her mind. She didn't mean to be unkind." Then he offers the heartbreakingly feeble proof of her sincerity and love for him: "Why, she even woke me up to say good-bye."

Resonating with blues-drenched dramatics and country rapport, "She Even Woke Me Up to Say Good-bye" was, in its own way, as good as the best of Lewis's rock recordings. The fact that the same man who bled emotion in ballads like this could also rip through the keyboards with such fierce abandon made a mighty profound impression on me.

The 1970s were a great time to be a Lewis fan. Not only could you hear his current material on the radio and see him on TV, but the import racks were stuffed with Charly label compilations of previously unreleased Sun material. My latent passion for rockabilly (i.e., hillbilly rock 'n' roll) exploded, which led me back to its roots in the music of Jimmie Rodgers, Hank Williams, Lefty Frizzell, and, of course, the blues.

Jerry Lee's music led me to all of that and much more, but in the end, I always return to the Killer himself. Lewis expressed the inexpressible for me. The way he played piano stirred me. He made his songs seem like personal experiences, which allowed me to feel empathy for a lifestyle I could only imagine.

So, just how intense was my mania for Jerry Lee Lewis?

Well, have you ever heard of a teenage boy subscribing to *Billboard* just so he could follow the chart progress of his favorite performer? That was me. I also developed the unshakable habit of looking through a music book's index for any mention of the Killer. My rule was steadfast: no Jerry Lee, no purchase.

Dad's reaction to my fascination with Lewis was mixed. Mostly he was happy that I wasn't listening to the drug-induced hard rock of the era. Other times he seemed vaguely embarrassed by my growing love of country music. One day, we were on the balcony of our apartment and I was playing Lewis's LP *Country Songs for City Folks*. On the sidewalk below, a pretty young woman was waiting for her beau to pull the car around. An up-tempo number filled the air, and she danced in place for a few seconds. My father, who had an eye for the ladies, was briefly amused. Then, his voice drenched with quiet shame, he admonished, "Boy, you know that's *hillbilly* music, don't you?"

Country music probably should have brought us closer together—the way cheering on the Detroit Tigers did when I was younger—but it didn't. He couldn't understand why I was attracted to a culture that he had tried so hard to escape. I enjoyed more comforts and advantages than he ever had, yet I reveled in music that constantly reminded him that he was, essentially, an undereducated plowboy masquerading as a middle-class suburbanite.

My high school peers were puzzled by my love of country music, too. While they were listening to all manner of 1970s pop, rock, and (shudder) disco, I only stayed current with country. When WKNR went off the air after 1972, my allegiance switched to WDEE. At first it was because WDEE (its call letters were rumored to stand for "We've Done Everything Else") was the only station to consistently play music by former rock idols Conway Twitty, Jerry Lee Lewis, Elvis Presley, and Freddy Weller. Later, I kept listening simply because that station featured the music I needed to hear to make my day better.

I remember the exact incident that made me realize that country music actually spoke for me. Driving somewhere with my girlfriend, we heard John Denver's "Please Daddy, Don't Get Drunk This Christmas" come over the radio. Mind you, this was a treacly performance of an especially cloying song by an artist I did not like, but when my girlfriend started to make fun of the song's sentiments, I snapped, "You know, to some of us that's not so goddamned funny."

The capper? A few months later, after my girlfriend and I broke up, my dad tried to cheer me up by taking me to a bar.

Since that moment my life has been different.

Fortunately, I never developed a serious thirst for beer or booze and, unlike many of my generation, I never experimented with drugs. I have the revulsion I still feel over my father's constant intoxication to thank for that. However, T. G. Sheppard's "Devil in the Bottle" and the emotional torpor of Gary Stewart's "Drinkin' Thing" helped me find some sympathy for his plight.

Yes, I'm aware that my musical hero Jerry Lee Lewis has all my father's flaws and many more besides. I've always said: I love Jerry Lee's music but I wouldn't live his life on a bet. I genuinely feel he is the best ever at what he does, but he has willfully pissed it all away. It makes me sad to see him now. Age and health problems—exacerbated by his rampant substance abuse, no doubt—have devastated his energies and zest for music. Regardless, if I want to lighten my mood or cleanse my mental palate, there's nothing like a good dose of the Killer's music. I'm still a fan.

❧   ❧   ❧

My first ambition was to become a stand-up comedian and impressionist. But music had so turned my head around, I spent a good deal of my twenties and thirties writing rockabilly and country songs. I can now pump the piano a little like Jerry Lee and of the four hundred songs I've written, one Roger Miller–like novelty tune called "The Dead Cat Song" seems to have found favor among those with strange tastes.

In 1985 I began writing the column "The Continuing Saga of Dr. Iguana" for Roy Harper's freebie broadsheet *Outer Shell*. As often as not, I wrote about rockabilly, early rock 'n' roll, and country music, and, bit by bit, I found more opportunities to write about music and fewer excuses to make my own. Now I work as a freelance reviewer and feature writer, and though I have covered all sorts of music, the vast majority of my writing continues to be about country.

The genre now is vastly different from when I first started listening to it. I believe, however, that the Dixie Chicks, Toby Keith, and Tim McGraw would've been stars in any era; the rest are rather soulless and bland. Mainly, I'm proud to cover the many up-and-coming roots artists who make small label country and rockabilly so worthwhile. (My recommendation to those seeking the return of true country music?

Support independent labels and alternative radio. The major labels and mainstream airwaves have forsaken you.)

So, when asked if I'd like to write a book entitled *Country Music Changed My Life*, my gut response was, "Hell, yeah. I've been in training for it all my life."

❧   ❧   ❧

Simply put, this is a book of as-told-to stories from performers about country music–related events that changed their lives. Some are straight bios, some are capsules of moments in time, some are inspirational, and some . . . well, some are just a little weird.

You may be wondering, "Where are my favorite artists of today?"

I couldn't get 'em.

Before I took on this project, I asked some folks from whom I regularly get review discs if they could line up interviews with some current stars. Some gave me a flat-out no, but I was answered in the affirmative by enough of them that I felt I'd be able to get a good mix of contemporary and classic artists. But when it came time to schedule the interviews, my calls, faxes, and e-mails were either ignored or dismissed with responses like "He's crazy busy right now." I'm trying like hell not to take these contradictions too personally. You see, artists and labels hire publicists to manage an artist's time, drum up interest in their projects, and shield them from the wrong type of coverage. So, my guess is that the PR folks in question rationalized that a book of country music stories wouldn't help sales of their client's current album and demurred.

Harder to stomach were the actions of a prominent alternative label. One flack promised me access to a famous beat poet/musician as well as to a member of an innovative comedy group, both of whom might have had something juicy to say about their respective experiences with country music. We were ready to set up interviews when suddenly the publicist left the company. Her replacement knew nothing about my request and couldn't set anything up because "they're crazy busy right now."

Worse? I actually got snubbed by a famous blues singer. A Phoenix DJ told me that this particular legendary figure just loved country music, was deeply influenced by it, and was a real good talker besides. The bluesman seemed to love the initial idea for this book—people from all walks of life talking about how country music changed their lives. He said, "I've got a gig right now, but call me next Monday and we'll really *talk*."

At the scheduled time, he told me he had just gotten home from a fishing trip and asked that I call back in an hour. When I did, a woman told me he had just gone out for the evening. Advised by my DJ friend to keep trying, I called again a few days later. That's when the same woman answered the phone again and sweetly reported, "[He] said to say that he's not home right now."

Rescue came in the form of the vintage country artists. It's important to note that while most of the artists assembled in this volume no longer rule the charts, they're still working as hard as ever playing shows, writing songs, and occasionally recording for small labels. So these people talked to me not because they were "at liberty"; they talked to me because, on their way up the country music ladder of fame, they learned that being a country star meant making personal connections with fans, disc jockeys, rack jobbers, vendors, and, yes, even writers. As a result, it was no problem for them to speak with me, no matter how "crazy busy" they were.

It was delightful conversing with some of the finest country artists of all time, and, frankly, our chats put me in the mood to go out and buy more of their music. I hope their stories will do the same for you.

The only living artist that I really wanted to talk to but couldn't?

You guessed it. Jerry Lee Lewis.

The Killer's sister, Linda Gail, and his best friend, guitarist Kenny Lovelace, speak for him, however—and maybe that's how it should be.

All the others speak for themselves about their tough times and triumphs—and how country music changed their lives, as it has mine.

Ken Burke
Black Canyon City, Arizona

1

RAGS TO RICHES

You can go to college and learn all about marketing the way Garth Brooks did, you can take lessons, or you can hire consultants, but if you want to be a country music star, no one can teach you the two things you need most: talent and desire. Sure, a great song, a creative producer, an involved label, and a hard-nosed PR firm can work wonders. But when audiences sense the innate human need behind a performer's talent, they tend to regard that performer as their champion—and spend their cash more readily.

A good example is Shania Twain. As a child she was so poor that she sang on barstools for tips, and her schoolmates felt compelled to give her parts of their lunches. From the depths of poverty, the former Eileen Edwards became a major music phenomenon who now resides in a genuine castle. While people still argue over whether she is truly country or not (in the southwest we say she is country "by Canadian standards"), few who know of Twain's poverty-stricken background begrudge her the fruits of stardom.

So while the immense scale of Twain's success may represent a relatively recent trend, her rags-to-riches story has had parallels throughout country music history.

Seven years old and singing on *TV Ranch*.

BRENDA LEE

Dubbed "Little Miss Dynamite," Brenda Lee became a star because audiences thought she might actually be a midget.

"That's true," Lee tells me. "They had heard me sing in France, but they had never seen me. So, because my voice was so big and all, they thought I was older. My manager thought it would just be a great publicity stunt to say that I was a thirty-two-year-old midget instead of the twelve- or thirteen-year-old girl that I was. It was great press. It really worked."

Parisian crowds flocked to her performances to see if they could tell if she was an adult or a child. While they were there, they found themselves thoroughly entertained by a major talent. She was held over for five weeks, then went on to perform for standing-room-only crowds in Germany, Italy, and the United Kingdom. By the time she returned to the United States, she was a big name, drawing wild ovations everywhere she went. Lee loved the applause, but she wasn't on stage for anything as petty as acceptance. The seemingly tireless performer with the desperate, hungry look in her eyes was her family's sole support and she knew it.

Born Brenda Mae Tarpley in Atlanta, Georgia, Lee was *the* country crossover child prodigy long before Tanya Tucker or LeAnn Rimes dazzled the world with their own youthful talents. One of four children of a binge-drinking, itinerant day laborer, she knew hunger and she knew shame.

The Tarpley family was always short on money. They ate grease sandwiches for lunch, didn't see oranges until Christmas, and had electricity but no refrigerator. When Brenda Mae wore out the few articles of clothing she possessed or required medical attention for a nasty fall, she felt plenty guilty. One of her earliest memories is of the profound disappointment she felt after being awarded candy instead of a cash prize at a talent show. "Well, it was tough," Lee told me. "We didn't have a lot of money, and we were poor! I was very conscious of it as a child." Circumstances worsened when her father was fatally injured on a construction job. Her mother's meager salary often couldn't cover their expenses; theirs was a family in crisis. But young Brenda had already started making the rounds at talent shows. At age five she won a trophy for singing "Take Me Out to the Ballgame" and Pee Wee King's "Slow Poke."

When she opened her mouth to sing, out came an unusual hybrid of gospel, country, and R&B. The only other performer around with a similar style was Elvis Presley, and he'd had years to absorb those genres and refine his sound. By contrast, Lee can't pin down her musical influences. "I don't know that I had any early influences, because we didn't have a record player or any way to play music. About the only music I heard growing up was through the church—the gospel music—and my mom used to sing me Hank Williams songs. But that was about it."

Like many poor southerners, she gloried in the sounds of the Saturday night *Grand Ole Opry* broadcasts, courtesy of an old-fashioned battery-operated radio. Later, she developed a deep appreciation for gospel legend Mahalia Jackson. "I loved her. She was absolutely one of my very favorite singers," she asserts. "I think I just accepted it as music that I loved. I wasn't looking at the color or anything. I was just hearing a sound that I loved."

Besides her stunning and powerful singing chops, which were capable of emitting raving rockabilly one moment and quavering country heartache the next, young Brenda Mae possessed another awesome gift: memory. Ever since she was three years old, she has been able to learn a song completely after hearing it only twice. Asked if that type of gift ran in the family, Lee shrugs it off. "No, I've just always had a good memory, and I can memorize things easily and quickly. I've just always been able to do it. It applied to my schoolwork and things like that. I can still pretty much do that."

She changed her stage name to "Brenda Lee" when she became a regular on Atlanta radio's *Starmaker's Review*. Then Red Foley's manager Dub Albritten saw her on WAGA's *TV Ranch*, a local country music variety show, and signed her as a client.

Albritten made things happen. Appearances on Foley's *Ozark Jubilee* led to higher-profile television gigs on prime-time variety shows hosted by Steve Allen, Red Skelton, and Ed Sullivan. She was just eleven years old, but her diminutive stature made her appear even younger. Although she was clearly booked for her curiosity value, Lee says she wasn't treated like some freakish little kid. "They showed great respect for me, and they treated me just like they would any other entertainer on the show, and I respected them for doing that."

The demands of live television created a high-pressure environment. Vintage footage shows her looking scared and joyless, but Lee claims she never got nervous. "No, I don't think I've ever been nervous, and I think when you're a kid you're not because you don't realize the enormity of what's happening at the time. All I knew was that I loved to sing and this was just another place to sing—on TV. I wasn't nervous at all. I don't think I even thought about the importance of it, what it might do for me, or what the outcome might be."

The outcome in this particular case was a recording contract with Decca Records. The company played up her girlish appearance, dressing her in baby doll clothes and pressing promo records proclaiming "Brenda Lee, Age 9." Her first minor hits, "Bigelow 6-2000," "One Step at a Time," and "Dynamite," made a little noise with American teens in 1956 and '57 but didn't suggest that she was anything more than a novelty attraction. She needed a gimmick to jumpstart her career as a big-time performer. That's when her manager spread the rumor that she was, in reality, a thirty-two-year-old midget, and the focus shifted from Lee's age and size to her talent.

She began to assault the pop charts in earnest with such major sellers as "Sweet Nothin's," "I'm Sorry," "All You Gotta Do," "Fool #1," "Dum Dum," "Emotions," and the ever-popular seasonal smash "Rockin' Around the Christmas Tree." Lee's records scaled the pop Top 40 an amazing twenty-nine times. Many of these hits featured B sides that charted strongly on their own merits. That rare display of consistent, dual-sided power put the young songstress in the same league as Elvis Presley, Fats Domino, and the Beatles.

Lee gives most of the credit to her producer, the late Owen Bradley. "He was just a genius at choosing songs, he was a fine musician, and working with him was a joy. It wasn't work like it is with some producers. He knew exactly what he could get from you and how far he could push you to get it. He was just a genius at what he did and whatever 'sound' Brenda Lee has, I owe to Owen Bradley."

The legendary producer, who also worked with the likes of Patsy Cline, Conway Twitty, and Loretta Lynn, earned Lee's trust by seeking her opinion on songs and production. As a result, when he assured her she could tackle more sophisticated, torchy material, she suppressed her doubts and gave him her best efforts.

"Well, he was always big on doing foreign songs and then having them translated into English, like 'All Alone Am I' or 'I Want to Be Wanted,'" explains Lee. "So those kinds of things, where the melodies were so beautiful, especially on 'I Want to Be Wanted,' I didn't think I could sing it. He said, 'No, I think you could do a really good job on that.' And it was my second #1 record. So he was right."

Bradley capitalized on Lee's European popularity by having her rerecord many of her hits in phonetically sung French, German, and Japanese. All of her success led to non-stop personal appearance tours, which are punishing for performers of any age. "They were very, very hard. One-nighters, five- and six-hundred-mile jumps [via car] every night, dealing with the elements, dealing with a state fair one day—out in the dust on a horse track—then dealing with an auditorium the next day. Then when I got old enough to do clubs I had to deal with that atmosphere and all the smoke. So it was just tough. Of course I was always very disciplined about my voice and I still am."

Lee's appeal bridged the generation gap of the early to mid-sixties. Adults marveled at her womanly vibrato and emotional command, while teens dug her as a talented version of their angst-ridden selves. "Well, yeah, because you know I could relate to that because I was always an overweight teenager. Oh, I was! I went through the acne stage and all that stuff, and I could really identify with girls that were having problems, and I was always the girl next door. Boys would come and talk to me about girls that they wanted to date but never wanting to date me. So, I could relate to 'All Alone Am I,' 'I Want to Be Wanted,' and all those songs I was singing."

When the British Invasion groups began to dominate American airwaves, Lee remained something of a force on Top 40 radio long after many of her contemporaries had been relegated to obscurity. Although Decca had consciously tried to steer her towards adult contemporary audiences, her best records were always as much country as pop. But after the 1969 single "Johnny One Time" received more airplay on country than pop stations, Lee took the hint and switched to that genre exclusively.

After years of being promoted by Decca/MCA as a chanteuse, Lee says, "I've been blessed to have a great country career." In the studio, little changed. Owen Bradley was still twisting the dials, and Nashville's "A-Team"—Floyd Cramer, Buddy Harmon, Bobby Moore, Ray Eddington, and Grady Martin—was still playing right beside her as she recorded the Top 10 smashes "Nobody Wins," "Big Four Poster Bed," and "He's My Rock."

Because of Lee's efforts, her family was completely lifted out of poverty and her brother and two sisters were able to get college educations. On the downside, she has suffered several exhaustion-related illnesses throughout the years, not the least of which includes a cyst on her vocal chords that kept her out of commission during part of the nineties.

Other former child stars speak about the awful pressure of supporting their families at such a tender age. That kind of talk doesn't make sense to Lee. "No, I knew that I was helping, and I knew that I had to help. It never was a chore for me. I was always glad to help my siblings and mom. We were close and had a lot of love. So it never was a job for me. I was just always proud that I was able to do it. I never got to the point where I said, 'Hey, I'm sick of this and you all have deprived me of my childhood.' I never went through that syndrome."

However, at a certain point early in her marriage, she realized that she was letting her ambition get out of hand. "When I had my first baby, I went out on the road when she was three weeks old. When I came back home, she was walking. So, I was gone all the time. Finally, I just had to say, 'Enough is enough! I've got a husband; I've got a family; I've got to be home some.' So I cut my touring schedule back somewhat—not a great deal, but enough to keep things together."

One of the few performers to be inducted into both the Country Music Hall of Fame and the Rock and Roll Hall of Fame, Brenda Lee still works thirty-five to forty gigs a year— a greatly reduced schedule compared to the old days. Which brings up the question: does all that free time after decades of hard, compulsive work make her uneasy?

"Well, my husband says I'm only unhappy twice in my life—when I'm working and when I'm not working."

And what about the midget thing? As an adult she measures four feet, eleven inches in heels. Is she sensitive about her height today?

"No," laughs Lee. She can afford to be gracious and lighthearted. Against all odds, she became a music industry giant.

In the early 1960s.

HANK LOCKLIN

"I was hungry."

That's Hank Locklin's comically timed yet completely accurate response to the question of why he decided on a career in country music. Along the way he learned that fame didn't automatically translate into fortune and sometimes people will try and trick you out of what you are due.

Born Lawrence Hankins Locklin, he grew up during the Depression, when hard times were the only times. Like many young men of his era, he helped support his family through backbreaking manual labor, eventually getting a hand up through FDR's Works Progress Administration (WPA).

At age ten, he won his first amateur talent contest and knew he wanted to make his living in country music—an ambition easier to dream than to live. Surviving on scandalously low wages and sometimes none at all, he sang on radio shows based in Panama City and Mobile, Alabama, before finding his first regular employment on WCOA in Pensacola, Florida. Local radio paid so poorly that his military induction actually represented a substantial raise in pay.

When contacted at his Brewton, Alabama, home, Locklin, a *Grand Ole Opry* member for over four decades, speaks candidly about the hardscrabble road he traveled to country music stardom after World War II. "I used to fool around on the guitar, and I was pretty good at one time. So, right after I got out of the service, I went to work with Jimmy Swan, and we were playing in Hattiesburg, Mississippi. These twin boys I knew had a radio show in Hot Springs, Arkansas, and we became the Four Leaf Clover Boys. We were on around noontime, and we played dates around, y'know, but I really liked to starve to death there."

Initially, Locklin was the band's rhythm guitarist, but that soon changed. "We were at a show in Arkansas somewhere, and I was testing the mic for somebody, and I remember singing a line or two of 'You Only Want Me When You're Lonely,' and I heard myself singing. I thought about it and realized that I could make more money singing than I could pickin' the guitar."

Eventually the Four Leaf Clover Boys sought more lucrative gigs in Shreveport, Louisiana. Working for KWKH's Harmie Williams, they'd stuff five men and a huge bass fiddle into a '41 Ford Coupe and race from barn dances to the *Louisiana Hayride*.

"There was a guy who wanted to start a big barn dance with me. He told me, 'Hank, I got enough money to fill a two-story building.' He made it during the war selling cars. That was Elmer Laird. We played [the *Hayride*] and then decided to break up when Clent Holmes got an offer to work with Hank Williams. So, I ended up on KLEE [in Houston], just my guitar and me. It was a five-thousand watt station and it went down all over Texas. I was on at 12:45 every day, five days a week. I really done good there for about ten years."

Pappy Dailey, still a few years away from launching Starday Records, hooked Locklin up with Bill McCall's Four Star label, on which he scored a national Top 10 record with his composition "The Same Sweet Girl" [#8, 1949]. This in turn led to appearances on the radio program *Big D Jamboree*. However, there were consequences to working for McCall, whose roster once held such luminaries as Patsy Cline, Ned Miller, and the Maddox Brothers and Rose. "I never made no money with him," discloses Locklin. "My understanding was that he liked to go to Vegas. I guess Bill was just a guy who liked to take everything. I did 'Let Me Be the One' [#1, 1953] while I was on the label, but he put his wife's maiden name on the song."

Wary, Locklin prevented McCall from diddling with his most famous tune, "Send Me the Pillow That You Dream On," by publishing it with Acuff-Rose. The Four Star version didn't chart nationally, but Locklin is still amused by the reaction the song got when he sang it on his radio program. "Pillows started rolling in like you'd never seen. Big ones and small ones. After I recorded it, everywhere that thing went it got the same response and people sent me pillows! I don't know what I did with 'em all."

McCall tried to fight it, but Locklin left Four Star when his contract was up. He then signed with Steve Sholes at RCA and began cutting juicier, more polished sides with producer/guitar virtuoso Chet Atkins. Locklin recalls his late friend with great affection. "Well, I loved the guy. That's the way it was. He kept a guitar in his office and we'd go and pick out songs. Then all of a sudden he'd pick it up and hit a chord or two on something or other that floated through his head. He was so good, and he really helped me a lot with RCA."

Locklin credits Atkins for moving the base for RCA's country recordings from New York to Nashville, which didn't exactly sit well with the company at the time. "So, there was some little misunderstanding with RCA because he was getting a lot of people down in Nashville making hits, and they weren't making them like they would've in New York. They had a better sound." That new sound helped Locklin rack up hits with his version of "Why Baby Why" [#9, 1956] and one of the first foreign-themed country songs, "Geisha Girl" [#4, 1957].

After returning from a successful tour of Japan, Locklin employed Atkins's sure commercial instincts and rerecorded "Send Me the Pillow That You Dream On." It proved to be a very fruitful session. "At that time a session was four songs, so I cut 'It's a Little More Like Heaven' [#3, 1958], the flip side 'Blue Grass Skirt,' and 'The Pillow.' Well, RCA first released 'Send Me the Pillow' [#5, 1958]. It was June, and I had just moved from Texas down to a place in Florida called McLellan, just a little wide place in the road. And there was a radio station in Montgomery, Alabama, that was *big* on playing country. So, I was riding along there listening and the disc jockey said, 'I've got twenty requests for this song. Here it is: "Send Me the Pillow" by Hank Locklin.' Man, I liked to climb out of that car! That thing took off like a scalded rat, and it just kept on going."

The song became a standard and, in one version or another, has been played over one million times on radio. Besides Locklin's version, which rode the charts for thirty-five weeks, hit renditions were recorded by Dean Martin [#10 pop, 1965] and Johnny Tillotson [#17 pop, 1962; #11 country, 1962]. Locklin is especially pleased with Dwight Yoakam's version on the platinum selling album from 1988 *Buenas Noches from a Lonely Room*. "That was really a thrill because that album he cut, it done good all over the world, and the first check I got from it was for about twenty thousand dollars."

Locklin today.

Locklin achieved his greatest claim to fame when he recorded a song rumored to have been a Jim Reeves cast-off, "Please Help Me, I'm Falling" [#1 country, 1960; #8 pop, 1960]. Though his yearning vocal set it apart from other hits of the era, Locklin is quick to give credit for the song's appeal to piano great Floyd Cramer. "You know that slip note thing on the piano? I said to Chet, 'If we could get Floyd Cramer to do that on this song, we might just have a big hit.' So, we went through it and said where Floyd should come in on this, that, and the other. Then he kicked it off, and the Jordanaires were with me there too, and we did it in one take. We didn't have to cut it again. Son, when that sucker hit the air, it exploded. Ain't no telling how many records it sold and it's still selling!"

It seems no late night record offer can be compiled wihout "Send Me the Pillow" and "Please Help Me, I'm Falling." Locklin, with shrewd business sense, has parlayed his two biggest hits into a comfortable lifestyle. He's been able to put his son Hank Adam through law school, and you can bet he and his family haven't gone hungry in decades.

Of course, when talking about the classic country music era, one must remember that the term "riches" is a relative one. To measure the gap between the salaries of today and of 1960, use as a yardstick the following reminiscence about the peak of Locklin's crossover success.

"There was a guy who booked us from Texas. Big guy, I can't think of his name right now. When 'Please Help Me, I'm Falling' came out, he called and said he had several dates out there and asked if I'd fly out there. Well, I wrote him a letter saying, 'Yeah, but it's going to cost you a little more money.' So he called me again asking if I'd come and I said, 'Well, you got my letter, didn't you?' He said, 'Yes I did and I'd like to fell out of my chair.' I think I was asking for three or four hundred dollars a night."

Did Locklin get the requested pay hike?

"I got it, all right. He hollered like a scalded rat, but I got it."

Al Downing today.

BIG AL DOWNING

Big Al Downing played and sang his way out of poverty, only to have racism stunt his country career. The versatile Oklahoma-born piano pounder had been dealing with race issues since his days with the predominantly white rock 'n' roll band Bobby Poe & The Poe

Kats. "When we decided to go on the road and back Wanda [Jackson], we went into places like Butte, Montana, and different off-the-wall places that we never even heard of," recalls Downing. "They didn't like it that I was on the stage with Wanda, a black guy on the stage with a white girl. That's how they saw it. They didn't see it as entertainment; they saw it as a black guy being uppity. So they would say catcalls and things like that. Finally, Wanda would say, 'Look, if he can't be here, I'm not going to play either because he's my piano player and we work together. So, if y'all want me, you'll shut up and let us do our show.' Several places she had to tell 'em that. I think there were even a couple of places we even walked out of because they didn't want to do it, so we just packed up and left."

According to Wanda Jackson, Downing dealt with the hardships without sacrificing one iota of his personal charm or dignity. "When he was in my band, in the first place, it was unheard of—especially in the Midwest and West—to have a black man in your group. We had some problems here and there. But Al was such a wonderful personality. People just loved him. When the others boys took their breaks, in a lot of the clubs Al could not go up to the bar, use the restroom, and things like that. So, he'd have to just sit on stage. That just breaks your heart. But after five minutes, you'd look up there and people would be standing around the piano talking to him. Then the guys would have to hide him in the backseat of the car when they'd check into motels and things, because he couldn't stay in them if [the motel own-ers] knew it. We'd have to bring him things to eat from the restaurant; he'd have to eat in the car."

When asked if those experiences ever made him feel like giving up, Downing is adamant. "No. I didn't like it, but I felt that the music was more important. Working with Wanda and taking the music to the people like that was more important than the two guys out of the whole audience calling names and saying something bad about it."

Maintaining his philosophical determination in the face of callous humiliation has helped Downing forge an international reputation as an entertainer's entertainer. His is not a household name, but he enjoys a sizable rockabilly following overseas, had a #1 disco hit, and scored a neat string of late-seventies/early-eighties Top 40 country hits.

A farm boy at heart, his work ethic and musical influences have their roots in the Oklahoma hay fields. "All my family, my brothers and everybody, we were all sharecroppers," explains Downing. "What we did was if somebody needed a field of hay brought in, we'd go out and mow it and stack it and put it in the fifty-foot-high barns or whatever they needed. Also, we'd go up and get permission from the big farms to look for herbs on their property, down by the river or whatever, and we sold those to the market in Coffeyville, Kansas, where they made medicine and things like that."

Downing was one of fifteen children (twelve of whom survived into adulthood) and most work was seasonal in nature, so food was sometimes scarce. "Oh, I've been hungry many times," he says. "Not only hungry, but sometimes during the school year we got laughed at because we had to go to school barefooted. Out of the five or six of them that was going to school, we only had one or two pairs of shoes. So we had to trade off. One day my brother would wear the shoes, the next day my sister would wear them to school. Then I'd go to school barefooted that one day. That's just the way we done it. We were very poor. But you know, we didn't really know it until we went somewhere like the store."

Downing's first musical experiences came via a gospel quartet his father and brothers started. Later, he learned to love the country music the truckers listened to while the family loaded the hay, but it was a discarded junkyard piano he and his brothers stumbled upon that caused his commitment to music to really take hold.

"We had a tractor trailer, not a flatbed, and one day we were coming home from loading that hay and we went by the junkyard and there was an old upright piano there," Downing recalls fondly. "So, we loaded it on the back of the old truck and took it down the road home. Once we got it there, we just started banging on it and we found that about fifty or sixty of the keys still worked. Then, we decided to put the radio on top of the piano. Dad would come in and listen to the *Grand Ole Opry* and everything with the radio blaring on top. Then I started liking that [disc jockey] John R. on WLAC out of Nashville because he would play Fats Domino and Louis Jordan and them people. So, we listened to that and I started picking out Fats Domino music. He'd come on and I'd start trying to find those notes on the piano and that's how I learned to play."

Impressed, Downing's parents wanted him to take piano lessons. "They paid this old black lady, about eighty years old, I guess she was then. I never will forget it. I was like thirteen or fourteen years old. I walked in and she had long, strong, bony fingers, and I said, 'Whoa man, I'll bet she can whip a piano to death.'

"She said very, very gruff, 'Play something for me.' So, I sat down and I played something for her. Then she said, 'Now get up and get out of here.'

"I said, 'I thought you were going to teach me.'

"She said, 'Look, that's a gift that God gave you what you're doing and I'm not going to touch it.'"

Encouraged, the young pianist played local dances and proms during his teen years, and all the money he earned went into the family coffers. After winning an amateur contest sponsored by radio station KGGF with his imitation of Fats Domino singing "Blueberry Hill," Downing was asked to join a group hoping to cash in on the rock 'n' roll craze of the late 1950s.

"Bobby Poe was a white guy in town that had a band called the Rhythm Rockers," Downing explains. "After he heard me win that amateur hour thing, he drove out to my house the next day. He said, 'Look, Al, here's what I want to do. I heard you last night on the radio and I'd like for you to join a band I'm going to be putting together. You'll be doing Fats Domino and Nat King Cole and Ray Charles and all them people and all us boys will do the Everly Brothers and people like Jerry Lee Lewis and we'll cover the whole spectrum of the music that way. Nobody has ever done that before.' He said, 'I want to warn you that it won't be easy. Because some of the places we're going to be playing, a black person has never been in or they've never seen a black person play music there. It's going to be kind of rough on you.' I said, 'Ahh, let's do it, man. I can take it.'"

Rechristened Bobby Poe & The Poe Cats, the band earned "pass the hat money" at local VFW halls before manager/producer Lelan Rogers got them into a studio to record for the Texas-based White Rock label. Combining Downing's Little Richard imitation and Fats Domino–inspired piano licks with Vernon Sandusky's wild rockabilly guitar riffs, they fashioned the classic rocker "Down on the Farm." Leased to the Challenge label, it only scaled the lower regions of the national Hot 100. Nevertheless, the record garnered gigs for the band on the *Dick Clark Caravan of Stars* and secured steady work backing Capitol rockabilly star Wanda Jackson. As a sideman, Downing played piano on Jackson's breakthrough hit, "Let's Have a Party," as well as on several other less successful sides. Downing had faced racial taunts before, but once he began touring with Jackson, the abuse increased.

Subsequently, he and the band latched on to a steady five-year gig in Washington, D.C., at Rand's Nightclub. They recorded for a variety of labels, including East/West, Carlton, V-Tone, and Kasoma, but the pianist learned that hit singles were an elusive commodity. Their lack of success was due in part to both bad luck and lousy timing.

Downing earned a small measure of renown by teaming with heroin-addicted soul singer Little Esther Phillips for the

Nashville-produced Lenox Records release "You Don't Miss Your Water" [#73 pop, 1963]. "She was a lot of fun to work with but even then I think she had a little bit of the habit," says Downing sadly. "It was kind of hard because sometimes she'd come in and be as happy-go-lucky as anything and other times she'd come in and be a little bit moody at the session and things. I loved her to death. What a great voice and we really clicked together vocally. We had planned on doing a whole album like Brook Benton and Dinah Washington, but I don't know what happened there, it just didn't work out."

The following year, Downing cut a blistering rock 'n' soul side called "Georgia Slop" for Columbia that came out just as the Beatles were pushing most American acts off radio playlists. Eventually, members of Downing's band departed to form a Beatles knock-off group called the Chartbusters, and the pianist became a solo act. Recording country-soul for Shelby Singleton's Silver Fox label, and also briefly for Columbia, he stayed active but didn't really taste commercial success until "I'll Be Holding On" became a #1 disco hit for Chess in 1975.

At a fruitless follow-up session, Downing was finally able to realize his lifelong dream of recording country music. "In the back of my heart I always had wanted to go back and do the simpler kind of country," he discloses. "Tony Bon Giovi, who is Jon Bon Jovi's uncle, was producing me at the time, and we couldn't come up with an idea for a new disco song. So they all took a break to have some lunch, but I stayed in there at the piano. I didn't know it, but Tony Bon Giovi stayed in the engineering room there with the mic open. So I sat down at the piano and started doing songs like 'Touch Me,' 'Mr. Jones,' and 'Let's Sing About Love,' and he was listening to it. All of a sudden I heard him say, 'Hey Al, what's that stuff you're playing?'

"I said, 'That's the kind of stuff I want to do if I ever do a country album.'

"He said, 'Well, the hell with disco, let's do that.'"

The sessions, featuring Dee Dee Warwick and Cissy Houston singing back-up, were released by Warner Bros. in 1978. Downing became one of the rarest of all performers, a black country star—one of only three in the baby boomer era (the remarkably popular Charley Pride and the lesser-known Obie McClinton being the other two). Even though several of the Warner Bros. releases made various chart entries, none rose higher than #18.

If asked, Downing will tell you why he believes his singles didn't rise higher on the charts. "There was a reason for that. That thing raised its ugly head again—the racism thing. Once I got in the Top 20, there was about twelve of the biggest radio stations around in the South and places that didn't want to play me, simply because I was black. They said, 'We're not going to play any black records on our show.' They're some of the same people who wouldn't even play Charley Pride. So, that's what stopped my records from going into the Top 10, because I needed these radio stations to do it."

According to Downing, the situation worsened when Warner Bros. decided not to issue an album and began delaying plans for future releases. "And then Warner Bros. said, 'We want to go a different direction,' so [Bon Giovi's company] bought my contract back from Warner Bros. and said, 'We'll put it out on our own label.'"

Downing's self-titled debut country LP on Bon Giovi's Team label hit a respectable #22 on the *Billboard* country charts in 1983. This, along with the Top 40 entry "It Takes Love," seemed to validate his talent and mainstream country appeal. However, follow-up singles on the Team, Vine Street, and Doorknob labels seldom made it out of the bottom third of country's Hot 100 and his promise as a commercial country artist withered.

"I've always said that the [fans] have not been the problem with my success, it was the people high in the business," says Downing today. "They were the problem with any success I didn't have."

It's worth noting that no black performer—not even Charley Pride—has graced country music's playlists since 1989, which is about the time when the genre became the destination for pop music's white flight from hip-hop. (This lack of diversity leads this writer to two possible conclusions: the executives running the record labels and radio outlets are a bunch of racists or, even worse, they think country's listeners are.)

Not interested in fanning the flames of controversy, Downing earns a more than comfortable living playing festivals and classic country venues. He is especially popular overseas where he plays 90 percent rock 'n' roll and 10 percent country. But that ratio is reversed at home.

Now comfortably ensconced in Leicester, Massachusetts, he believes one word alone is responsible for his escape from poverty. "I think that the whole word that describes what I'm about is *dedication*. I've been dedicated to this music since the beginning and it has taken me all over the world. It really has been great to me."

Guitar virtuoso and entertainer.

GLEN CAMPBELL

Between shows at the Andy Williams Theater in Branson, Missouri, I get a chance to talk with the Rhinestone Cowboy himself, Glen Campbell.

After years of touring, Campbell says he likes the lengthy sit-down gigs in Branson. It allows him to get in a little golf, sing with Andy Williams, and see his old buddy Jim Stafford. "He's got a theater here, and man, he's funny. It's the best show in town, I think."

Campbell is pretty funny himself. He quips about his early years, "We didn't have electricity . . . we had to watch TV by candlelight." It's an oldie, but the joke is funny because it reflects a deeper truth.

Despite his famous disclaimer—"I am not a country singer. I am a country boy who sings"—Campbell *is* one of country music's greatest success stories. The son of an Arkansas sharecropper, he became one of the most recognizable personalities in the world, and, along the way, expanded the horizons of what was once a largely rural genre of music.

Campbell, born outside of Billstown—just four miles away from the slightly more populous Delight, Arkansas—was never exactly in rags, but his formative years were anything but middle-class. "I was one of twelve kids," Campbell reminisces. "I was the seventh son of eight boys and four girls. You worked and you worked on the farm. Whether it was picking cotton for someone else to make a little money, or plowing and driving the cultivator for Dad, you worked growing up. Now, setting out trout lines on the Little Missouri River, that was kind of fun. Fishing was OK because you were just sitting there with a pole in your hand. But, doing some of the other stuff, like picking cotton, gathering the corn, cutting the wood for the winter . . . we didn't have electricity, so you had to cut the winter wood and get it all in before then. It usually all ran out. Mama never could can enough food to last until the garden got started."

When asked if his family had indeed ever gone hungry, Campbell responds, "Oh yeah! There weren't any fat kids in the bunch." He laughs, then turns serious. "However, you learn to fend. There were always squirrels, rabbits, and whatever Dad brought home. We didn't eat possum or coon though. We ate possum until Dad saw one crawl out of the belly of an old dead cow who had been there about a week. But we ate squirrels, and we fished. Daddy had trout lines set out all the time, and we raised our own vegetables—the potatoes, sweet potatoes, corn, onions, turnips—and Mama would can. Boy, I don't see how they did it. Lord, it was amazing."

Some of Campbell's childhood memories were blocked out when he nearly drowned in the muddy Little Missouri River, an experience that, during adulthood, would haunt him in the form of panic attacks. "We lived right next door, across the old slough from a black family; he was one of my buddies growing up from I'd say age three 'til five years old. I don't remember exactly because that's when I drowned. I fell in the slough and Mama pulled me out and Lindell did the respiratory thing that he learned in the CC camps [Conservation Corps camps], and he revived me."

Like other Arkansas luminaries Johnny Cash, Conway Twitty, Charlie Rich, and T. Texas Tyler, Campbell sought relief from the farm grind in the region's raw mix of hillbilly music and gutbucket blues. "We listened to whatever we could get on the old battery radio we had because we didn't have electricity. Dad had a battery radio, and he put the battery on the old potbellied stove to heat it, so he could get a couple more days out of it.

"I really loved Hank Williams's stuff, Eddy Arnold, whatever pop was going on at the time, the old blues, and just whatever we could get on the radio. But I do remember Hank Williams being a big influence. Gene Autry and the movies were a big influence. [He sings] 'I'm back in the saddle again. . . .' You learn a lot from things like that."

Presented with a five-dollar Sears-Roebuck guitar at age four, Campbell proved something of a prodigy, able to ape the disparate styles of Grady Martin, Hank Garland, Barney Kessel, and Django Reinhardt. By high school, he was ready to hit the road with his uncle Dick Bills's western swing band.

"I went out to New Mexico first, then I went back home, but I left for good to go work in Albuquerque when I was seventeen or eighteen," Campbell explains. "I was working with a guy who was married to my dad's sister. They had a radio show on KOB [the K Circle B] and boy, I never looked back, because that was a whole lot better than plowing. Manual labor, that just don't get it. When I was in Albuquerque, I was with my uncle up until 1960 or '61. That was like five or six, maybe seven years. It was fun; we had a little radio show, and we played a lot of joints. Also, a lot of county fairs and state fairs too, playing the cowboy dances. That was my whole thing growing up, all I did was play and sing."

Campbell's mettle as an instrumentalist was tested working on radio, in dance halls, and on the local television program *Hoffman Hayride and Country Store*. "We did everything from Glenn Miller's stuff to the Sons of the Pioneers to pop stuff. It was amazing doing the big band stuff. We did 'In the Mood' and lots of different things. It was fun."

This versatility provided the key to Campbell's success. He moved to Los Angeles in 1960 and joined up, for several months, with the Champs, of "Tequila" fame. When that group dissolved, he, Dave Burgess, and Jerry Fuller formed the nucleus of Ricky Nelson's studio group, playing on such Fuller-penned hits as "Travelin' Man," "Young World," and "It's Up to You."

"I toured with Ricky over in Asia and Japan," Campbell fondly recalls. "I played bass and sang harmony with him because Ozzie got mad at Joe Osborn and fired him for about three weeks." Burgess, Fuller, and Campbell in turn made Nelson an honorary member of two short-lived Challenge Records groups, the Fleas and the Trophies. Burgess is quoted in the notes of Bear Family's Nelson boxed set saying, "We'd do anything he wanted us to, but what cracked us up was that Ricky was in awe of guys like us; he thought Glen Campbell farted through silk."

With his reputation as a studio ace growing, Campbell recorded "Turn Around, Look at Me" for the tiny Crest label. A solid hit in L.A., the single stalled out nationally, but accomplished two things: it got him on *American Bandstand* and got Capitol Records interested in buying his contract.

Campbell hit the bottom third of the pop charts with a slick rendition of "Too Late to Worry, Too Blue to Cry," and, with a collective known as the Green River Boys, cut the Top 20 country hit "Kentucky Means Paradise." Looking for a niche, he recorded a disc with the Dillards as The Folkswingers, and later picked with Gary Usher, Bruce Johnston, Terry Melcher, and Kurt Boetcher in a group called Sagittarius. Nothing really clicked for very long, and it seemed that Capitol didn't know what aspect of Campbell's immense talent to focus on.

"Well, I was with Ken Nelson at Capitol Records, and they had bought my contract from this little company that put out 'Turn Around, Look at Me.' Ken wanted to do some stuff and I just told him, 'I just like to sing what I like to sing. Don't aim 'em at anybody.' It's like when the country woman called up the doctor and said, 'Doctor! Doctor! My son swallowed a bullet, what should I do?' The doctor answered, 'Give him some castor oil and don't aim him at anybody.' [Laughs] That's the way I was back then. I didn't want to aim it at anybody; I just wanted to play it, and see if I could get it played on the air."

To pay the bills, Campbell did an incredible amount of session work: 586 dates in 1963 alone. At that time, Martin Margulies (aka Johnny Legend) was under the impression that the guitar ace had given up on a solo career. Margulies explains, "Once I ran into Glen and started talking about how much I liked 'Turn Around, Look at Me.' That became a running joke between us. He'd see me hanging out with my band the Seeds of Time, and he'd say, 'Hey, there's that guy who knows who I used to be.' The more he said it, the less I thought he was kidding."

Asked how he managed to have a solo career and do so much session work, Campbell laughs. "Well, I didn't. Boy, that was good money doing sessions. Tracking especially. The union made them pay more for tracking. It was just amazing. It was fun, and it was a lot of work, but every session was different. It was a very busy time, and I really enjoyed it. I got to work with some of the biggest guys in the business, the best musicians, and I was really enjoying it. I was known as the country guy who could play. I'd play on a Merle Haggard session and then play on a Frank Sinatra session and that was really cool. Because I didn't see any of the stuff that you see at a Haggard session that you see at a Sinatra session. Or, like all the old Bobby Darin stuff, that was the Wrecking Crew guys. They were the coolest dudes around, and they could play anything. There was about fifteen guys there like Joe Osborn who could flat make a record for anybody there."

One of the acts he did session work for was the Beach Boys, who asked him to tour with them when Brian Wilson began his famous retreat into the studio. Occasionally, the hired hand would be placed in the middle of the power struggles between Wilson and Mike Love, as was the case with the session for "Guess I'm Dumb."

"Well, I played on the track for Brian and the Beach Boys, and the guys didn't want to do it. They didn't want to do 'Guess I'm Dumb,'" Campbell exclaims, astonished. "So Brian says, 'Glen, you want to sing it?' I said, 'Sure I do.' Because I kind of liked it. It was a great track and the guys already had some background on it. But that's when Mike Love thought he was the star of the show. If he hadn't had Brian Wilson to write, I don't think anything would have ever happened." Wilson's production of the song, much prized by collectors, is one of Campbell's rarer solo releases.

Campbell's thoughts flea-skip to a far more famous recording session. "Brian was just a total genius. When we were doing the sessions in there he got everything just the way he wanted it. On 'Good Vibrations,' I remember him sitting there doing that—" and he imitates the record's psychedelic hook. "That's all I remember about the session. It was something unusual."

Embracing the folk-rock trend, Campbell returned to the charts in 1965 with a version of Donovan's "Universal Soldier," and appeared as a regular on the ABC teenfest *Shindig*. However, things didn't really start to turn his way until he demanded that Capitol let him record and release what he pleased, including John Hartford's "Gentle on My Mind."

"I really did like 'Gentle on My Mind'—it was that kind of thing [a folk song]. The bums, the railroad guys sitting around the fire, boiling something in the pot. I think that Hartford wrote that out of a lot of experience, and I really did think that was a fabulous song. I heard it on the radio, I got John's recording of it, and that's why I cut it. I think if it hadn't been for John Hartford, I probably wouldn't be where I am today because 'Gentle on My Mind' was such a huge crossover, and it became my theme song on the *Goodtime Hour*. I'll always be thankful to John for that."

Campbell's years as a session player had taught him how to get the sound he wanted at a recording date. Along with producer/arranger Al DeLory, he fashioned a series of monster hits, including stellar renditions of Jimmy Webb's "By the Time I Get to Phoenix," "Wichita Lineman," and "Galveston."

"Jimmy, he just knew he was writing a good song," bubbles Campbell. "He has got songs that I haven't recorded, that nobody's ever recorded, that are totally fabulous. I could probably sing you ten or twelve of them that I just took and never recorded. I'll probably do an album of this stuff. When I get off the road, I just might do that. I've got some Pro Tools set up in my house, so I can get off my lazy rump and do it."

When he began hosting the *Glen Campbell Goodtime Hour* as a summer replacement for the *Smothers Brothers Comedy Hour*, his career really went into overdrive. "It seemed like everything I was cutting back then was on the pop, easy listening, and country charts. That really pleased me, and I'm glad it did, because I guess I kept enough twang or country in it. But I really just wanted to cut good songs. That's the whole ticket right there. Like 'It's Only Make Believe,' Conway [Twitty] had a #1 record with it in 1958, and I had a #1 record with it in '69–'70. That's a great song that can do that. But the TV show helped, I would say that. I think I sold maybe three or four times as many records as I would've sold had I not been on TV."

Apple-cheeked, sporting well-groomed long hair and sideburns, Campbell became mainstream America's idea of what country music was all about. It wasn't unusual to hear someone say, "Well, I don't like country music, but I do like Glen Campbell." His prolonged success set a precedent for other artists who wanted to widen the genre's parameters.

Would Willie Nelson have enjoyed mainstream success if Campbell hadn't paved the way? Garth Brooks? It doesn't seem likely.

That was really only the first wave of a career that has surged forward, subsided, and surged forward again. Does he like this particular wave of his career?

"Oh yeah. I am not picky. Believe you me, I could retire. So, if I wanted to do something I'd do it, if I didn't want to do something, I wouldn't. I tend to lay back and do some stuff with my kids now."

There's so much more to talk about. John Wayne and *True Grit*, the awards, designing his own guitar, the comeback days of "Rhinestone Cowboy" and "Southern Nights," not to mention the spiritual reawakening he credits with saving his life. However, it's showtime at the Andy Williams Theater and there is time for only one quick final question. How has country music changed his life? Campbell responds with humor and truth.

"Well, it got me out of the cotton fields and got me into Hollywood."

2

CLOSE ENCOUNTERS
OF THE COUNTRY
KIND

Sometimes a chance encounter will provide a lasting memory, forge a lifelong friendship, or provide an opportunity to build a career. This is especially true in country music, where many of today's neo-traditional performers are not only ardent fans but also archivists and historians looking to glean valuable insights from their heroes.

For instance, Dave "Smelly" Kelley—the mustachioed, gravel-voiced singer for the San Francisco–based honky-tonkers Red Meat—remembers the day he and his band's whole creative outlook was changed by legendary songwriter Harlan Howard. "Our radio promotions guy in Nashville said, 'I'll take you to lunch at this place. Harlan Howard's got a special seat at the bar. He usually comes in and smokes two cigarettes and has a draft beer for lunch. We'll just go and lurk.' So [the band] ended up getting our picture taken with him and one of us asked, 'What advice would you give me?'"

The band leaned forward, waiting to be regaled with pearls of wisdom from the man who wrote such classics as "I Fall to

Pieces," "Heartaches by the Number," and "I've Got a Tiger by the Tail." As he stubbed out his second cigarette and rose to leave, Howard growled, "Try to write it better!"

The band laughed. For them it was a perfect Harlan Howard moment, complete with a sardonic snapper. Whether the band ever makes it to national fame or not, they were thrilled to have met one of their idols. Moreover, his advice is something Red Meat's chief songwriter Steve Young continues to take to heart.

These are stories of chance meetings that turned into friendships and sometimes into career-defining opportunities.

Teacher by day, king of rockabilly bass by night.

RAY CAMPI
on Ken Maynard and Walter Matthau

I f you are a fan of old movies, you may have heard of Ken Maynard, a forgotten cowboy star of yesteryear. It's less likely you have heard of Ray Campi, who was able to supply the drunk and cantankerous Maynard with one last, fleeting moment of recognition.

Campi has been playing his special brand of rockabilly, western swing, and straight country for over fifty years. Despite an international following, dozens of albums released worldwide, and helping Ron Weiser's Rollin' Rock label get off the ground during the 1970s, Campi is not a big star. In fact, most of his income comes from working as a teacher in the Los Angeles school district.

Also a film buff, Campi has audiotaped hundreds of hours of interviews with celebrities ranging from George Raft and William Holden to Bud Abbott, the Three Stooges, and Walter Brennan. While compiling interviews of movie cowboy stars, he met one of his childhood heroes, Ken Maynard.

Maynard started his film career in the silent era. When talkies came along, the former *Buffalo Bill's Wild West Show* rider lucked into becoming the silver screen's first singing cowboy. During an era when movie serials and westerns were extremely popular Saturday matinee fodder, Maynard was a major star, with a major salary to boot. Today he's noted for giving another singing cowboy, Gene Autry, his first break in pictures. Autry costarred with Maynard in the serial *Mystery Mountain* and the feature *In Old Santa Fe* in 1934. A better singer and evidently a smarter businessman, Autry soon eclipsed Maynard, who ended his movie career playing second fiddle to younger, thinner cowboy stars.

By the time Campi met Maynard, the former star was experiencing hard times. "He lived in the filthiest trailer you ever saw," remembers Campi. "It was old and it was in the worst trailer park in San Fernando, just a terrible place, and his trailer hadn't been cleaned in years and years. The water faucet didn't have a washer so the water would run all the time and the cat would jump up and get a drink from it. Ken would spend all day smoking cigars and reading cowboy books in his old age. So I'd get him dressed up and take him somewhere for Chinese food or take him to the store. I don't think he had any way of making a living. I think Gene Autry sent him a check every month. [Autry was renowned for such acts of generosity.] Maynard was a millionaire at one time with a big ranch, his own plane, and a new Packard every year given to him free just for being Ken Maynard. He had a big poster above his sofa of the circus he owned with a hundred people in it and all kinds of animals. He drank it all up and just threw it all away.

"Of course, Ken was a good friend of mine," Campi states with an implied "but." "Funny thing about Ken Maynard, he wasn't a nice person. He was a real mean drunk. But he liked anyone who would butter him up like I used to. I bought him whiskey and got him underwear when he'd shit his pants."

Campi was instrumental in providing the down-and-out Maynard with some sorely needed ego inflation. "One time he told me, 'I want to go to the grocery store.' I took him out to Thrifty Mart and as I walked in, I saw that Jack Lemmon was walking out. I'm with Ken, and he's got on a little Western shirt and a red bandana and jeans with a nice cowboy belt. So, he grabs a cart and says, 'I'm going to get what I need.'

"Well, I see that they're filming a movie in there, *Kotch* with Walter Matthau starring and Jack Lemmon directing [1971]. It was five o'clock and they had just stopped shooting, and Lemmon was walking out the door. So we went over there and Walter was wearing the wig he used in the movie, and he was at the frozen food counter. He's still in costume and I go up to him and say, 'Um, Walter? Would you like to meet Ken Maynard?' I explained that Maynard lived nearby, and I was a friend who brought him up to do some shopping. And man, Matthau turned into a six-year-old kid. 'Are you kidding?' Matthau said. 'Meet him? He's my *idol*. I went to every one of his movies when I was a kid!'

"I said, 'Well, he's here.' So me and Walter—who never took the wig off—went through one aisle after another looking for Ken and I'm thinking, 'Isn't this wonderful? This big movie star is just a fan like me.'

"We found him, and Walter was very humble and shy. 'Ken, my name is Walter Matthau. I'm a big fan of yours, and I saw many of your movies when I was growing up, and it's so wonderful to meet you.'

"Then Ken gets all full of himself [Campi imitates Maynard], 'W-e-l-l-l son, I'll tell ya. . . .' Really funny. Ken is a talker, you know, and Walter was just eating it up, but honestly, *I* don't think Ken had any idea who [Walter Matthau] was.

"When it was over, Walter said, 'Ken, would you mind if I had a picture taken with you?' There was a still photographer there, and he called him over and took a picture with his arm around Ken. Then he came over to me after Ken went on and said, 'Oh, thank you! That was so wonderful for you to bring me over to meet Ken Maynard.' So, we're all the same, we're just fans."

Maynard died in 1973.

Campi's experience with the fallen cowboy star was one of many that helped form a philosophy that allowed him to cope with his own show business frustrations.

"If you stand in the back of the hall, not being in the business, not dying, and being healthy so you can still go out and meet people, you can see memorable things and people. I have been in the company of Hank Williams, Elvis, Hank Snow, plus all the actors I've interviewed, George Raft, Mae West, my idols Roy Rogers, Gene Autry—I've had breakfast with him a few times. My whole music career is based on fandom because I've always done things that I heard and liked as a kid.

"I've done a lot to revive music, but mainly I've seen a lot. I've seen so many people come up and go down. I remember the staff band at the Palomino when it was the biggest club in town. You couldn't get in there. Hugh Hefner and all these people were there during the *Urban Cowboy* era. I was in the back of the hall wondering, 'Gee, could I ever get to play the Palomino club? Wouldn't that be great?' But what happened to all those guys I looked up to? They're either dead, gone, washed up, or drugged out.

"Look where I am. Going full blast. My head is still straight, and I can still make records. A lot of other guys just got burnt out by the business and didn't get a chance to meet or notice people on their way up."

Rocking out in Freddie Blassie's wrestling-ring jacket.

JOHNNY LEGEND
on Wesley Tuttle

Half-jokingly, Johnny Legend refers to himself as a "full-time rock 'n' roll beast and part-time everything else." However, he also acknowledges that "country music has influenced 50 to 75 percent of everything I've done." Among those influences is western swing bandleader and onetime Sons of the Pioneers member, Wesley Tuttle.

Johnny Legend's career virtually defines the word eclectic. Born Martin Marguiles, he was a folk rocker with Seeds of Time, a heavy metal front man with Shadow Legend, and transformed himself into a rockabilly ace at Ron Weiser's Rollin' Rock label during the 1970s. As a songwriter/producer, he convinced wrestler Freddie Blassie to record the classic novelty record "Pencil Neck Geek." Eventually, he became a wrestling manager himself, at one time holding a belt as the A.I.W.A. *women's* wrestling champion. Moviewise, he has scored porno movies and directed the first and only X-rated rockabilly feature, *Teenage Cruisers*. In legitimate film he has appeared as a bit player in *Rat Race* and *Man on the Moon* and directed Andy Kaufman's final film, *My Breakfast with Blassie*.

Legend explains how country music came down the pike for him.

"I grew up in San Fernando and I had no idea that I was in a hotbed of country music activity. It was all around me, but it took several years for it to sink in. This place was like a little Bakersfield. Roy Rogers, Gene Autry, people like that lived out in the valley. We also had a lot of local TV shows that were priceless, like *Cal's Corral*—that's the famous Cal Worthington of Worthington Dodge—and other country people who had hours and hours of TV programming every week, usually Saturday and Sunday afternoons. To me it was just part of the weird, cosmic local programming thing that I watched.

"Originally I was a bit of a snob. I kind of laughed at this stuff, like, 'Look at these weirdos.' Then at some point in the late fifties, Wesley Tuttle, the famous bandleader, moved in about four doors down from me on Orange Grove. Apparently their family had suffered a major tragedy, the daughter had drowned or something. So they had gone completely religious and basically left the showbiz world. His family actually opened up a bookstore called Tuttle's Religious Supplies, and they also had a local TV show that was kind of country/religious. They had a son that was about my age, Wesley Jr., who played in some rock bands around the same time that I did."

Tuttle had amassed an enviable track record in country music before he took the saved route. With his band the Texas Stars, the Colorado-born bandleader scored solid hits during the mid-forties with his Capitol recordings of "With Tears in My Eyes," "Detour," "I Wish I Had Never Met Sunshine," and "Tho' I Tried (I Can't Forget You)." He also appeared with the Sons of the Pioneers in some B movie westerns and provided the sound of Dopey's yodel in Disney's animated classic *Snow White and the Seven Dwarfs*.

Legend remembers well the day he met the born-again bandleader. "One or two days after he moved in, my brother and I were climbing a tree in front of his house and cussing. [Wesley Sr.] suddenly came walking out to us with this stern look on his face and said, 'We don't use that kind of language in *this* neighborhood.' I looked at the guy with amazement and said, 'Hey buddy, I've been living here all my life, and this is the first time I've ever seen you. Who the fuck do you think you are?' I was a belligerent kid."

Wesley and Marilyn Tuttle in their heyday.

Seeing Tuttle being visited by people such as actor/song-writer Stuart Hamblin gave Legend the idea that making country music was not only admirable, but also a goal he could achieve. He began quietly nurturing his love of old-time country music by practicing Hank Williams's songs in his bedroom and watching Ernest Tubb on television. "At one time he had the two best guitar players in the world," Legend explains. "The lead guy and the steel guy. So, in the middle of the drug-induced Doors, Pink Floyd, and that whole sitting-around-at-night-getting-stoned-and-listening-to-Fugs era, I would wait religiously each week for Ernest Tubb's syndicated TV show to come on."

The Sons of the Pioneers reunions further stoked Legend's country music passions. The only person in attendance of hippie visage, Legend was deeply gratified when he gained easy access to Marty Robbins and Dale Evans without a trace of scorn.

"Everyone was there, all the original singers who were still alive like Roy Rogers, Gene Autry—he could barely talk. I didn't realize that he was going to live another fifteen or twenty years. He got up with tears in his eyes, but his speech pattern was breaking up. But Gonzales Gonzales was there, Cal Worthington was hanging around, all the local people in the know were at this thing. It was just breathtaking because I sort of fit in, got in with the whole crowd, and just had a great time.

"At this time, Wesley Tuttle still lived down the block from me, and I would occasionally run into him. I'd try to talk to him and say, 'Hey Wesley, I'm into this whole country music thing now.'"

When the second Sons of the Pioneers reunion was scheduled at the Palladium in 1972, Legend informed Tuttle, and, figuring that his neighbor's religious convictions precluded him from attending, thought no more about it.

"By the time I got to the second reunion, I was feeling more like a honcho, like I knew my way around. Then, I heard some rumor that Wesley Tuttle Sr. was out in the back. There was a typical artist's entrance with a guest list and a lot of old codgers out there trying to come in, and this buffalo-headed doorman wasn't letting Wesley in. So I went back and said to the doorman, 'Hey, this is Wesley Tuttle, the famous bandleader and Pioneer. Give us a goddamned break!' They brought him in, and he started seeing a lot of people he hadn't seen in twenty, thirty, forty years because he had gone into this religious thing.

"So, he had one of those really great nights. Every now and then I'd yell over to him, 'What about this Wes, isn't this great?' He said, 'Yes, I'm having the time of my life.' He was one of the few people I knew at this event, just one of my neighbors who I only saw once every few years."

While chasing down his own dreams of stardom, Legend wouldn't see Tuttle again for many years. However, the country influence that Tuttle represented kept cropping up in the zany singer-songwriter's work. "One of the places you can find it is my crowning achievement, 'Pencil Neck Geek,'" Legend proudly states, "which was a pure country-spoken nightmare, with a few trappings of Sergio Leone tossed in there."

"Pencil Neck Geek," long a favorite on Dr. Demento's radio show, was a piece Legend conceived exclusively for bleached blond wrestler Freddie Blassie. Incorporating one of Blassie's favorite wild-eyed interview catchphrases, the record became a hilarious anthem of misplaced macho braggadocio.

According to Legend, the cult hit's underlying theme came from an odd source. "I had also listened to all those Klan records we had discovered during the early seventies, because I was just astounded that they were pure country in that they harkened back to the authentic country trappings of Hank Williams and Ernest Tubb. Unfortunately, they were the purest form of hatred I had ever heard in my life. You might say it was the darkest side of country you could possibly get, but it was still pure. So 'Pencil Neck Geek' was like taking that level of hatred in the Klan records and finding a way to place it in a nonracist context. We had an enemy that everybody could identify with, which were pencil neck geeks, a totally nonethnic, nonracial ditty that you can relate to right up to this day. Equal opportunity hate is what it is . . . crosses all color lines and denominations. In that way it was kind of brilliant. Even the victims like Regis Philbin who think of themselves as pencil neck geeks could join in the cause and say, 'Well, you know, I'm the one that they're all looking for.'"

It can be argued that Legend's greater musical contribution was his association with Ron Weiser's Rollin' Rock label, which recorded fresh sides by such forgotten rockabillies as Ray Campi, Johnny Carroll, Jackie Lee Cochran, Tony Conn, Mac Curtis, and Charlie Feathers. Legend, who recorded prolifically for Weiser, had the idea of starting an actual rockabilly group with Campi, Conn, and Billy Zoom (later of the punk band X) to play behind the legendary Gene Vincent on some West Coast gigs. Although the Black Leather Rebel died before the new group could back him, that band idea lived on.

The Rollin' Rock Rebels hoped to play nothing but straight rockabilly and hot bop gigs. However, it was Legend's and Campi's knowledge of country music that kept them out of trouble during one memorable early gig. "When we first started the Rollin' Rock Rebels in the early seventies, we had only done two shows at that point. So one night, [R&B saxophonist] Chuck Higgins called us up. He'd been playing this club and he had double booked himself by accident and he says, 'It's a pretty great place. We just do an oldies show out there. They'll probably like you guys even though you're doing that rockabilly thing. Just tell them it's oldies and they'll go for it.'

"So we took this gig sight unseen in this town called Belle Gardens, and we got out to this place, and it turns out to be one of the rowdiest lowbrow dives. This place was near a prison, so half the people in the place were ex-cons who had just been out for a little while. It was like they had just been released that weekend, and the first place they'd go was that bar. As soon as you walked in there, you could tell. I remember Dr. Demento came and he was horrified. Within ten minutes one guy grabbed another customer and smashed his head through the jukebox, and the guy's head was sitting on the turntable with blood pouring out.

"Naturally Billy Zoom panicked. He grabbed his amp and took off out the side door: 'I wouldn't play here at gunpoint.' This was a place where the bar was built so that the bar itself went right up to the stage. So these guys had their drinks, ashtrays, and weapons right where our feet were. They could pound on our feet if they wanted to. So, as soon as Billy Zoom left, about five or ten of them started looking at us saying, 'Oh, wait a minute. If these guys think they're going to get out of here, they got another thing coming.'

"We couldn't even think of leaving. So we suddenly had to remodel the band on the spot. Tony Conn, who is just a singer, became a bass player. Ray Campi, who played stand-up bass, had to become the lead guitarist, and I had to become a rhythm guitarist. Basically we just told everybody we were pure country. We had to do three hour-long sets that night, and we just did everything that we could possibly do, under the guise of country music. Even if it was something like Johnny Carroll's 'Hot Rocks,' we'd say, 'Here's a little thing Conway Twitty had out in '59.'

"As long as we kept knocking off references, and Ray kept doing a lot of Johnny Horton songs, we were able to get through it. They all loved it. That's something that's saved my ass a few times, where I've had to do a slightly bogus, surprisingly authentic country music thing on the spot with a gun to my head more or less."

Talking at his customary stunningly fast clip, Legend mentions that someday he'd like to form a full-fledged country band called Johnny Legend and His God-Fearin' Galoots. For that enterprise he plans to switch from wearing one of Freddie Blassie's gold lamé robes to an old Hollywood studio Confederate soldier's uniform. Before his mind flea-skips to another quicksilver mental thread, I ask him whatever happened to Wesley Tuttle.

"It's really funny," reports Legend. "Wes Sr. is still down the block. He's in his nineties and people say he's blind and senile. He walks his dog around seven every morning. I was walking by there one day a few weeks ago, and he suddenly said, 'Hey, by the way Johnny, I meant to thank you again for that thing.'

"I said, 'What?'

"'You know, that thing at the Palladium. I really wanted to thank you for that.'

"This was like thirty-something years later, and he was thanking me for getting him in. So, he's a little sharper than some people think. I guess he's forgiven me for swearing at him."

Wesley Tuttle Sr. died September 29, 2003.

The modern-day master of the double-neck guitar.

DEKE DICKERSON
on Rose Maddox and Hank Thompson

Deke Dickerson remembers well his calamitous gig backing the legendary Rose Maddox. "Well, that was with [my previous combo] Dave & Deke, the same day we backed up Hank Thompson. That was just a day of abuse for us," he laughs today.

One of the finest of the new-breed roots musicians, Dickerson imbues everything he attempts with droll humor and instrumental flash. Moreover, he is a renowned archivist and technician who knows how to re-create the sounds of classic rockabilly and vintage country records. The Missouri-born Dickerson told me that finding the LP *The Two Guitars—Country Style* by Speedy West and Jimmy Bryant changed his life. An equally big influence is Joe Maphis, whom Dickerson emulates every time he picks up his double-neck Mosrite guitar.

Dickerson has plied his trade playing surf 'n' turf with Untamed Youth, hillbilly rock 'n' roll with Dave Stuckey as the Dave & Deke combo, and the "snak-rock" parody band the Go-Nuts. Under his own name, he has prolifically cut his own zingy mix of country, rockabilly, and western swing for Hightone and his own Eccofonic label. Although not a mainstream star, he is popular in clubs and festivals at home and abroad.

Part of a touring roots band's responsibilities includes providing backup for legendary names who occasionally headline the show. Some acts hate doing it, others like having the honor of saying they backed a star. Dickerson, who has never exactly needed the extra work involved with such doings, remembers why he started playing for some of the veteran acts.

"I remember seeing [fifties rocker/sixties country star] Jack Scott in Switzerland and the guitar player had never even heard Jack Scott, didn't know who he was. I was squirming watching the guitar player who didn't even know the chord changes to 'The Way I Walk.' I said, 'I can't take this. I physically can't take being in the room when this is going on.' So, a lot of it for me is wanting to hear these older artists being able to put it out the way it needs to be put out, and not embarrassing themselves. I'm not saying this to be patronizing or derogatory towards them, I think a lot of times all they need is just a focused lens to be stunning. But you can't put a band behind them who doesn't know their songs and expect them to be good."

Most of the time, the older artists Dickerson and his group play behind appreciate their efforts, as in the case of "the female Elvis," Janis Martin. "That was a lot of fun because there are a lot of solos on her records that are really hard, because it was all Chet Atkins and George Barnes, people like that. And when I played with her, during the solo to her version of 'Ooby Dooby' she turned around and said, 'It's George Barnes sitting right behind me.' That was cool. I was operating at about 40 percent of George Barnes, but that was cool."

That said, not every backing gig proved to be as pleasurable. His and Dave Stuckey's experience backing up Rose Maddox and Hank Thompson is a prime example. The Maddox Brothers and Rose recordings are the spirited prelude to the fifties rockabilly era, and Dave & Deke genuinely looked forward to playing with the legendary lady.

According to Dickerson, it didn't go well. "Because Rose, God rest her soul, man, was the meanest woman you've ever met! I could tell she liked us, she liked my guitar playing. But she had this thing which probably went back to the Maddox Brothers stage shows, that centered around one person being the brunt of her hate. That wound up being Dave. His was the least used musical instrument because he was just playing acoustic guitar, and everybody else was kind of integral.

Whenever there'd be a guitar solo, she'd walk right up to Dave and just hit him. She was *really* mean! It wasn't joking around. She'd yell at him and Dave would be like, 'Well, I don't know . . .' and then she'd just hit him! By the end of it, Dave looked like he had just gone through World War II."

Things went from painful to painfully puzzling when the diminutive eighty-something songstress started calling for material unfamiliar to the band. "We had worked up all these great Maddox Brothers songs. But she had a set list which included songs that we had no idea what they were. This song called 'Shelly's Winter Love,' that apparently is by somebody like Eddie Rabbit from like 1976. We had no idea what this song was. We didn't want to play it and we said, 'Rose, we don't know that song.'

"She's like, '"Shelly's Winter Love," key of D.'

"'O . . . K . . .' So we tried to follow the chords just by her vocal inflections and it was such a train wreck, man, it was unbelievable."

Yet that was nothing compared to the embarrassment they suffered on stage with one of their true musical heroes, Hank Thompson.

"Like I said, that was our day of abuse," Dickerson remembers. "Hank Thompson had sent us this tape which was pretty funny because it was really poorly dubbed, sounded like it was done on one of those high speed jambox dubbers. He goes, 'Howdy friends, this is Hank Thompson, I'm really lookin' forward to workin' with ya.' All the while the tape is going—" and Dickerson imitates heavy tape noise. "So he says on this spoken part, 'Now the way we do my songs is we start off with two verses, then a chorus, then another verse, a chorus, and then out. No solos or turnarounds.'

"We were like, 'He can't be serious about that. Jesus, you've got to have the solos and turnarounds, these are his signature songs!' Myself and Jeremy Wakefield, who played steel guitar that day, we learned all these Hank Thompson turnarounds. They're all pretty simple twin guitar things that we felt were very integral to the songs. We didn't have any musical discussions before we hit the stage. He pulled up in this rented Lincoln Continental, popped the trunk, pulled out his guitar, walked on stage, and plugged in.

"We had done all these things to make it seem really special. I brought out all of my Standell tube amps, because his band used them in the fifties, but he didn't even make a comment on it. Thompson pulled this ornately engraved Gibson Super-400 leather case from his trunk; it had his name engraved in it and all this fancy Western stuff. Then, he pulled out this guitar. It's a Super-400, top-of-the-line, best arch-top electric they ever made. It has this hand inlaid armrest, his name on the neck, gold hardware and everything. This guitar is probably worth at least ten thousand dollars. Then Thompson pulls out a Radio Shack, four-foot long, molded-end guitar chord. He plugs the guitar in and plugs into the Standell, walks up to the mic and discovers it's not long enough. So I have to move the Standell, which is really heavy, forward enough so his guitar chord will reach. I was thinking 'God damn man, this is like the living epitome of Hillbilly Flash. He spends ten thousand dollars on his guitar and a dollar ninety-nine on the cord.'

"Anyway, the first song we launched into was 'Whoa Sailor,' and it's got this turnaround right after the first verse. So, JW and I just instantly launched into the turnaround. We figured, once he heard we're competent on these tunes, he'd be relaxed and enjoy it. So, three notes into this turnaround he starts waving his arms wildly and yelling 'No! No! No!' and stops the song. Then he turns around and says to us 'No turnarounds or solos!' There are like eight hundred people watching this whole thing. Then he just goes, 'bom-bombom-bom Whoa Sailor.' Me and Jeremy are just like these wooden robots because we've just gotten a total lashing by Hank Thompson."

It took a while for Dickerson and Stuckey to get a perspective on the incident. "It was obviously just a case where he had worked with so many hack bar bands that he just didn't want to mess with anything unrehearsed."

However, since then, Dickerson has made a point of running through set lists with artists as much as time will allow. As a result he has forged strong working relationships with many established acts who respect his musicianship and archival knowledge, such as fellow double-necked guitar-slinger Larry Collins (of Collins Kids fame), another of Dickerson's heroes.

"We were playing with the Collins Kids, and we were all sitting in the room together and this guy was doing an interview with Larry and Laurie. He asked them some really technical questions like, 'How did you record this and that?' And Larry pointed to us and said, 'Man, you need to ask them about that sort of stuff. They studied it. All I did was live it.'"

Cross Canadian Ragweed, Canada second from right.

CODY CANADA
of Cross Canadian Ragweed on Nick Benson

Nick Benson was a fan. He never contributed a note of music, but to alt-country combo Cross Canadian Ragweed, he was an essential and beloved member of their extended family. To illustrate his close ties to the group, bandleader Cody Canada talks about a college town party during which Benson helped bring the singer-song-writer closer to his future bride, who was hoping to be a part of the band's inner circle.

"[Nick] and my wife Shannon were really good friends too. Probably closer than I was to Nick. I never will forget, I lived with seven guys at this big two-story house. But we had a big party—we knew it was going to be a big party because we were musicians—and we invited everybody in town. We had the football team, basketball team, professors. It was big. The bigger guys and the guys who lived at the house had to wear these sleeveless undershirts or, as they're called nowadays, 'wife-beaters.' As in, 'Hey, you got a wife-beater?' Nick was like the biggest guy there, so Nick wore an undershirt.

"My wife showed up, she wasn't my wife then, we'd just started dating, and she goes, 'I want a wife-beater.' I said, 'OK,' and the only thing I could think of was this beautiful woman in a wife-beater. I ran up to Nick and said, 'Shannon O'Neil is in my bedroom right now in a bra. She wants to wear a wife-beater.' Then he gave me the high-five and said, 'Hell yeah, man!' Then he just stared at me, and I said, 'Give me your damned shirt!' 'Oh! Yeah, *yeah*.' Shannon hates that story, but I think it's funny because we're married now."

Formed in Stillwater, Oklahoma, in 1994, Cross Canadian Ragweed consists of Canada, Randy Ragsdale, Grady Cross, and Jeremy Plato. They specialize in the "Red Dirt" sound, which draws heavily on such influences as Steve Earle, Bob Dylan, and the Great Divide while incorporating bits of Van Halen and seventies Southern rock.

Although more melodic and soulful than eighties cowpunk, the group's efforts were still initially a tough sell.

Canada recalls those early days. "We played a million roadhouses. Some places, we didn't know if we were going to make it out of there without getting hurt. But to club own-ers it was like, 'Well, it's not country enough.' Same with the radio—'It's not country enough.' Or then we go to the rock bar and they'd say, 'You're too country.' At the country bar it'd be, 'You're too rock.' There was no in-between with them. So the roadhouses became the in-between. These were the places that had both George Strait and Molly Hatchet on the jukebox. A lot of them heard the Southern rock influence, and there were bar audiences who would scream out for Skynyrd and Marshall Tucker. We'd deal with it by saying, 'What about this song?' Then, we'd play one of ours. Our motto is if you cram it down their throat long enough, they're going to recognize it. Not necessarily like it, but they'll recognize it."

Discouraged by the lackluster audience response in Texas, the band formulated a sure-fire plan to get the cus-tomers on their side. "Lubbock, Texas," recalls Canada. "We played that town four times and we did everything to get these people into it. It'd be a busy bar, but the people would be standing on the dance floor in a horseshoe around the stage just looking at us, like 'I don't get it.'

"One night we jumped back in the van, and we all agreed, 'The next time it doesn't work, we're not going to come back to Lubbock for a long time.' So, the next time we played, we didn't make a dime. We bought the entire bar shots of Jager. Just to try and win them over. We wanted to just invite them in and encourage them to loosen up. So we had fun that night. The next time we showed up, there was a line wrapped around the building, and there was a whole tray full of shots of Jager on the stage. It was sort of a payback, saying, 'Here, now it's our turn.' And it went on from there. Lubbock is now one of our best towns. We play big places in Lubbock now. That's when we knew, 'Now we can do it. It just takes time.'"

Generally, Cross Canadian Ragweed's young fan base has been supportive of their blue-collar approach to songwriting and rock-edged rural sound. But compared to Nick Benson, the group's growing legion of admirers was merely hopping on the bandwagon he helped build.

"I met him because I was doing acoustic gigs at the Wormy Dog Saloon, our headquarters," explains Canada. "That's a great bar. We call it 'the best little shithole in Oklahoma.' It's like, if your dad's an asshole, he's *your* asshole, y'know? You don't want nobody else to say it. I got to know Nick while playing acoustic up there, and he hired me and my friend Jason Bowen to play every Thursday at the KA house for burgers and beer. No money, just come over, eat some burgers, play some music for two hours, and have a good time. It wasn't about money, it was about the songs. We got to be really good friends with Nick, went out a million times with him in Stillwater."

Beside being a benefactor and friend, Benson supported the band by attending their local shows. "He was the guy who was just always there," recalls the still appreciative Canada. "Every time you went to the Wormy Dog, you'd see Nick."

Canada never expected that to change, but it did. Swept up in the patriotic response to the tragedy of 9/11, Benson joined the Air Force. Canada, who was proud of his friend, recalls, "He came back from training and I saw him at the Wormy Dog one night, and he said, 'Man, I did it. I'm going to live my dream and fight for America, and I get to fly a superjet. This is what I've lived for all my life.' Then he said, 'You might not ever see me again.' I said, 'Man, don't say that.' Then he said, 'If I never see you again, I want you to know that I'm proud of you. I believe in your music and support you.' He always did support me and the band. I saw him one other time after that, and then we got a phone call."

It was bad news. During a training mission, Benson's aircraft crashed, killing him instantly. The band was emotionally devastated.

"We were actually about to hit the stage in Austin at Stubb's Barbeque when we got the call that said he had a head-on collision," remembers a somber Canada. "It really reminded us of when Randy's dad died—we were in the middle of a gig when that happened—and we didn't quit. Well, that night was for Nick. It was a great show, and I think people got more than their money's worth, because we had a different thing about us that night. We weren't playing for three thousand people, we were playing for one person."

Since then Cross Canadian Ragweed's career has been on the rise. In 2002, they signed a deal with Universal South

Music and their fanbase has expanded outside the Southwest. Despite the newfound success, the band has no intention of forgetting their late friend.

"I guarantee that we think about him every day," affirms Canada. "We've got his picture hanging up in the bus and a newspaper article over him. I got a pair of blue Converses that I wrote 'Big Nick' on the toes of. He was this big dude that had so much passion and so much love for his friends. After 9/11 had happened, he had wrote on a bomb, 'This is for the guys in Ragweed and everybody at the Wormy Dog Saloon.' He was going to drop it on Al-Qaida. Now, we have people who come up to us in military towns and say, 'Yeah, I knew that guy.' His spirit will never leave this band."

The Comets today, Marshall Lytle at right.

MARSHALL LYTLE
on Bill Haley

Marshall Lytle was Bill Haley's bassist long before the spit-curled singer conquered the world with "Rock Around the Clock." Haley changed Lytle's life by giving him his first job in country music. In turn, Lytle was an integral part of the musical revolution known as rock 'n' roll.

"My career started around 1946 or '47," begins Lytle. "Bill Haley had moved into the area [Chester, Pennsylvania], and he had a band called the Four Aces of Western Swing. His guitar player became a roomer at our home. I had an older brother who had just gotten out of the navy. He was a country singer, and he used to listen to Bill Haley in all the local bars. He brought the guitar player home one time and said, 'This guy needs a place to stay.' My mother said, 'Well, we can rent him a room here.' His name was Tex King, and he played guitar and sang with Bill Haley and the Four Aces of Western Swing."

In case one doubts Haley's credentials as a country singer, Lytle offers testimony. "Haley was actually one of the best yodelers in the country; he won the Indiana state championship in yodeling. A lot of people don't realize that he was a yodeler. There is a CD out called *Hillbilly Haley* that has Bill doing some trick yodeling and everything. He learned that from another yodeler named Kenny Roberts, one of the greats. Bill used to do that in our hillbilly nightclub act before we switched over to rock 'n' roll; he'd yodel just about every night."

Lytle, an aspiring musician, would occasionally talk to Haley about music when he came over to pick up his guitar player. The youngster wasn't looking for anything to come of it, but one day Haley dropped by the house and made him a surprising offer. "Bill's original bass player quit. So, Haley came to me one day, I was just about to turn eighteen years old, and he said, 'Hey Marshall, my bass player quit. How'd you like to be my bass player?'

"I said, 'I'm a guitar player and singer; I don't play bass.'

"He said, 'Well hell, I'll teach you. It'll just take thirty minutes.'

"We went out to the radio station where he did a one-hour radio show every day. He had an old bass fiddle there, and he taught me how to slap a bass.

"I said, 'Well, that ain't that difficult.'

"So, I went out and bought one and went to work for him that night. I was the only percussionist in the group along with Bill playing the chop guitar. We had steel guitar and accordion, that was pretty much standard instrumentation for country and hillbilly bands in those days. No drums, saxophones, or anything like that. That came later in our career.

"[Haley] was a big fan of the *Grand Ole Opry* stars, Bob Wills, and all the big bands that played western swing. He really had a good feel for that music. In the country field everybody played a kind of slap bass and Bill had a sound that he wanted from the bass called a shuffle beat. He taught me how to play it and it was a very, very physically demanding type of bass playing, especially back in those days when we had no amplification."

Asked if Haley and the group made the transition to rock-a-beatin' boogie overnight, Lytle responds with the story of how rock 'n' roll got its name.

"It was a gradual thing. How it really transpired was like this: Dave Miller at Essex records had a great feel for what was going on in the music world. He was a competitor of Sam Phillips and they were pretty much equal as far as being innovative and knowing what the public was going to buy. The first thing Bill Haley did for Dave was a song called "Rocket 88," which was a cover of an R&B song [by Jackie Brenston]. It got a pretty damn good sound and Dave Miller really liked the shuffle beat on the slap bass, and he re-created the sound that we got in the nightclubs. People loved it.

"Then, we recorded '(We're Going To) Rock This Joint,' and it started taking off in certain cities. In Cleveland, Ohio, in 1952, we were doing a disc jockey show with Alan Freed. We were known at the time as Bill Haley and the Saddlemen, and we still wore the cowboy suits when we performed. That night, around midnight so, we were doing an interview with Alan Freed. He had a switch on the wall which turned the mic on and off, and while 'Rock This Joint' was playing he'd turn the microphone switch on and yell, 'Rock 'n' roll everybody! Rock 'n' roll!' The people started calling in and saying, 'Play that rock 'n' roll song again.' So, he played it again and again. [Freed would] say, 'I'm going to play that *rock 'n' roll* song one more time. Here it goes!' He played it about twelve times that night. I truly, honestly believe that was the night he gave rock 'n' roll its name. Up until then he was known as 'King of the Moondogs,' and he played rhythm and blues music. But that night, there was rock 'n' roll in the air, and I believe that's when it was really named, and I was there."

The band, renamed Haley's Comets in 1953, changed the course of music history in the days before Elvis. Yet at the peak of the group's success with "Rock Around the Clock," Lytle, Dick Richards, and Joey D'Ambrosia quit when they learned they hadn't been made equal partners in the band as previously promised. The departing members formed the Jodimars, who scored a solid hit with "Now Dig This" on Capitol in 1956.

Today, Lytle has re-formed the original Comets group with Richards, D'Ambrosia, Johnny Grande, and Franny

Beecher. An English Haley soundalike, Jacko Buddin, handles most of the vocal chores, and the group of seventy- and eighty-year-old veterans surprise audiences the world over with their fiery, ever-youthful rock 'n' roll prowess. One of their most notorious and well-received numbers is Lytle's original composition "Viagra Rock."

"I test marketed it here in Florida and I had a #1 on five radio stations," Lytle proudly reports. "I did interviews with people on network radio shows, and they just loved that song, and it was so timely. I originally wrote the song to use as a commercial to sell that little blue pill because we, the Comets, are in that age bracket. We're not the thirty-five-year-old baseball players they're using in their ads now."

But what about Bill Haley? Was the Father of Rock 'n' Roll happier playing country music than he seemed to be playing rock 'n' roll in the years before he died in 1981?

"I think he was," speculates Lytle. "That's where Bill's real true love lay. Gene Autry was his idol. After he became a star he built a house and named it Melody Manor after Gene Autry's ranch."

Haley's last days were sad. By most accounts, he was sick and felt bitterly unappreciated by the rock press who didn't know it was he, not Elvis, who popularized rock 'n' roll. By contrast, his old bandmates are alive and kicking, grateful for a fresh chance to strut their stuff.

"We're having the times of our lives," says Lytle. "We were meant to rock 'n' roll and when you've got that going for you, age doesn't mean a thing."

Clement at right with rockabilly legend Ray Smith.

JACK CLEMENT AND BILLY LEE RILEY

J ack Clement's eclectic career as a hit songwriter and respected producer would not have started at Sun Records if Billy Lee Riley hadn't picked him up hitch-hiking a few hours after he had gotten out of jail.

Riley recalls: "One Christmas, I was back in Jonesboro [Arkansas] visiting my folks, and, on the way back to Memphis, I picked up these two guys flagging down a ride. It was Jack Clement and his partner! That's where I first met him—on the highway. We got to talking music, and they told me they were building a studio over there called Fernwood studios, and they had a band that played every weekend in Arkansas. When I picked 'em up, I was only going to take them a couple of miles to where my mother lived, but we got to talking, and it got so interesting, that I drove 'em all the way to Memphis."

Clement went on to write and produce some of Johnny Cash's biggest hits, produced Jerry Lee Lewis's "Whole Lotta Shakin' Goin' On," and brought country music powerhouse Charley Pride to RCA. The self-proclaimed World's Greatest Rhythm Guitarist (and unofficial King of Nashville Polka) is also the Executive Tour Guide and Scenic Consultant for the Country Music Hall of Fame and Museum.

The story of how a hitchhiker possessing a good line of gab but no apparent recording experience became such a prominent country music figure requires some untangling.

A native of Memphis, Tennessee, Clement had actually been playing music since he was a teenager. At seventeen, he joined the Marines, where he honed his country music chops during off hours and acquired a much-treasured memento: "I've got a picture of me on the Capitol steps with Queen Elizabeth," Clement quips. "She was only a princess at the time."

Upon discharge, Clement made some unsuccessful bids to get his bluegrass band, which featured Jimmy and Scott Stoneman, on the *Grand Ole Opry*. Pursuing the random pattern that would define his entire life, Clement also studied architecture at Memphis State while working as an instructor for the Arthur Murray Dance Schools. (When I told him that a friend of mine had danced with him and proclaimed "he's still a wonderful dancer," the portly producer replied matter-of-factly, "that's true, I am.")

In 1953, Clement and Buzz Busby auditioned for Virginia radio's *Wheeling Jamboree* as Buzz and Jack—The Banjo Boys. Initially, they were rebuffed, but an opportunity did exist for them. "They said they already had acts like that, the only thing they needed was a comedy act," explains Clement. "Sort of like Homer and Jethro. So Buzz went back to D.C. and got some joke books and some silly little outfits, silly little vests, silly little hats, multicolored. Anyway, we got up this act, and we went back and auditioned, and they took us that time. We did a lot of Homer and Jethro type things. I wrote a few things like 'Lady Insane.' [Singing to the tune of "Lady of Spain."] 'Lady insane how you bore me . . .' That kind of stuff. But we weren't into that thing. I wanted to sing Marty Robbins songs and Webb Pierce songs. Stuff of the day. I'd do those every once in a while, but mostly we were a comedy act."

The team gathered a little steam when Hawkshaw Hawkins's manager got them a well paying regular radio gig on Boston's *Hayloft Jamboree* on WCOP. "We were doing pretty good there," reminisces Clement. "In fact, we were doing better than the [*Hayloft*] *Jamboree*. The *Jamboree* folded—well, it didn't completely fold, but they decided to discontinue our salaries. By this time it had gotten really cold in Boston."

After Clement returned to Memphis, he soon discovered that Elvis Presley was taking the city by storm with his first Sun single, "That's All Right Mama" backed with "Blue Moon of Kentucky." "I loved it; it was like, 'Hey, why didn't I think of that?' It was like going on the radio and fartin', letting it all hang out. It wasn't a strange sound to me; I had made a lot of the same types of sounds slapping bass in my bluegrass stuff. It was sort of like, 'Hey, somebody's doing that on the radio now.' So I was hooked from the first day and before that day was over everybody in Memphis was talking about Elvis."

Clement also holds the distinction of being one of Presley's first imitators. "After I moved back to Memphis this guy had me come back to Boston to play a fair one time. Elvis had just started and no one had ever heard of him up there. I said, 'There's this guy down in Memphis, the people are loving him, and he sounds like this.' Then I imitated him doing 'Blue Moon of Kentucky.' I could do it, everybody around Memphis could do it after a while. So, I did those two Elvis songs and a couple of other rocking things for a couple of weeks, and then I went back to Memphis."

Billy Lee Riley entered the picture in late 1955. The Arkansas singer-songwriter had come to Memphis to start a restaurant with his brother-in-law. Their chance meeting on the highway changed the course of both men's lives.

"I was going to college at that time," recounts Clement. "In my spare time I was building a little studio in Slim Wallace's garage. Slim Wallace was a truck driver, but truck drivers made a lot of money and Slim had a nightclub in

Memphis. Then he bought one over in Periogule, Arkansas, where he grew up. He'd go over there and take the band every Friday and Saturday night.

"So, this was on Christmas Eve. Slim was driving and his wife Dorothy and some girlfriend of hers came along. Well, we got over there and this dizzy little dame got really drunk and I didn't. I was playing all night, I might have had a beer or two, but I was eating and playing, so I was not drunk at all. So, we were heading back to Memphis after the gig, and we stopped in Jonesboro at a place called the Coffee Cup. Well, I wasn't real hungry and this girl was real drunk, so I said, 'I'll tend to her, y'all go on in.' We're sitting there, and she got out of the car and starts walking around, and the cops come along. I got out of the car thinking that I could tell them that I would take care of her, but they put us both in jail. So, Dorothy drove his car back and Slim stayed over so he could bail me out. But you talk about pissed, angry, mad? Here I am in jail on Christmas Eve, and I can't even call my new bride or anything.

"Slim gets me out of jail about six in the morning, and we go down to the bus station to see if we can get a bus to Memphis. We found out the next one was at three that afternoon. So we messed around in Jonesboro for a while and then decided to start hitchhiking. We were out on the highway when along comes Billy Lee Riley. He recognized Slim and Slim knew Riley.

"Once we were in the car, Slim started telling me how great Riley was and I'm believing it. So, we invited Riley to come visit us in our little studio. He showed up one day and got to picking, and I really liked what he did. He was great then, and he's still great. He should've been a big star."

Armed with a small Magnacord tape recorder purchased from WHBQ disc jockey Sleepy Eyed John, Clement and Wallace planned to make Riley's "Trouble Bound" and "Think Before You Go" their first release. "At that point, we were just using that garage studio to rehearse in," explains Clement. "We worked it up there and then took it down to radio station WMPS. So we rented that and cut two or three sides on Billy Lee Riley. We were going to press it up on Fernwood [Records]—which was the name of the street Slim lived on.

"So I took the tape to Sam [Phillips] one day [to have it mastered], and he told me he'd have it ready for me when I picked it up the next Wednesday afternoon. When I came back in to pick it up, he was sitting in the front office there by himself. He said, 'C'mon back to the control room, I want to talk to you.' We got back there and he said, 'I really like that record. I'd like to put it out on Sun, I'll pay you a penny a record. That's the first rock 'n' roll anyone has brought me around here.' That's exactly what he said."

After Clement said he would talk to Wallace about the lease deal concerning Riley's record, Phillips offered him a staff position. "He said, 'What do you do?'

"I said, 'I'm working at Clark and Faye right now. I don't like it very much.'

"He said, 'Maybe you ought to come to work for me.'

"I said, 'Well, maybe I should.'

"I gave my notice and two weeks later I went to work there. It was June 15, 1956. Elvis was already gone. Johnny Cash's big hit record at the time was 'I Walk the Line.' That's sort of where I came into the picture. Sam was getting tired of running the board is what it was. He was looking for somebody to come in there and do that stuff. He found me and I was in hog heaven. Here's all this gear. By then I didn't care about singing very much, I wanted to produce."

Clement made a lot of changes at Sun. He brought in superior equipment and hired a house band that included Riley, guitarist Roland Janes, pianist Jimmy Wilson, and drummer J. M. Van Eaton. He also instituted a musician-friendly payment policy. "I was always trying to take care of the boys."

The results he got working with Johnny Cash on "Ballad of a Teenage Queen," "Guess Things Happen That Way," and "Down the Street at 301" (which Clement also wrote) were his most consistent commercial achievements at Sun. However, the material he cut with Sonny Burgess, Barbara Pittman, and several others proved to be the best those cult artists could deliver.

Even today Clement feels the atmosphere at the Sun studio was extraordinary. "People would go in that room and they'd just let loose. That's what you were supposed to do in there. Elvis did it. Jerry Lee, he was the best I ever saw at just walking into a room with a piano and an audience of one and do a whole show. Give him one or two people and a piano and he'll do the whole thing—give you the whole show and not hold anything back. It was great—especially when you've got the tape machine running. Like [Lewis's 1957 breakthrough hit] 'Whole Lotta Shakin' Goin' On'? That was one take, besides that we hadn't even run it down. We'd been working on another song ['It'll Be Me'] and I got tired of it, and I went out in the studio and said, 'Let's come back to that. Let's do something else.' The other song was my song 'It'll Be Me,' which wound up on the back of 'Whole Lotta Shakin'.' Sam thought it was an A side."

Phillips fired Clement in March of 1959 for "insubordination," but his career was in motion and there would be no stopping it. He has written hits for George Jones, Porter Wagoner and Dolly Parton, Bobby Bare, and his dear friend Johnny Cash. On the production side he has turned the dials on projects by Waylon Jennings, John Prine, Charlie Pride, Townes Van Zandt, Hank Williams Jr., and polka veteran Frankie Yankovic among others.

"I'm an unlicensed psychiatrist," says Clement of his role as producer. "I've heard a lot of stories and dealt with a lot of egos, prima donnas. Hell, I'm not afraid of prima donnas; I chew 'em up and spit 'em out for breakfast. I picked that up from dealing with all these people for all these years."

But what of Riley, who is mentioned along with Clement in Johnny Cash's 1979 hit "I Will Rock 'n' Roll with You"?

Riley never scored with anything beyond a regional hit. He left Sun a year after Clement and embarked on a music industry odyssey that continues to this day. The Arkansas native has cut a Grammy-nominated blues album, toured the world as a rockabilly icon, and cut jingles, novelty albums, and harmonica instrumentals galore. However, it wasn't

Billy Lee Riley, still rockin' in style.

until 2003 that he recorded and released his very first, full-fledged country album, *Hillbilly Rock 'n' Roll.*

How has country music changed Jack Clement's life?

"Well, I guess it's kept me a music bum almost all my adult life," he says, half-joking. "It's allowed me to turn my hobby into my business and vice versa. And it's allowed me to think that if you cut the right record, you can get played once on one radio station, and it could be a hit. It's been a propelling force. It has given me the feeling that I need to stay true to certain things musically, do what I like to do, and make a joyful noise unto the Lord. Make happy music and not too serious. Fun, like country music's supposed to be. It's a communal thing, stuff that people do in kitchens, libraries, and in their backyards. I've always tried to keep that feeling in there some way."

Elvis had his guitar, Pat had his ukulele.

PAT BOONE
on Red Foley

Although Pat Boone will tell you that his biggest vocal influences were relaxed pop crooners Bing Crosby and Perry Como, the man who personified professionalism for him was Red Foley.

One of the biggest stars of the 1940s and '50s, Kentucky-born Foley did more to spread the popularity of country music than any performer of his era. Regular appearances on the *Grand Ole Opry* and the WLS *National Barn Dance* made him a star, and he was the first country artist to host his own network radio show, *Avalon Time*. Featured in several motion pictures, Foley also successfully brought country music to network television with the six-year run of his *Ozark Jubilee* on ABC.

Foley's recordings of such numbers as "Smoke on the Water," "Shame on You," "Birmingham Bounce," "Alabama Jubilee," and "Chattanooga Shoeshine Boy" were huge country crossover hits before that term even existed. In addition, he was the first major artist to record regularly in Nashville, as opposed to New York, and was instrumental in changing the labeling of his genre from "hillbilly" to "country."

Initially, none of this made an impression on the young Pat Boone; he was more interested in Foley's daughter Shirley. "I had no interest in country music at all until Shirley Foley transferred from West High to David Lipscomb High School in Nashville, Tennessee, a Church of Christ denomination school. As soon as this sixteen-year-old beauty transferred to Lipscomb, I had an *immediate* interest in country music! And I became a big Red Foley fan overnight. I had not paid much attention or realized what a big star he was, but I was really smitten with Shirley. I visited their home a good bit and got to know Red, and I went down to the *Grand Ole Opry* and got to watch him perform from the wings at the Ryman Auditorium.

"I saw this consummate performer that people just loved from the instant he walked on stage until he left. He was so at ease with the musicians, and he had that warm, deep, rich voice, and he had that warm way with the people. He seemed to love them as much as they loved him, and it was genuine. Then I saw that same attitude towards people backstage and out on the street. Red really loved people, and he was always polite and friendly with them even when he was tired, even when he was under pressure. He felt that he owed them his success, which is true. He showed appreciation to them always.

"So then, as I studied his singing, I noticed that he didn't have any gimmicks, that he sang songs with real enthusiasm, but mostly with real feeling. He seemed to deeply mean whatever song he was singing. I thought that was a very important thing. So for the rest of my whole career I automatically used what I learned from Red. I did my very best to mean every syllable even if they were almost nonsensical. I've recorded at least twelve or thirteen hundred songs and over a hundred albums, and I've sung some songs that I didn't care for, that the recording director put in front of me to sing, but I tried to mean them and sing them with great sincerity and with no particular gimmicks.

"Sammy Davis Jr. told me once, 'I can imitate anyone in show business but you, because you don't have any gimmicks, you don't have any hooks. I can't take a slur or a buh-buh-boo or a trill like other singers do to try and imitate you. All I can do is sing "Love Letters in the Sand" and wear white shoes.' I think that's probably been a real bonus, a real plus for me. What I learned from Red was to mean every song I sing."

Boone also got to witness Foley's spiritual side in an especially telling moment. "He told Shirley and me in later years that he missed going to church most of his life. He said, 'You know, I'm on the road most weekends. So my show is my church and my songs to the people like "Just a Closer Walk with Thee" and "Peace in the Valley" are my prayers.' That really was accurate. He meant every gospel song that he would sing. He would close his eyes while he sang the songs and what he sang was communicated to the people. That was one of the reasons people loved him so much—because he made them feel something.

"I did a fair with Red in Denver one time. My career was hot and he'd been around for quite a while, so the promoter made me the headliner. Red went on first, which I didn't really want, that's just the way it fell. But he went on. It was outdoors in late September and it's pretty cold, and he did 'Chattanooga Shoeshine Boy,' 'Tennessee Saturday Night,' and all these great hits of his. Then he got around to doing the gospel songs. You could feel a palpable hush and reverence in the fairgrounds as he sang these gospel songs. I was in the wings and when he came off, I saw that tears had rolled down his cheek and frozen. There were little icicles on his cheek, it was that cold. So, if I ever needed any tangible proof that he really meant every word when he sang them, there it was.

"So, that's what I learned from Red, to be totally earnest and always appreciative and always be professional and knowing your music so you can give the people the very best you're capable of. That shaped my attitude and my thinking. When I first learned all that, I wasn't much of a performer, so it was like being poured into a mold.

"My other idol was Bing Crosby and he made everything look so easy, but he was just as professional as Red. As a matter of fact, I read a quote about Red from Bing—he had had a record of 'Chattanooga Shoeshine Boy' out, but Red's version went #1, and it was a more popular record than Bing's. And Bing said at that time, 'Red Foley is the best all-around singer in the nation.' Red studied classically, he could actually have sang opera if he wanted to; instead he went to the *Opry*.

"In the past, I asked some of the most popular singers like Gene Autry, Eddy Arnold, Roy Rogers, Webb Pierce, some of the real giants, who they thought was the best singer ever in country music. Without exception they all said, 'Red Foley.'"

Foley has been largely forgotten since his death in 1968, a fact that rankles the normally easygoing Boone. "I've chafed about that because some of the guys like Hank Williams and Jim Reeves have been more lionized. Right at the last he was inducted into the Hall of Fame but there's not been nearly the retrospective compilations of Red Foley out that there should be."

Boone saw the impact of his late father-in-law's work one final time while making a tribute album. "I recorded some of his most favorite songs in a CD called *I Remember Red*. I used the same musicians that he had used. When we were in

Hilltop studios outside of Nashville there were a number of moments where we would play his record for the musicians to write down the numbers on the charts, and a great number of times when we would finish listening to a record, guys were sniffling and not wanting to look at each other. They missed him and he touched them even then."

3

COMING BACK AND COMING HOME

Country music has often offered performers who became famous in pop or rock an opportunity for a career revival.

Think Kid Rock's ill-conceived foray into country is unique? Look at the post–Urban Cowboy boom of the late 1980s. Before he scaled the country charts with such monster hits as "Bop," "Everything That Glitters (Is Not Gold)," and "Love on Arrival," Dan Seals plied his trade with the seventies rock duo England Dan and John Ford Coley. Likewise, the band Exile had recorded the infamously sleazy disco-era number "(I Wanna) Kiss You All Over" before hitting the top of the country charts with "Woke Up in Love," "I Don't Want to Be a Memory," and "She's Too Good to Be True."

Contemporary acts are routinely given the heave-ho by record companies after an album stiffs. But during an earlier age, when expectations were lower and a #1 album might sell fifty thousand copies, labels were more supportive. To the rocker making a comeback, this security, along with country's intensely loyal fan base, provided potent compensation for the relatively diminutive sales. Moreover, in the case of many former rockers, turning to country meant coming home.

The best example is Conway Twitty. A natural born country singer, he was the nation's #1 rock 'n' roll star while Elvis Presley was in the army, riding the crest of such big hits as "It's Only Make Believe," "Lonely Blue Boy," and a rocked-up version of "Danny Boy." The Arkansas native wanted to return to the country fold as early as 1961 but neither his management nor his label at the time, MGM, would permit it. Prospects brightened when Ray Price hit the country Top 10 with Twitty's song "Walk Me to the Door" in 1963, but it still did not persuade the singer's next two labels, ABC and ABC-Paramount, to let him switch genres.

While playing at an eight-week run in Summer's Place, New Jersey, Twitty finally had had enough. In the notes for the excellent four-disc set The Conway Twitty Collection, *the singer talks about the decision that changed his life. "I guess I thought the only way out was to just cut it clean. I was right in the middle of a show that night. And all of a sudden, I just couldn't sing another song. I just couldn't. I finished with a song, took my guitar, set it down and told the band to finish up the set. I had never done anything like that in my life. I went out and told the club owner, 'I can't take it no more.'"*

Returning to the south, he played country music in clubs for a fraction of what he had been earning as a rock performer. Twitty told Alanna Nash for Behind Closed Doors: Talking with the Legends of Country Music *that songwriter Harlan Howard was responsible for his big break in country music in late 1965. After Howard played Twitty's country demos for famed producer Owen Bradley under the guise of a song pitch, the Decca Records honcho asked who was singing. Howard responded, "Well, you're not going to believe it, but it's Conway Twitty."*

Bradley gasped in disbelief, "Awwww, Conway Twitty, the rock singer?"

Once assured that Twitty indeed wanted to go country, Bradley told Howard, "OK, he sold me. If he wants to do country music, tell him to come on in and we'll do some."

After two years of less than stellar chart action, Twitty broke into the Top 5 in 1968 with "The Image of Me." The following year his "Next in Line" became the first of his astounding forty-one #1 hits.

One of country's most successful singer-songwriters, he quickly developed a reputation as the singer who knew what women needed to hear. Employing some of the sexy growl and dragging bass vocals from his rock days, he imbued such classics as "Hello Darlin'," "You've Never Been This Far Before," and "I See the Want To in Your Eyes" with shocking eroticism.

By the time Twitty died from complications of an abdominal aneurysm on June 5, 1993, the man they didn't want to go country had scored eighty-eight hits. In the process, he opened the doors for many of his rock 'n' roll contemporaries.

In 1976.

JOE STAMPLEY

Joe Stampley clearly recalls how his megaselling partnership with Moe Bandy came about. "I was doing the Wembley Festival over in London, England, and so was Moe. So, one night Moe and I, [producer] Ray Baker, and my piano player Ansley Fleetwood went out to supper at the

Hard Rock Café. Waylon & Willie had just come out with 'Good Hearted Woman.' I said, 'It's amazing how the name 'Waylon & Willie' rings a bell. It's a man and a man singing together. I'll bet you if 'Moe & Joe' recorded a song we would register with the fans out there.'"

Stampley never suspected this wildly successful idea would eventually slow the momentum of a career that was hotter in country than it ever was in rock.

One of country's most consistent hit-makers of the 1970s, Stampley earned his first measure of fame doing "blue-eyed soul" with his band the Uniques. Like many Louisiana natives, he mixed blues, country, and pop as if they were a natural extension of his environment. "I was born in Springhill, Louisiana," Stampley states. "That was a little town on the Arkansas border. Northwest Louisiana, one mile from Arkansas, thirty miles from east Texas. Just fifty miles south of Springhill is Shreveport, where I would listen to Red Sovine and Hank Williams Sr. on *Johnny Faire's Syrup Sopping Show*. We lived in Springhill until I was about seven years old. We moved from there to Baytown, Texas. Right down from where I lived was a radio station that played country music."

At the age of nine, Stampley received some good advice from one of country's most legendary figures. "One morning, Hank Williams Sr. and Johnny Horton were being interviewed at this radio station right down the street from our house. My mom took me down there to meet them. I was a big Johnny Horton fan too. They were going to go fishing out on the bay out there, they were both big fishermen.

Anyway, I told Hank Williams Sr. that I loved his songs. I could sing every song that he put out. He said, 'Well I'll tell you what, don't try to sing like me or anybody else. Just be yourself and sooner or later it may pay off for you.' That was quite a long while ago, but boy what a thrill to meet him! A year or so later he passed away."

In addition to the classic country artists of the fifties, Stampley grew up hearing tunes by the great New Orleans R&B artists Art Neville and Clarence "Frogman" Henry while digging the rock-drenched offerings of Jerry Lee Lewis and Elvis Presley. By the time he began high school, the youngster was especially keen on Ray Charles.

In 1959, Stampley got a leg up in the business from songwriter/disc jockey Merle Kilgore, who now manages Hank Williams Jr. "When I was fifteen years old, Merle Kilgore had been a disc jockey there in Springhill, he would work at the radio station during the week, and on the weekends he would do the *Louisiana Hayride*. He was known as the "Boogie King" of the *Louisiana Hayride*. So I would go down, and I would play Merle some songs on a piano they had at the radio station. He'd listen to them and he'd say, 'Look, you've got a couple of things here that I really like. I've got a friend in Hollywood, California. He's got a label called Imperial Records.'

"I said, 'Imperial Records! That's got Ricky Nelson and Fats Domino on it!' He somehow or other got me a deal with Imperial Records while I was still a sophomore in high school. They cut four sides on me. Ernie Freeman produced 'em, but the song just didn't happen. One side was called

'Glenda' and the other was called 'We're Through.' I wrote them with a high school buddy of mine, Ronnie Campbell."

Stampley's second solo opportunity came with the subsidiary of a classic blues label. "I had a little record out on Chess Records ["Creation of Love" backed with "Come a-Runnin'"]. Leonard Chess had the Chess, Checker, and Argo labels. Dale Hawkins was on that label along with another guy named Lucky Clark who had a record that went, 'Made me sick, oh so sick, I'll have to get a little better to die.' He was from out of Shreveport, Louisiana. So I had a one-shot deal with Chess and it just didn't happen."

Despite three flop singles, Stampley was something of a star in high school, and his notoriety as a local singer resulted in his first blush of fame. "When I was in the tenth grade, a little band came down from Magnolia, Arkansas, and played our rec center down in Springhill," he recalls. "Some of the kids said, 'Hey, you ought to get Joe up to sing a song or two with you.' The name of the band at that time was the Cut-Ups. So they said, 'Man, would you like to join up with us and be our front man?' I said, 'Yeah, I'd love it!' Later on, we changed our name from the Cut-Ups to the Uniques."

The band quickly developed a solid local following. Smelling opportunity, Stampley felt the band's next step should be recording. "So, I went to Stan's Record Shop over in Shreveport and I told Mr. Stan Lewis, 'Hey, we've got a band and we're hot right now and I'm writing a lot of songs.' He said, 'Well, I'll be honest with you, my label is a rhythm and blues label and you're kind of pop. Look, go talk to Dale Hawkins—

he's my A&R guy for the labels I have here.' Which were Jewel and Ronn Records, which were rhythm and blues.

"So I walked up to Dale Hawkins and said, 'I'm Joe Stampley, I'm from Springhill, Louisiana, I write songs and I sing.'

"He said, 'OK, sing me something you wrote.'

"That's when I cracked down on a song that me and Merle Kilgore had written a few years back called, 'Not Too Long Ago.' I got about halfway through with the song and Hawkins said, 'I'll tell you what I'll do. Get your band together and meet me in Tyler, Texas, at Robin Hood Brian's Studios next Thursday. I'll record that song on you and one more.'"

Asked if he remembers producing the Uniques' debut hit, Hawkins, who recorded the 1957 rock classic "Suzy Q," is effusive. "I guess so, I wrote a hot check to record him," he laughs. "I've even got the old hot check on the wall here. Stan Lewis wouldn't give me my money and I had to go hustle it up. I finally got that money back. I pressed up five hundred copies, four hundred for sale and one hundred for the DJs, then I sold the DJ copies out the back of the store. But all the disc jockeys and promotion people liked me a lot, man. I left Shreveport and I hit Vicksburg, Monroe, bam-bam-bam all the way to Atlanta, and by the time I got back to New Orleans that son of a bitch was a hit. It was a song called 'Not Too Long Ago.' I don't know how high on the charts it went, but it was about a 700,000 seller, which was a pretty good record at that time, man. Then, old Joe just took it on from there!"

The Paula label, whose logo featured a cameo of Stan Lewis's wife, also had Stampley and the Uniques provide backing for Nat Stuckey's first Top 5 country hit "Sweet Thang." "But the big record on that label was 'Judy in Disguise with Glasses' by John Fred & the Playboy Band," recollects Stampley. "Number one in thirty-six countries! By contrast, the Uniques had a little success there with Paula Records. We had four or five Top 40 hits during that period. 'Not Too Long Ago' was one of them, 'All These Things,' which was a ballad the way we did it, 'How Lucky Can One Man Be,' and I think 'You Ain't Tuff' charted for us. We thought we were *somebody*." He chuckles.

Stampley is especially proud of the band's 1967 Christmas single "Please Come Home for Christmas," which still garners seasonal airplay. "What's funny is, I heard it for the first time on WNOE in New Orleans, Louisiana, by Charles Brown, who wrote the song. Great singer! I said, 'Boys, we're going to work that song up and we're going to record it.' I think our version of 'Please Come Home for Christmas' will stand up with any version of that record."

From 1960 to 1970, the Uniques were a popular show-band who appeared on television on *American Bandstand* and L.A.'s *Lloyd Thaxton Show*. Their danceable blue-eyed soul and tough, grinding garage rock sound made them a perfect fit for clubs, teen centers, and college dances. At their peak, they played the *Soupy Sales Easter Show* at the Paramount Theater in New York and shared a bill with the likes of the Kinks, the Hullabaloos, the Hollies, and Little Richard.

When pop music changed from something to be danced to into something to be listened to while staring at posters under a black light, it spelled the end for the Uniques.

"When it started going psychedelic and metallic, it wasn't danceable type music and we were a dance band," explains Stampley. "So, when that happened, some of the guys started making other plans. Mike Love the drummer said, 'You know, I want to start a boat business and sell boats and motors. I love that.' My brother wanted to do something different, Ray Mills had a painting business. So, it wasn't like we were mad at each other or that type of deal. They wanted to go their own individual ways."

One of the Uniques' last deals came via an association Stampley had made through longtime friend Kilgore. "During the sixties, Merle Kilgore had introduced me to Al Gallico, a publisher from New York City. I had written some country songs and I presented them to Merle and he said, 'Shoot, I think that Al would sign you as a writer.' When our deal ran out with Paula Records, Al Gallico had put the Uniques on Paramount Records to see what would happen, and he had put me on ABC-Dot as a country singer. My third or fourth single was 'If You Touch Me You've Got to Love Me,' and it went Top 10. That's how it all happened."

Was there any resistance from the country establishment towards the long-haired, former blue-eyed soul singer?

"No, not really, because a lot of these people didn't even know where I came from in the first place," chuckles Stampley. "They just enjoyed the music I was doing. I was the first male country act Norro Wilson produced, and so we kind of worked it up together. There I was fresh into it and Norro was a fresh producer, and he kind of liked the soulfulness of my voice, so he wrote a lot of songs that were especially made for me.

"But I'll never forget my first show after 'If You Touch Me You've Got to Love Me' became a hit. They put me on a package with Lefty Frizzell, Carl Smith, and Don Gibson. I was the new baby boy on the block and I was scared to death. I never will forget Carl Smith telling me, 'Man, you ought to get yourself some fringy jackets with the leather hanging down. You like to move on stage, so just be yourself and do your thing and just sing 'em out there.'"

Stampley's 1972 #1 record "Soul Song" outsold anything the Louisiana native ever did as a rock performer and created a path for other country vocalists with soul leanings, including T. Graham Brown and Terri Gibbs. "Yes it did," affirms Stampley with pride. "It crossed over and hit #37 on the pop charts and was #1 in country. I was presented a Gold Mike Award, which was big back at that time."

Stampley gives Al Galico and Norro Wilson most of the credit for his country breakthrough and sustained success, the key to which was great songs. "[Al Galico] is a great song-plugger and publisher and he knew a great song when he heard it. He found a lot of the songs that I had approval of and I would bring a lot of the songs in too, but I think that was the secret to our success. The way I did it was, if I heard a song that really just killed me, and my producer said, 'No, I don't think so,' I still fought for just that one song. I'd say, 'Hey, you can have your way on all the others, but I really believe in this song.'"

However, one of Stampley's biggest hits almost slipped by him. "When Norro Wilson presented 'Roll On Big Mama' to me I said, 'I don't think so. I just don't get it.'

"He said, 'Well, if you just trust me. I'm going to put in airhorns, a truck cranking up, get the guitar going, and it's going to *feel* good. You just wail it out there. I guarantee you that we've got a hit here.' He was absolutely right. It's one of those songs that will last forever. It's in the Top 5 of all trucking songs ever. It's in there with 'Six Days on the Road,' 'Convoy,' and all those songs like that."

Was there a substantial difference between being a rock act and finding country stardom?

"Yeah," observes Stampley. "I'll tell you, unless you have that magic 'Judy in Disguise'–type hit, it's hard to sell a lot of records on an independent label. When you get on a major country label, they've just got it all laid out so you can sell more records. Promotion and distribution, that's the key. Plus, you've got independent promotion people who are working your record all the time, they're screaming your name to all the stations, and that's what it takes. It's a war out there is what it is."

Travel was also different. During the sixties, the Uniques drove many hard miles pulling a little trailer to their helter-skelter schedule of gigs. With the advent of a string of hit records, Stampley bought a touring bus and lived in relative style while taking on 250 live dates a year. The money was better, the fame was greater—the only things left were better deals and bigger labels.

Gallico moved Stampley from ABC-Dot to Epic Records in 1975, but the artist's former label had some material left in the can and used it. "During 1976 I think it was, I won the Billboard Singles Award because I had four charted singles in one year. The reason for that, after I left ABC-Dot, every time Epic would put out a single, ABC-Dot would throw out a single and they would all chart. There's only been two people to have a #1 record after they've left a label. Charlie Rich and me. RCA put out Charlie's 'There Won't Be Anymore' and it hit #1 after he had struck with 'Behind Closed Doors' and 'The Most Beautiful Girl in the World.' Mine was 'All These Things,' that was put out after I left the label."

Working with producers Billy Sherrill and Ray Baker, Stampley continued racking up hits throughout the 1970s and into the early '80s. He is especially fond of his ballad work on "Ten Minutes to Fall in Love," "Red Wine and Blue Memories," "Do You Ever Fool Around," and "Put Your Clothes Back On." But today's mainstream audiences best remember Stampley's collaboration with Moe Bandy on a string of novelty hits, which benefited greatly from the duo's lighthearted personal rapport.

"Ray Baker picked up on it, came back to Nashville and approached the label with it and they said, 'We'll try three songs and see what happens.' My piano player Ansley Fleetwood picked up on it and when he got back to Nashville, he wrote 'Just Good Ol' Boys,' and that's how it all came about. When Moe Bandy and I teamed as Moe & Joe, Ray Baker was producing those songs. We won three vocal duet awards as Moe & Joe; we were kind of the early Brooks & Dunn."

Stampley feels that his collaboration with Bandy, while fun and profitable, signaled a premature end to their respective solo careers. "Here's what happened. Moe & Joe became bigger than Moe by himself and Joe by himself, because of the three vocal duet awards that we won. We only had one #1 record together and that was 'Just Good Ol' Boys.' But we had about six or seven Top 10s together, like 'Tell Ole I Ain't Here (He Better Get On Home),' 'Tell A Lie,' 'Holding the Bag,' 'Hey Joe (Hey Moe),' songs like that. So, it became a deal where Moe & Joe were kind of like a little cult thing. Then when we put out that spoof on Boy George, 'Where's the Dress?' and won a lot of video awards—gosh, we were pretty high on the totem pole. But it affected both our solo careers because people became more interested in hearing just a Moe & Joe song."

As a result, chart success eluded him after 1984, but Stampley himself never really stopped. Now working in Nashville as a songwriter and independent producer, his 2001 album on his own Critter label, *Somewhere Under the Rainbow*, demonstrated he could still both rock and croon soulful country. As a live act, he also benefits from playing country nostalgia shows—as a solo act and with Bandy—and reunion gigs with the original Uniques. No longer constrained by the expectations of a specific genre's playlist, he enjoys a certain sense of creative freedom. "Whether it's country music or rock 'n' roll music, whatever sounds good to my ear, I'm going to appreciate it because I'm not going to get clogged up in one area of music."

Not surprisingly, it's Stampley's rock work that has earned him acclaim with the overseas rock 'n' roll fanatics. With a sense of awe in his voice, he recalls how at the peak of his fame as a country singer, his days as a rocker were validated by a particularly high-profile fan.

"I was working in England in '78 or '79," discloses Stampley, "and of all people to come and get an autograph from me, because he was a fan of the Uniques, was Elvis Costello. Isn't that amazing? At the time I didn't really know much about Elvis Costello, but he had worked his way backstage and he told me that he had the *Uniquely Yours* album."

In 1972, at the peak of his country fame.

FREDDY WELLER

"Everyone advised me, 'Man, this is the greatest thing that could happen. You've got to quit this Raiders thing and take advantage of your country career.' But one thing that they didn't know was that Revere and I had made a little agreement before I went in to record. That agreement was that he wanted to let everybody do different things to add to the power of the group itself, but he said, 'If for some reason you should have a big hit, I'd like your word that you won't leave me.'"

So says Freddy Weller, best known to fans of 1960s pop as the guitarist who replaced Phil "Fang" Volk with Paul Revere and the Raiders and the cowriter of Tommy Roe's 1968 #1 hit, "Dizzy." Yet country music wasn't so much a stretch for him as it was a spirited return to his roots.

Laughing, Weller says, "I don't know how [country music] changed my life because I started out with it. The earliest memories I have are in Atlanta, where I grew up. Atlanta was more of an R&B town, if you really think about it. There wasn't a country station in the city limits of Atlanta. So, I would listen to WTJH in East Point, Georgia, on my little radio. It didn't come in too well. I would listen to the likes of Hank Williams as he did Luke the Drifter stuff, Hank Snow, Johnny Cash, and all those type things. It changed my life from an early age, but it wasn't something that came along later in my life, because it was always with me. It was the first thing I ever learned."

As a teenager, Weller parlayed his abilities on the guitar and bass into a semiregular spot on the *Georgia Jubilee*, where he worked alongside fellow up-and-comers Jerry Reed, Ray Stevens, Billy Joe Royal, and Joe South.

"I kind of got my start with Joe South," explains Weller. "He probably still is my favorite songwriter. I played in his band for a while and with whoever was in his band or the studio group at that time. We did sessions in Atlanta on just about everything. I don't know if you remember a group called the Tams? I played on a bunch of their hits and did some of the background vocals on their things. The first thing I did that ever landed with any degree of success was when I played rhythm guitar on 'Down in the Boondocks' by Billy Joe Royal. Once that record was a hit, I played guitar on the road with Billy Joe for about a year and a half. He didn't carry a band. He just carried me, and I showed the band how to play the songs. So one of the many shows that we played was the *Dick Clark Caravan of Stars,* and Paul Revere and the Raiders were headlining. I'm thinking that was in Canton, Ohio. We just did our normal thing that we did every night, and we played everything from little bitty clubs to the big *Caravan of Stars*–type shows.

"Unbeknownst to me or anybody else, Paul Revere, for whatever reason, was needing another guitar player, and he was privately looking for someone. When he saw me with Billy Joe, he let a couple of months go by. I never even met him really because they flashed in and flashed out. I worked clubs sometimes in Atlanta, and I didn't get home until around 2:30 in the morning, and I had a note that my mother had left me: 'Paul Revere of Paul Revere and the Raiders would like you to give him a call when you come in.' Well, it was three hours earlier out there, so I went ahead and called him. He told me he had seen me, and he was wondering if I would be interested in talking to him about this job as a guitar player with the Raiders. I had seen *Where the Action Is,* and I knew what they did was rather outlandish and that was not really me. Especially the dance steps. So, I told him, no, I didn't think so."

Besides the uniforms and dance steps, Weller had another reason for turning Revere down: he had begun to make some progress as a songwriter. "I lay claim to the fact that I wrote the follow-up that killed the Swinging Medallions," jokes Weller. "I wrote the follow-up to 'Double Shot of My Baby's Love' called 'She Drives Me Out of My Mind.' All this was in Atlanta; I also wrote a lot of country stuff. I had a Del Reeves album cut and a few things like that. So, I was very much into the country thing, and there was starting to be a little groundswell of country music being recorded in Atlanta. That was one reason for my hesitation in taking the job with Revere—I wanted to be part of the country thing that was happening in Atlanta. But Revere called again and asked, 'Would you mind just flying out here and talking to me about it?' The following weekend I flew out and talked to him about it, and I still turned it down. A couple of weeks went by, and by now they were on tour.

"He said, 'If you don't have anything going, just come out and join us on tour and travel with us for a couple of days and get a taste of it. Let's see if we can change your mind.' With that, I did kind of get caught up in what they were doing, and I realized it was like a Harvard education if you're going to be in the music business. So I took the job as the guitar player. They modified the dance steps some, and they were going through some changes anyway."

The very first time Weller stepped on a stage with Paul Revere and the Raiders was for an appearance on the *Ed Sullivan Show*. He finally got used to the costumes and the band's zany physical shtick and became a Raider in good standing and appeared with them on their ABC television series, *Happening '68*. However, he still harbored dreams of a solo career. A combination of efforts from associates both old and new provided the opportunity.

"Joe South had always been my hero and he had written songs that I thought were just terrific. When I would go to Atlanta, I would hear his demos and the things that they would cut, and it was my biggest treat to listen to the new Joe South stuff. So when I heard 'Games People Play,' I just went crazy. I guess I had been with the Raiders about a year and half. I started with them in '67 and in '69 Joe had cut 'Games People Play,' and it had come out by him, but it was kind of hovering around, it wasn't setting the world on fire. So I learned it and played it on bus tours. I played it so much that everybody in the band knew it.

"Mark Lindsay, who was the lead singer and producer, got the idea that we would go in and cut some country things on me. He kind of did it under the guise of a Raiders session. We used a couple of outside musicians who were more country. On my record of 'Games People Play,' there was no lead guitar. I played rhythm guitar. Keith Allison played bass, Archie Francis from the Palomino Club played drums, Red Rhodes from the Palomino Club played steel, and Glenn D. Hardin played piano. So there was just five pieces on it.

"We recorded two songs and Mark got really excited and flew to Nashville and talked to Billy Sherrill about signing me as a country artist. Billy had a couple of suggestions about the mix, but to make a long story short, they signed me to Columbia in 1969 as a country artist.

"'Games People Play' went to #2 in *Billboard* and #1 in *Record Row*, which was a pretty prestigious magazine back in those days. We were touring Europe opening for the Beach Boys when we found out that 'Games People Play' was doing so good back home."

Immediately, Weller faced the conflict that defined his career.

The winner of the ACM's Most Promising Male Vocalist award in 1969, Weller kept his word to Revere and only pursued country offers when he wasn't working with the Raiders. At the same time that he was recording such solo hits as "These Are Not My People," "The Promised Land," "Indian Lake," and "Another Night of Love," he was also appearing on the Raiders hits "Mr. Sun, Mr. Moon," "Let Me," and the band's only #1 hit "Indian Reservation."

The temptation to go it alone niggled at him, but Weller remained grateful. "Here I am having country hits, some big ones there at the start, and I couldn't leave the group. And I wouldn't if I could, because they were so nice to me and they were so influential. I never would've had that opportunity had I not been with Paul Revere and the Raiders. That opened the door."

Style-wise, Weller was the perfect cross between down home country and good ol' rock 'n' roll. "Oh yeah. I tried to get country rocking years before it really was," he chuckled. "I was trying to do Travis Tritt when the engineers didn't know how to turn up the buttons. A lot of them wanted Eddy Arnold and that was it. So when they would hear it done louder and harder, to them it wasn't country music. Of course, then the younger generation came into it; the early Waylon stuff was starting to happen around that time. The younger people loved it, and they realized what I was trying to do even though it took a while to catch up with itself from the very concept of recording. To turn the bass drum up a little bit or put a little more treble on the guitar, the engineers didn't know how to do it. It was an evolution that took quite a while."

When asked if the country establishment hassled him about his rock 'n' roll associations, Weller laughs at his own recollection. "Well, most were oblivious until I got there, and then all of these Raiders fans would show up, and they would notice that they had a whole houseful of people that they'd never seen before. Back in those days, people who listened to country didn't know that much about rock, and vice versa. It was like two totally different things. The only thing that I really caught a lot of flack from was my hair, which was too long for most of them. When I would go out and do my country shows, they would all want to give me a hair cut. It wasn't six months later until Waylon's hair was down past his shoulders."

Weller, who won a BMI award for his coauthorship of the Bob Luman hit "Lonely Women Make Good Lovers," stayed with the Raiders until 1973. By then the "new" was off him and his chart momentum was sharply diminished. As a solo act, he recorded nine more Top 40 country songs before he became a full-time songwriter. Creative and prolific, he has crafted material for Reba McIntire, Confederate

Railroad, Vern Gosdin, George Jones, and Pirates of the Mississippi, among many others.

"It's a whole new ballgame out there, writing and pitching songs and trying to get them cut. It's a very hard business but it's very satisfying. But when you do get a song on an album, it means something these days. The money is a whole lot better."

Speaking of money, when asked how he feels about "Dizzy" being used as a Nabisco Double Delight Cookie jingle, Weller chuckles appreciatively. "I love it. I hope they use it on every product that comes along."

The Desert Rose Band, Hillman third from left.

CHRIS HILLMAN

Chris Hillman helped change both the pop and country music landscapes with folk-rock groups the Byrds, Flying Burrito Brothers, and Stephen Stills's Manassas. However, Hillman considers his country success with the Desert Rose Band more an arrival than a comeback. After all, in one form or another he has been playing country music all his life. It just took him a little time to come up to the front of the band.

"I grew up in a very rural area of Southern California called San Diego County," recalls the affable and articulate singer-songwriter. "It was twenty-five miles north of the city of San Diego. I grew up with horses—not a ranch, nothing like that, but just a one-acre little ranch house—and we had a horse, a burro, and various animals.

"Spade Cooley was the West Coast equivalent of Bob Wills. It was western swing, and he had a weekly television show. I watched him and another live show going on at that time, Johnny Otis, which was rhythm and blues. So, I had the two shows that I used to watch as a ten-year-old kid.

"When my older sister went off to college in the fifties, she came back with folk music albums under her arm. Not the Kingston Trio, not the Brothers Four, but the Weavers, Leadbelly. I started listening to that and that got me started playing the guitar. But then I heard the New Lost City Ramblers, which was old-time string band music, and *that* really got me. I started playing mandolin after hearing Mike Seeger play mandolin in the New Lost City Ramblers.

"I heard bluegrass on an album for the first time in 1960. I said, 'Boy, that's it!' I just loved it. My dad could never understand why I liked it, but he was supportive, as was my mother. He used to kid me all the time, 'We've got a hillbilly—what happened?' He died in '61. But here was this music that struck a nerve with me, and it carried me right on through high school."

Hillman's first notable band association was with a contingent known as the Scottsville Squirrel Barkers. While playing a bluegrass festival in Los Angeles, he was spotted by the Golden State Boys, one of his favorite acts on the *Cal Worthington Country Time* television show. "When they had an opening for a mandolin player, they called me and I took the job. I worked for them for about six or seven months. Don Parmley, the banjo player, had come out from Kentucky; the Gosdin Brothers [Vern and Rex] were from Alabama and these guys were in their early thirties and I was eighteen years old, and they were *real guys* who played that kind of music. That was my window on authenticity, and I really got a great education from the vocal standpoint and on the instrumentation."

By 1964, Hillman had joined with Roger McGuinn, David Crosby, Gene Clark, and Michael Clark to form the Byrds, the eclectic band for whom the term folk-rock was coined. "Everybody who ended up in the Byrds was interesting. Here I am a bluegrass mandolin player who happened to love Muddy Waters and John Lee Hooker too. Roger McGuinn was quite an accomplished accompanist to Bobby Darin and all those people. He had a great sense of time, and he honed his whole craft while backing people, which takes a lot of focus and a lot of skill. Then Crosby came out of a folk singing group. Gene Clark was in the New Christy Minstrels. Michael Clark, the drummer, probably had more of a rock 'n' roll background than any of us. We all came out of a traditional acoustic folk and roots background. [T]hat background lent itself to the fine line between folk and country."

Combining rich folk harmonies, McGuinn's distinctive twelve-string electric guitar, and a pop production sensibility, the Byrds scored a major hit right out of the box with their classic rendition of Bob Dylan's "Tambourine Man." "Everybody was a bit hesitant at first when that song was brought to us, and it worked lyrically, and it still stands up," says Hillman. "It's a great set of lyrics. It's probably when Bob Dylan was peaking as a lyricist, and it's a good record. That's all you could ever hope for, that whatever you do at that moment can be looked at thirty or forty years down the road and say, 'I did it right.' We did that one right. We did 'Turn, Turn, Turn' right. We did '8 Miles High' right, and 'So You Wanna Be a Rock 'n' Roll Star.'"

As early as 1966, the Byrds made a conscious move to include more country music in their sound. They cut Porter Wagoner's "A Satisfied Mind" for their second album and moved further into the genre with their album *Younger than Yesterday*. Crosby's 1968 departure, among other group changes, led to the arrival of Gram Parsons and the birth of another new hybrid sound: country rock.

One of that genre's early milestones was the album *Sweetheart of the Rodeo*, recorded at a time when most young fans of mainstream music had a knee-jerk dislike for country. Consequently, it was one of the group's weakest sellers. Did the Byrds feel they were putting their fan base at risk by recording such a thoroughly country project?

"I think the music business at the time was such an open, creative arena that we didn't think about that," says Hillman. "You really were given free reign to do stuff, and it was such a period of experimentation in the studios. In all honesty, *Sweetheart* is not my favorite Byrds album. It's OK. It was a noble experiment. We did it, we enjoyed it, and over the years it seemed to have left quite a good legacy. It opened up a lot of people to this kind of music. I remember some of the guys in the Nitty Gritty Dirt Band say they had heard *Sweetheart of the Rodeo* and they immediately learned how to do this and that. So, that has to somehow outweigh the critical or monetary benefits."

Hillman and Parsons left the Byrds shortly after *Sweetheart of the Rodeo* to form the Flying Burrito Brothers, the group that laid the groundwork for the country rock movement. "Parsons and I knew exactly what we wanted to do and how we wanted to do it. We knew how to do this type of music; it was beyond *Sweetheart* as far as execution goes. We had some great material and so the first album [*The Gilded Palace of Sin*], although technically I would have recorded it differently in hindsight, had magical moments. It was straight country, some tongue-in-cheek, but really straight country music. I give Gram credit for bringing 'Do Right Woman' and 'Dark End of the Street,' two radically R&B songs, to a country format. That was brilliant, I thought."

Although the Flying Burrito Brothers LPs are somewhat profitable now, during their initial run they garnered little in the way of sales or airplay. "Well, the Byrds couldn't get played on the country stations, they weren't going to go with it. We got played on the FM rock stations. The Burritos were so country, but weren't recognized by the straight Nashville radio–styled stations, and we weren't getting on the rock stations. So we were caught in the middle there."

Eventually, Parsons drank and drugged himself out of the band and died from an overdose in 1973. Asked for his

The Byrds, circa the recording of *Sweetheart of the Rodeo*, rereleased in a deluxe edition in 2003.

favorite memories of the Flying Burrito Brothers, Hillman brings up the early days with his late partner. "Oh gosh. Gram was a focused, coherent guy for about one year. The beginning of the journey is always more interesting than the destination, if you follow me. When we put the band together, that was a lot of fun. Gram and I shared a house in Los Angeles, and we'd get up and write every day. We wrote some really good stuff. That particular six-month to a year period, when we were launching the band, was probably the best. That was one period, and after Gram left—where we had to actually get rid of him because—well, we lost him at that point."

He lacked perseverance?

"That's the one thing Gram Parson didn't have. He did have the talent. He had a God-given talent, but he didn't have the discipline for hard work or the focus. For one brief period he did, but after that it was gone. It was a talent wasted. At twenty-six years old he dies . . . bang.

"The Burritos were never good live when we started. We were pretty sloppy. But when Gram left around 1970, and Bernie Leadon and I built the band back up, it was a good live act. Even after Bernie left we had a good live band. We did the *Last of the Red Hot Burritos*, which was a very good record. So, there's some moments."

Seldom idle, Hillman plied his trade with Stephen Stills's band Manassas, briefly reunited with former Byrds bandmates McGuinn and Clark, and formed the Souther, Hillman, Furay Band. The latter produced the album *Desert Rose*, which became the inspiration for Hillman's most successful country music project, the Desert Rose Band.

"With the Desert Rose Band, I used to coin the phrase, 'the highly evolved Burritos.' It was more for me. It was me coming from the back of the lineup as a bass player and learning how to do this, learning how to sing, and learning to write songs properly, and then putting together the best players. We had a really good run, about seven or eight years. Longer than any other band I was in. It was a great band and yes, it did validate years and years of apprenticeship."

Formed in 1986, during the height of that decade's neo-traditional movement, Hillman's band released a string of solid country hits, including "One Step Forward," "He's Back and I'm Blue," "Summer Wind," and "I Still Believe in You."

Boasting a crowd-pleasing live show, the Desert Rose Band won the Academy of Country Music's "Touring Band of the Year" award in 1988, 1989, and 1990.

"Well, what was nice was that we had actually become really successful in country music and most of the people who accepted us had no idea who we were in a past life. They didn't know who the Byrds were and couldn't care less. They said, 'This is a great country band,' and it didn't matter where we came from or what."

In 1987 the Desert Rose Band received the ultimate vote of confidence: an invitation to appear on the *Grand Ole Opry*, where they were given some sage advice by none other than "Whisperin'" Bill Anderson. "We had a mild hit with 'Ashes of Love,' which was an old Johnnie & Jack song. It was our first Top 20 hit and Bill said before we went on, 'Chris, I think if you did "Ashes of Love," that'll open up these people right away.' He was absolutely dead on the money, and they loved it. We did 'Ashes of Love,' and the people recognized the song, saw these guys with rhinestone suits on, and it took 'em right back."

The country music soundscape changed radically during the early nineties. Line dancing and megaselling crossover acts such as Billy Ray Cyrus and Garth Brooks ruled the day, and the labels wanted more of the same. Bands with the accent on traditional country were phased out.

"They switched from what they had, which was successful in its own right, over to this thing where they wanted nine guys with hats," explains Hillman. "That's where it went. They got greedy, and it still hasn't been the same. We started to lose our radio accessibility around '91 or '92. We just weren't getting played. We retired the band in '94. It was the only band where we just walked away as friends, and I said to the guys, 'I've been on the road for thirty years and my family is suffering from me being gone.' In country music you work all the time, so I made that decision, but the other guys were pretty into it too. So we just stopped. I said, 'If we continue to go and not get radio play, we won't be playing the main grandstands anymore at the state fairs, we'll be doing a different kind of work. I can't take it anymore. I'm going to take a break.'

"It was a real wise choice, and I still work with Herb [Pedersen] and Bill Bryson, and I'm still very close with Jay Dee Maness and all the guys in the band. We're all proud of the band and I'll tell you, I'll hold it up against any of those bands out of Nashville right now. I thought we were very unique and put on a really good live show. But we walked off at the right time."

Pederson and Hillman continue to record when they can and have toured the world with a show that contains material from all the facets of their respective careers. In most cases, the instrumentation is spare. "It's amazing what you can get away with on mandolin and guitar," laughs Hillman. "We just played the *Opry* in September [2002], and we have a standing invitation to go back as guests, as Chris and Herb. That was pretty interesting. We did one song with the *Opry* band. We did an old Wilburn Brothers song, and then with just mandolin and guitar we did this old Monroe Brothers song 'The Old Crossroads,' and the people went nuts!

Because it was so pure. It was down to the pure essence of what this music is."

Hillman felt a special pride when a member of the *Opry* band congratulated him on his set and said, "Do you know how nice it is to play country music again?"

As relaxed as a morning cup of coffee.

DON WILLIAMS

Unless you're a 1960s folk fanatic, chances are you've never heard of the Pozo Seco Singers. Yet if they hadn't broken up, Don Williams might not have become one of the biggest stars of the seventies and eighties.

Discharged from the army during the height of the Beatles era, Williams and Lofton Kline played the hootenanny circuit as the Strangers Two. At one of their gigs they met Susan Taylor and they became the Pozo Seco (*dry well*) Singers, an acoustic pop/folk ensemble.

Williams explains their sound: "All of us really appreciated Peter, Paul, and Mary, and Joan Baez, [Judy] Collins, and all those people. We didn't really try and copy anyone." Sharing lead vocals with Taylor, Williams was the titular head of the group. "They elected me to that position," the singer chuckles, "which meant that I had to take care of all the headaches, you know?"

Folk was one of the great musical undercurrents of the 1960s, and the group's Edmark recordings were picked up by Columbia. A few of their better efforts ("Time," "I Can Make It with You," "Look What You've Done") flirted with the pop Top 40 before the trio's commercial prospects died on the vine. They officially disbanded in 1971.

However, songwriter Bob McDill helped provide Williams with a star-making opportunity at Jack Clement's JMI label in Nashville, under producer Allen Reynolds. "My first encounter with Allen Reynolds and Bob McDill was the last single that the Pozos put out," laughs Williams today. "Bob McDill was the writer of it. When I came back [to Nashville] and we started working together, I told him he owed me a lot because the last single the Pozos had was a flop." Williams merely intended to be a staff writer for the publishing company, but his rapport with Reynolds was strong: "It got to the point that Allen didn't want to go into the studio on any of the projects he was doing unless I could come in and work with him."

Clement remembers how a particular demo session led to Williams's transformation into a solo recording star. "Allen Reynolds had hired him and I had a studio at that time, and I had booked every Thursday with my band. Then we'd go in there and do something. Well, this one Thursday, Reynolds wanted to cut a bunch of demos with Don Williams. . . . They went in there and in one day they cut six really good sides, including 'We Should Be Together,' which was actually his second release. We got six sides in that one day, two sessions."

Despite the rush of productivity, Williams didn't get his hopes up. "We thought, 'We'll just go in, get the musicians together that would understand my treatment the best. Worst-case scenario, we'll come out with, hopefully, some really good demos that'll help get these songs cut.' That first day constituted about 95 percent of the first album. It was like it was supposed to happen, I guess."

That one session put a career in motion that, between 1973 and 1991, produced an astounding forty-five Top 10 records for MCA, Capitol, and RCA—seventeen of which hit #1.

Williams says he can't remember a time when he didn't listen to a song and try to figure out what the artist was trying to say. Though he never attempted to emulate anyone in particular, the Floydada, Texas, native cites Brook Benton, Perry Como, Johnny Cash, Johnny Horton, and "a bit of Elvis" as his earliest musical influences. As a result, his best records were as popular with crossover listeners as country audiences, though he is at a loss to describe his sound and appeal.

"I guess the vision that I had for myself was that I really wanted to appeal more to the country fans, but I think a good bit of what I've done is anything but traditional country. With every album that I've made, I've hoped I haven't made such a departure that people listening to it would think, 'Well, what'd he do that for?' When I think of people like Hank Sr., I don't feel like I'm anywhere close to that. But, at the same time, when I first started, I had people come up to me and say, 'Man, you're the most country thing that's come down the pike since Hank Sr.' I just do what I do and I try to be as honest about it as I know how to be."

When Williams first moved to Dot/MCA, Reynolds and Garth Fundis helped him produce his distinctive laid-back sound. But eventually the artist began producing many of his own biggest hits, which put a strain on his friendship with Reynolds. "I had some hard feelings between Reynolds and myself for several years, but that's all history. Everything's cool with us," assures Williams. "We worked through all that."

Not that Reynolds was hurting for people to work with. His creative efforts helped establish the careers of Crystal Gayle and Garth Brooks, among others. Reynolds told *Encyclopedia of Record Producers* contributor Melinda Newman that working with Williams taught him a lot. "One of the most powerful things I learned [from Don] was that the microphone is like an ear placed that close to the singer's mouth, that you didn't have to project or 'let them have it in the balcony,' that you could convey powerful emotion and achieve subtle nuance without raising your voice or trying too hard. Working with Don also furthered my confidence in the power of songs to define careers."

Indeed, great songs and songwriters have defined Williams's career. Although capable of writing his own hits (notably "Love Me over Again"), it was his association with such Nashville tunesmiths as Waylon Holyfield ("You're My Best Friend," "Some Broken Hearts Never Mend") and McDill ("Turn out the Light and Love Me Tonight," "Say It Again," "It Must Be Love," "If Hollywood Don't Need You") that shaped his image as a sensitive country troubadour. He also saw the promise in Danny Flowers's composition "Tulsa Time" (later a massive pop hit for Eric Clapton), and employed his keen writer's instinct to redraft "I Believe in You" into his most enduring hit.

"Roger Cook and Sam Hogin had written it, but didn't have it completely finished and gave Garth Fundis what they had at the time. I listened to it, and I told Garth instantly, 'Man, tell them to get on that and finish it up!' But Roger had some words in it that were a bit rock 'n' rollish that I didn't feel would be that palatable to my fans. So, I changed some of the words so it would fit me better." A perennial favorite that works as both a romantic pledge and philosophical statement, it's the one song he cannot leave off his live set list.

At the peak of his early success, Williams appeared in two Burt Reynolds films, *W. W. and the Dixie Dance Kings* and *Smokey & the Bandit II*. While working on the former, Reynolds gave the singer the hat that would become his trademark. The original item was stolen, returned, and "retired" in 1985, but Stetson made him an exact duplicate that he wears faithfully to this day.

Yet, despite an impressive run of hits that had turned him into a major concert draw, Williams found that it was still possible to occasionally suffer at the hands of a skinflint promoter. "I drove all the way out to New Mexico," he laughs ruefully. "I was supposed to do a week's worth of work at this place and I got there, and the guy had not advertised at all. It was just a funky little joint—it was just horrible and the first night we had three or four people there. I told him, 'Unless we have more people here tomorrow night, we're going to go on back to the house.' 'Oh, you can't do that!' 'Well, then you have more people than this tomorrow night.' He didn't, so we just packed it up and came back to the house. That was horrible. I guess he just thought if he paid for me to come out there, he didn't have to say anything, that the word would just spread or something. That was my worst."

During the early 1990s, Williams's records just weren't zooming up the charts as they had before. That's when the man they call the "gentle giant" decided to take a break. "I pretty much dismissed my band and my manager, my road manager, and just kind of got away from all of it for about two years. There were a lot of things behind that, one of which was my back was really giving me a hard time at that point. But it didn't have anything to do with radio."

In the later stages of his career, Williams's vocal resonance is as pure and expressive as ever, and he records and writes only when he feels like it. Still, he plays between seventy and eighty concerts a year and finds it deeply gratifying when audiences the world over sing along to such country classics as "Amanda," "You're My Best Friend," "Lord, I Hope This Day Is Good," and "Till the Rivers All Run Dry." "I still don't believe that I can go out and do the shows that I do and wherever I go, I still have the crowds that I do," he states with shy amazement. This sustained popularity triggered the 2001 Collector's Choice reissue of his early material with the Pozo Seco Singers.

Asked if the Pozos would have stayed together had their chart success been greater, the self-effacing star, who sometimes misses singing group harmony, answers in the affirmative. "I think it's entirely possible—if everybody held everything together."

Imagine what country fans would have missed if they had.

Jerry Lee and his "Keith Richards," Kenny Lovelace, in 1969.

LINDA GAIL LEWIS AND KENNY LOVELACE
on Jerry Lee Lewis

Of all the performers who went from rock into country, Jerry Lee Lewis got the most attention. Opinions varied. Teddy boys and aging greasers felt he betrayed the sacred cause of true rock 'n' roll, which, at that point in the late 1960s, was under siege by psychedelia, art-rock, and bubblegum music. But, Lewis had always exhibited a special rapport with country audiences, even back in the fifties, when his fiery rock hits "Whole Lotta

Shakin' Goin' On," "Great Balls of Fire," and "Breathless" were heating up the airwaves.

Lewis's sister Linda Gail, who sang on his show for thirteen years, explains. "Basically what happened with Jerry was, of course you know he had the rock 'n' roll hits which were also country hits. 'Whole Lotta Shakin' Goin' On' was a #1 country record and so was 'Great Balls of Fire' and so was the flip side, [Hank Williams's] 'You Win Again.' He always did some country music, but it was more traditional country."

The Killer's fall from grace is well documented. His short string of hit records and piano-kicking stage performances made him one of the hottest acts in popular music in 1957, and when Elvis was inducted into the army, it seemed Lewis was poised to be crowned the new King of Rock 'n' Roll. Then in 1958, he married his thirteen-year-old cousin Myra Gale Brown before the divorce from his second wife was official. With a mix of backwoods naivete and rock-star arrogance, Lewis took his new bride on what should have been a triumphant tour of England. The British press discovered the union and the public furor it provoked forced the tour to an abrupt end. The rocker and crew were sent packing.

Back in the United States, rock 'n' roll was under fire for allegedly corrupting our nation's youth, and Lewis's marriage to the barely teenage Myra Gale made him the perfect whipping boy for the self-righteous. Radio stations were discouraged from playing his records and *American Bandstand* host Dick Clark, in an admitted act of cowardice, dropped Lewis from his *Caravan of Stars* tour. As a result, Lewis's "High

School Confidential," possibly the best teen rocker of the era, stalled out at #21 on the charts. Sun Records stupidly tried to laugh the situation away with the comedy paste-up single "The Return of Jerry Lee," and Lewis's version of Charlie Rich's "Break Up" barely limped into the national Top 60.

Rebellious to the core, Lewis issued, through Sun, a record that expressed his defiant sentiments: a rock version of Moon Mullican's "I'll Sail My Ship Alone." That too sank, as did two of the finest records of his career, "Lovin' Up a Storm" and "Let's Talk About Us." At his lowest point, sloppy management and the artist's own recalcitrant attitude got him kicked out of the musician's union, so he couldn't even play piano at his own sessions.

Although he cut a little country at almost all of his marathon sessions, if Lewis had any intention of trying to regain his popularity by appealing to country audiences then, he didn't let on. In fact, during the recording of the country-pop number "It Hurt Me So" (documented on Bear Family's boxed set *Classic Jerry Lee Lewis: 1963–1976*), he can be heard pleading, "I want to cut one more rock 'n' *roll* song before we go."

Lewis almost got back on track in 1961 with a rhythmically potent reworking of Ray Charles's "What'd I Say." The record, which hit the Top 30 on the pop, country, and R&B charts, proved impossible to follow up. Many disc jockeys flipped his next single, "It Won't Happen With Me," over and played his version of Hank Williams's "Cold Cold

Heart," but neither Lewis nor Sun took the hint, and his subsequent rock records floundered during the era of the Twist.

Linda Gail Lewis was with her brother as he tried to rebuild his career one spectacular, piano-stool-kicking show at a time. "After the controversy over Myra, he wasn't on the radio anymore. So he went from making $10,000 a night to like $200 a night. He had a pretty tough time, but he had to get out there and just keep working until he built his career up again. He did such great shows and people remembered all of his big hits from the fifties. So we really did become very successful just from playing."

In late 1963, Lewis began recording for Smash Records, a division of Mercury. The first release from his new label, a revival of another Ray Charles tune, "Hit the Road, Jack," flopped. But, once again, disc jockeys flipped the record and the ballad "Pen and Paper" reached the country Top 40. Immediately, Lewis's manager and boyhood friend Cecil Harrelson wanted Smash boss Shelby Singleton to pursue the country audience. As Harrelson tells it in the documentary *I Am What I Am*, he was rebuffed. "Shelby told me, 'Aw, I don't want no 40–50,000 seller for a #1 record!' I said, 'But Shelby, all I want is the airplay.'"

Lewis recorded prolifically for Smash. His live performance of Buck Owens's "Together Again," included on one of his best-ever albums, *The Greatest Live Show on Earth*, brought cheers from the predominantly rock crowd. Out of desperation, Smash hedged their bets and had Lewis record an album of pop-coated cover songs titled *Country Songs for City Folks*. Welsh belter Tom Jones took "Green Green Grass of Home" off it and turned it into a major pop hit, but few others were buying.

Linda Gail Lewis remembers the frustration of that era. "Jerry Kennedy and Shelby Singleton had cut a lot of albums on my brother, and they just didn't make it. I don't know what you really call those kinds of albums, what kinds of music they were. I loved the stuff myself, because I'm a huge Jerry Lee fan. I loved 'City Lights' and all that stuff he did on *Country Songs for City Folks*. But it wasn't a hit."

According to Linda Gail, one man was responsible for changing Lewis's career fortunes. "Eddie Kilroy had a position at Mercury Records . . . and they were getting ready to drop Jerry Lee's contract because nothing was happening. Years go on by, no hits. Selling very few records. So Eddie Kilroy sold them on the idea of Jerry doing more of a modern country type song in Nashville with a more contemporary type sound. Well, they said, 'Jerry Lee will never do it. He's temperamental,' and this and that. Eddie Kilroy said, 'Well, I'll ask him.'

"So, Eddie Kilroy came to see us while we were on the road and asked my brother, 'Jerry, would you come in and cut a more contemporary type of country song? Maybe we can get it on the charts.'

"Jerry said, 'Well sure, I'll do it.' Jerry liked Eddie. He's a really nice guy and we'd known him for a really long time. So we went in and Jerry did 'Another Place, Another Time,' a Jerry Chesnut song. It was a big hit, so we did a whole album, and we did a duet on 'We Live in Two Different Worlds.' It also had an Ernest Tubb song, 'Walking the Floor Over You,' and that great Glenn Sutton song 'What Made Milwaukee Famous.' That was a big hit, but it was kind of sad what Jerry Kennedy did to Eddie Kilroy. He just fired him because he had so much power at Mercury Records. He had taken Shelby Singleton's place and Eddie's success was kind of embarrassing to him, so he just fired him. What's worse is that he took all the credit, didn't give Eddie Kilroy any credit for anything, and he started producing Jerry after that."

Kenny Lovelace, Lewis's guitarist and fiddle player since 1967, played on that first full country session and had a good feeling about "Another Place, Another Time." "There was something about it that you just knew it was a hit record. It just had that feeling and Jerry phrased the song so good, man, and he sings country so good. 'To Make Love Sweeter for You,' 'What Made Milwaukee Famous,' 'She Still Comes Around to Love What's Left of Me'—man, he just had hit after hit after that first song."

Producer Kennedy had the magic touch with Lewis. He chose songs, such as "Once More With Feeling" and "Touching Home," that fit the singer's persona as well as his unique interpretive gifts. Subsequently, after a decade of struggle, Jerry Lee Lewis was once again a hot commodity.

Yet according to Linda Gail, the Killer's newfound success did not sit especially well with some of Nashville's old guard. "We were accepted by most of them, because most of them are great people, but. . . . Once Connie Smith actually apologized for being on the same show with us. Kitty Wells and Mother Maybelle Carter were whispering about us as we walked by them backstage.

"Well," she admits, "we were pretty far out. Me with a very tight dress and Jerry had removed his jacket and then his shirt. It was a wild rockin' show that night, and they didn't approve. Ernest Tubb didn't like the way Jerry did his song 'Walkin' the Floor.' He said he appreciated him doing it, but did he have to rock it the way he did?"

Lovelace recalls that some overseas fans had issues with his boss's new emphasis on country music. "We used to work places like Germany, and at first they didn't want to hear the country. They said, 'We want rock 'n' roll!' Of course, Jerry would do his country anyway. Later they loved the country, but there was that period where he had to break the ice. Jerry would do the rock 'n' roll but during that show he'd sing a country song. Then it just grew and grew and grew and they loved his country after that."

Lewis's career benefited from both his fresh blast of country hits and the growing rock 'n' roll revival of the late sixties/early seventies. The story of how he'd been victimized by a hypocritical press made him seem sympathetic, and he received the most glowing coverage of his life. Even *Rolling Stone*, largely counterculture-oriented at the time, covered him warmly, winking at his drug use and admired his rebellious redneck nature.

Like many other country performers, Lewis made sure his family reaped the rewards from his great success, as Linda Gail proudly attests. "Jerry shared everything he had with us. He'd call my mama up and say, 'Mama, I want you and Daddy and Frankie Jean and Linda Gail to have everything that I have.' And we did! He had a Cadillac—we had a

Cadillac. He had a beautiful home—we had a beautiful home. I don't think anybody has ever been that generous to his family. If they have, I don't know who they are. 'I want my family to have everything that I have.' I don't know how many people would say that. He meant it too."

After hitting #1 with a Grammy-nominated version of the Big Bopper's "Chantilly Lace," Lewis's comeback had reached its zenith. He returned to the rock 'n' roll charts in 1973 with the all-star double LP *London Sessions* and worked out a four-album-a-year deal with Mercury. His stated intention was to cut as much rock as country.

That's when things started to crumble.

Divorce, family deaths, lack of strong management, and self-destructive behavior beyond quantification nearly killed all the fine work Lewis had done. Touring for months without end began to burn out his voice. Once a studio workhorse, Mercury now had trouble getting him in to record.

Stan Kesler, a former Sun Records associate, recalls how he landed producing chores for two of Lewis's Mercury albums *Sometimes a Memory* and *I-40 Country*. "Well, Jerry Kennedy was just tired of fooling with him. Those sessions with Jerry Lee are hard. He's just kind of hard to work with and Kennedy had just reached his rope's end. He just couldn't cut it anymore and Jerry Lee was drinking a lot, doing things, and wasn't getting any rest. He was hard to record. It took me a long time to get it on tape, get his voice on there and get him right. I went to Atlanta where he was playing. Charlie Fach called me and wanted me to go down there. He said, 'Go down there and see if you can get him in the studio after the gig,' which I knew was a bad idea to start with. But I went down there and about four o'clock in the morning, he finally quit playing at the club and came over to the studio, and he just couldn't do anything. His voice was just so weak and hoarse.

"[We] went back to Nashville, had him back in up there, and he still didn't do it. Finally I said, 'Well, if we're going to do this, we might as well do it at home.' He came to Memphis and we got him to come in down to Sam Phillips's studio and finally got him to overdub his vocal to where it was satisfactory."

When asked if he was brought in because Mercury thought the singer would respond better to an old friend, Kesler responds, "It might have been. I was never in on Jerry Kennedy's sessions. But he really didn't respond to anybody. He did what he wanted to do. When something wasn't right to him, he'd just buck you, he wouldn't do it. He is a remarkable talent though."

Occasionally Lewis would get his act together and validate his fans' faith in his God-given talent. His 1974 *Southern Roots* album is inspired rock 'n' soul that has gotten better with age, and his 1977 hit "Middle Aged Crazy" is a penetrating, angst-filled anthem. The switch to Elektra records in 1979 gave his country career its final chart boost. Yet before he could build on the momentum of such hits as "Over the Rainbow" and "Thirty-Nine and Holding," his stomach lining tore open and he nearly died. As he recuperated, his label dropped him. (In his autobiography, producer/label exec Jimmy Bowen openly brags about dumping Lewis from two labels he was associated with.)

And then his fifth wife died of an accidental methadone overdose, and, during a period when most men would have been allowed to grieve, Lewis was forced to defend himself against the accusations of foul play proffered by Geraldo Rivera and *Rolling Stone*. Cleared of any wrongdoing, the tragedy still permanently derailed his recording career and scarred him in the public mind.

He fled to Ireland in the 1990s, looking to take advantage of that country's artist tax exemption program, after the IRS asked him to pony up the millions of dollars in back taxes and penalties he owed. Lewis returned to the United States after they came to an agreement that he could pay the exact amount due with only minor interest. In the meantime, the one bright spot in a tempestuous sixth marriage was the arrival of his only surviving son, Jerry Lee Lewis III.

Yet, when allowed to flourish, Lewis's prodigious talent prevailed. His work on the soundtrack from the semiautobiographical movie *Great Balls of Fire* was the best thing about that poorly acted flop. His eponymous album for Sire in 1995 was a brilliantly distilled cornucopia of roots and rock that drew enthusiastic reviews from even baby boom–hating *Entertainment Weekly* magazine. By then, thanks in part to his influence, country radio had started to allow juicy hunks of southern-fried rock and boogie onto their airwaves, but, alas, Lewis had committed the unpardonable sin of being over fifty years old.

As of this writing, Lewis is going through another divorce, his sixth, and is managed by Phoebe, his daughter with Myra Gale, whom he calls "my heart." Suffering a myriad of health problems ranging from bad teeth to painful circulatory problems in his legs, he continues to book live gigs and to make recording plans when perhaps he should stay home.

Despite Lewis's trials and travails, Lovelace continues to stick by him. "It's really been a joy being with Jerry; we're like brothers, really. We have a good rapport with each other and I love Jerry. He's been good to me and he's got a great heart."

Linda Gail, who makes her home in both Tennessee and Wales and plays Jerry's songs to enthusiastic international crowds, thinks she understands the forces that drive her brother and the price he has paid. "Playing music always meant more to him than anything else in the whole world. I think his private life suffered because of it.

"I remember when they came out with those little Casio keyboard things. He had one of those in the limousine and he'd be playing that. When we would get to the Holiday Inn where we were staying, he always had a suite with the piano in it, and he'd play and sing a while before he got to the gig. Then, he'd go to the gig and do a real long show, and then after the gig he'd go back to his suite and play the piano for anybody who wanted to listen.

"I mean, there was just nothing left for anybody else. You give everything to the public, you give everything to your music, and you don't have anything left for anybody else. It's a hard way to go off and it's a hard life. If he hadn't had a lifestyle that he had by just strictly focusing on the music, would we have ever had a performance like 'She Even Woke Me Up to Say Good-bye'? There's so many incredible Jerry Lee Lewis performances on record and he did it for so long without any regard for his private life. He ended up not ever really being happy with that part of his life. It's a shame. But I guess if you don't have that time to give to a relationship, you just can't have one."

4

SPIRITUALITY

In 2003, Randy Travis scored a hit country single off a collection of sacred songs and brought country gospel back into the spotlight. Viewed as something unusual, Travis's rebound smash elicited a penitent admission. "I went to church for a very short time as a kid, but, as they say in the South, it didn't take," Travis told Peter Cooper of the Tennessean. "My dad wasn't a person who went to church in those days. He was a wild man. And you can't party, drink, get in fights in front of your kids and tell them not to do it. That don't work. My mom and dad had six kids, and four of the six went the same road: drugs, alcohol, running completely wild. I had no knowledge about the word of God to draw on. Good thing there is forgiveness, 'cause I had a police record longer than I am tall. By man's law, I have no right to be walking upright and feeling halfway decent."

However, even before gospel music became a mini-industry complete with its own awards show and controversies, the sacred song was extremely important to country music. Many performers—Tammy Wynette, Connie Smith, Gene Watson, and Travis Tritt to name but a few—discovered their chops singing in church. Others considered themselves honor-bound to use their secular appeal to help spread the Lord's word and have included gospel numbers and testimony during concerts.

During country's golden age, recording a sacred album was considered the natural right of an established country star. If a label tried to deny an artist's commercial expression of faith, it was deemed an unforgivable snub. Example? Johnny Cash. When Sam Phillips nixed a proposed gospel release because his independent company couldn't afford to absorb the genre's notoriously low sales, the Man in Black bolted the legendary Sun label for Columbia.

Sometimes an artist's personal life worked against him when it came time to record songs of praise. At the peak of his renaissance as a country singer, Jerry Lee Lewis went through a painful divorce from his wife Myra Gale, and decided to win her back by cleaning up his act. Returning to the Assembly of God church he was raised in with cousin Jimmy Lee Swaggert, he publicly renounced liquor, loose women, and venues that trafficked in both. Lewis's spiritual reaffirmation reinvigorated his love of gospel music, an obsession he shared with longtime friend and rival Elvis Presley. Subsequently, the Killer recorded a collection of sacred songs titled In Loving Memories, which sold poorly.

Years later, Lewis talked about the album during a 1983 session captured on the European CD That Breathless Cat. After wondering why he'd never recorded his own Christmas album—another rite granted to most country stars—Lewis claimed his gospel album was "doing great and they just chucked it clean off the market!"

The explanation: "Mercury records said, 'It'll ruin your image.'"

Talking to his wife at the time, Kerrie, Lewis brought up another wrinkle in the story. "Jimmy Lee Swaggert tried to buy it, you know. Offered 'em $250,000 for the masters. You know what they told him? They said, 'We wouldn't take two hundred and fifty million for it!' [Laughs.] And they won't even release it."

Mercury sat on most of Lewis's gospel recording sessions— some of the best straight country singing he ever did, including one particularly riveting outing cut during a church service. (All of Lewis's Mercury work has been released by the German Bear Family label in gigantic boxed sets.) "All I want to do is get in a good revival somewhere and talk about Jesus," the piano pumpin' star can be heard to say.

It never happened.

Myra Gale never truly believed in her husband's conversion and went ahead with the divorce. On top of that, touring as a secular act proved too lucrative to resist. As a result, Lewis's days as a born-again Christian, however sincere, were very brief.

Other artists had a tougher battle to fight: personal perception. Some country stars feel like every time they sing a country song they're sinning, and others have been chastised because they left the gospel field to make secular music. Here they tell a few of their stories.

"Christians can have fun, too."

WANDA JACKSON

Roy Clark, in his 1994 autobiography *My Life—In Spite of Myself*, paid tribute to the woman who gave him his shot at the big time, proclaiming, "Wanda Jackson was more than just a great singer, she was an inspiration to a whole generation of singers. Brenda Lee and

Tanya Tucker are just two among the many whose style has been influenced by her."

While that's certainly true, Jackson was also one kick-ass rock 'n' roller whose early style shone a guiding light for modern-day rockabillies Marti Brom and Rosie Flores, and predated the hard-edged histrionics of Joan Jett. Whether growling odes to frustrated sensuality such as "Mean Mean Man" and "Hot Dog! That Made Him Mad," hiccuping lusty braggadocio such as "Fujiyama Mama," or joyously whooping through "Let's Have a Party," Jackson imbued every up-tempo song she sang with searing, hot-tempered sexuality. Boasting a unique, rasping vocal style that embraced humor, pathos, and rebellion, Jackson and producer Ken Nelson forged the last great body of work to emerge from the original rockabilly era.

Much of her country work also asserted the fiery, sometimes violent persona heard on her rockabilly sides. Long before the Dixie Chicks created a sensation with "Good-bye Earl," such Jackson hits as "The Box That It Came In" and "Big Iron Skillet" threatened death and/or brutal assault upon a lying, cheating spouse. A third number, "This Gun Don't Care Who It Shoots," did not chart. "Nobody played that one," the singer laughs today. "Those were different times and we didn't take the songs as seriously, I guess." However, the raven-tressed Oklahoma native's most consistent success came while trilling the sweet and pure ballads "Right or Wrong" and "In the Middle of a Heartache."

Jackson, a two-time Grammy nominee, was a consistent chart presence until she and her husband/manager Wendell Goodman found religion. This is her testimony.

"Well, we don't always know what leads us to make that decision about seeking salvation. But Wendell and I—this happened in 1971—by then we had our two kids and we were still traveling. We were gone half the time from 'em and they were being reared by their grandmas, and of course we always had a governess live in. They were being well taken care of, but we knew we were missing out on a lot and our marriage wasn't in real great shape because of our lifestyle.

"Let's face it, the drinking, the late hours, the partying, always on the go. We could do whatever we wanted in a town and leave the next day. We didn't have to face the consequences. We weren't all that wild, but our marriage was in trouble, and we didn't know what to do about it. We knew we were in love still. We didn't want a divorce. That was never talked about—murder a couple of times, maybe—but never divorce.

"Anyway, I was a member of this church already and my mother kept my children in church because she knew it was important. Well, the kids just begged us to please join them and their grandma at church one Sunday when we were home. Just to get 'em off our backs we said, 'OK.' We got up late and started rushing around, didn't care anymore about going to church anymore that day than any other time, but we promised the kids. We weren't bad people. If we promised something, we kept our promise. So we went.

"It was during that service that God spoke to my heart, and of course you can only speak for yourself as to what's happening in your own heart. But it seemed like God was just saying to me, 'Walk with me, Wanda. Walk with me.' So when they gave the invitation, as they do in our churches, to make a public profession that you're giving your life to Christ, I turned to Wendell back in the pew and said, 'Honey, there's just something I've got to do.' I expected him to just to move out and let me by, but he said, 'Well, me too.' His feeling was that God was dealing with his heart at the same time. So, we both gave our hearts and lives to Jesus Christ at the same moment, which was the greatest thing that ever happened.

"From that moment on, everything was different. There's something about giving your life to Christ and giving him the control, taking your hands off the wheel and letting him do it, even though you don't understand what you've just done. Something definite has happened and all of your priorities in life just flip-flop and all of a sudden everything is just orderly. From that day on, Wendell was never jealous anymore and everything was different. So, certainly our souls were saved in that moment, but also our marriage and our relationship. That's not the reason we did it, we wanted to get right with God. But once we both did that, then he was the boss of our life. No longer was it 'Is Wanda the boss or is Wendell the boss?' all the while banging heads and fighting and fussin'. It was now 'What does Christ want us to do?' People try to make salvation hard and it isn't. It's just about relinquishing the control."

Brimming with the zeal of conversion, Jackson wanted her work to reflect her spiritual changes. However, she had no intention of quitting her secular music career. "That's been a myth some people believe. Of course I was more excited about telling the world about what had happened to me, and the only way I could do that was through music. I wanted to start recording gospel. My first gospel [album] was with Capitol and that was fine. Then I went in six months later and said, 'I'd like to do another gospel album because I'm doing a lot of gospel concerts. The word's getting around that I've become a Christian, and I'm singing at churches and revivals and I need another album out there for people to buy.' Well, Capitol wasn't interested. Ken Nelson finally talked to Wendell and me. He said, 'Look, I understand where your heart is, and I think it's wonderful. But Capitol is not that kind of a company. You were signed as a country artist.' Then he said, 'I think you should pursue a recording company that would allow you to do all the gospel that you need to do.' So, he got me my release from Capitol, which was almost unheard of back then."

Jackson signed with the Christian label Word, with the understanding that she'd use their distribution setup to help sell her country music too. It seemed an ideal situation.

"Well, as soon as we got that all worked out, they sold the company to Dot Records. At that time they were the biggest conglomerate, and I just got lost in the shuffle. They knew nothing about my agreement with Word. They didn't honor it if they did. I could've rightfully sued them. Even our pastor said, 'I think you should.' Because my career was just going down the toilet. There was nothing out there for anybody to buy or radio stations to play.

"Eventually we decided that we were Christians, and they had been a Christian company, and the Bible tells us that brothers shouldn't sue brothers. So, we didn't, but we got compensation from them. Then, from that point on, I just kind of bounced around and did my own recordings as so many of us have had to do."

Recording on her own, Jackson still faced some obstacles. While the gospel community in general was excited that the performer had given up recording for a secular label to sing songs of praise, they never treated her as one of their own. "None of the Christian stations would play my records. I could draw huge crowds in the church venues—and I'm not on a pity potty here—it's just a matter of fact that I was never nominated for anything in their circles. It was as if I was a stepchild, and it kind of hurt me at the time, but I remembered, 'Hey, that's not the reason I'm doing this. I'm doing this to get the gospel message out.'"

Jackson hosted her own religious program on TBN, but around 1985 a new generation of fans wanted to know about Elvis, rock 'n' roll, and that scary, sexy growling voice on those old Capitol records.

"A recording company in Sweden asked me to come over there and do rockabilly music with the new sound they have now. We prayed about it, and it seemed like God was saying, 'This is the way I want to use you now.' I could reach a hundred thousand times more people by appearing in those venues and giving my testimony, which I still do on every show. I don't bore people, and I don't preach. I just tell 'em the good news about what happened to me and sing a gospel song. So that's the way God is using my husband and me at the moment. Y'see, Christians can have fun, too."

Freddie Hart contemplating another world.

FREDDIE HART

Freddie Hart says he got his first practical lesson in faith as a fifteen-year-old marine in World War II. "I guess you learn a whole lot about God when you're in a war. You know, when trouble comes, that's when people pray most of all. When you get scared, all you can look up to is God. If you don't believe, then you're in bad shape, my friend."

Hart, who turned to making gospel music in semiretirement, doesn't miss much about his days as a major recording act. "Number one on my hit parade is Jesus Christ. I wasn't always a Christian, but I am now. I have contentment. You don't get that feeling from fame or fortune. You always get it from Him." Living in Burbank, California, the composer of

"Trip to Heaven" ("I just took a trip to heaven, I didn't even have to die") has a special way of dealing with atheists. "I've gotten a hold of some people who didn't believe. I'd get them in a car and go about a hundred miles an hour. Then, when I came close to something or other, they'd cry out, 'Oh God!'

"I'd say, 'What did you say?'

"When people are scared, the first thing they do is cry out for God. It's an instinct."

Oak Ridge Boys, Sterban second from right.

RICHARD STERBAN
of the Oak Ridge Boys

Now that gospel and religious music are considered just another crass branch of showbiz, it's hard to believe that the Oak Ridge Boys put their livelihood at risk when they first began performing secular music. But, as bass singer Richard Sterban recalls, it's true. "When some of the gospel music promoters saw that we were actually playing in Las Vegas, all of a sudden they felt we were too hot to touch, so to speak. They started dropping us like hotcakes. For a while there, we were kind of like in limbo. Our gospel dates had fallen off, and we had not established ourselves with many hit records in country music. In fact, there have been times when we were the subjects of preachers' sermons, talking about the Oak Ridge Boys becoming 'worldly.'"

So why the uproar? Well, long before they had the top-selling country hits with "Elvira," "Bobby Sue," and "American Made," the Oak Ridge Boys were one of the guiding lights of the southern gospel movement.

Named after a Tennessee nuclear facility where they regularly entertained, the Oak Ridge Quartet first formed in 1945, becoming the Oak Ridge Boys in 1961. Along with the Statesmen Quartet, the Oak Ridge Boys, in various incarnations, were the most popular act in country gospel. So it caused shockwaves throughout the gospel industry when the group—comprised of Joe Bonsall, Duane Allen, William Lee Golden, and Richard Sterban—began incorporating flashy clothes into their shows.

"Back when we were still singing gospel music," explains Sterban, "we stopped wearing suits and ties and tried to dress more in the current fashion. We allowed our hair to grow down over our ears a little bit. We did get some negative comments about that and there was a certain perception amongst some of those real staunch gospel music followers that you had to fit a certain mold. You had to have a certain look about you and a certain attitude or you were not a 'Christian,' so to speak, or you were not a gospel singer."

The situation was exacerbated when the Oak Ridge Boys began recording both sacred and secular material for Columbia, a groundbreaking, genre-blurring move. Before them, the Statler Brothers had changed their group name (from the Kingsmen) in deference to their gospel following when they went mainstream. By contrast, many in the gospel community were scandalized when the Oaks didn't also create a separate identity for their secular sounds.

With all the negative reaction from peers and bookers, why didn't the group just meekly return to the fold? "At the time, singing just gospel music, we felt that we were being marginalized, and we wanted to expand our horizons and take our music everywhere," Sterban discloses. "So we started to work a few secular dates. In fact, our good friend Johnny Cash, he understood what we were trying to do, and he actually put us on some of his dates. . . . People like Johnny Cash really helped us survive during that time, and we owe him a debt of gratitude. . . . "

Another star who aided the group during its transition was Kenny Rogers, who not only gave them valuable exposure on tour but also offered helpful advice for their secular recordings. "One of the things that Kenny Rogers stressed to us was, 'The most important thing you can have is a good song. Good songs are so important to success in the music business. There's nothing like that three minutes of magic on the radio. That will do more for your career than anything else that you can possibly do.' He constantly preached that to us, and I think we learned that from him."

The quartet found the right song after manager Jim Halsey placed them with ABC-Dot Records. "We acquired Ron Chancy as our producer, and he found a song called 'Y'all Come Back Saloon' for us, and it became our first #1 country record. That started us on our way toward establishing ourselves in country music, and then a lot of things changed. Once we achieved some success in country music, we found out that the fans we had all along in gospel music were still standing by us and supporting us. They supported us throughout our country music career as well. I think it was mainly the gospel industry that had turned its back for a while. It was never really the fans. They stayed with us."

Wildly successful, the main thrust of the Oak's career became country music, but they didn't completely forsake spirituals, nor did they only preach to the converted. "We always made it a point, wherever we were, even at the height of our career in country music when we were doing the stadiums, coliseums, and even while headlining the biggest places in Las Vegas, to include at least one gospel song during the course of the show.

"We feel like we have been blessed with our success in secular music, which allows us to do some good in places where it would not normally be done. I don't know that you could actually call it a ministry, but in some ways it really is. Also, there's really no guilt feelings on the parts of any of us about playing, say, a gambling casino, or a place where they do serve alcohol, because I think we're taking the message where it really does need to be taken."

In 2001, the Oak Ridge Boys were inducted into the Gospel Music Hall of Fame and released their first new collection of sacred material since 1976. If gospel's prodigal sons harbored any fears about their return to Christian music circles, they were quickly allayed. "We went to the Dove

Awards for the first time in twenty-five years, and it blew our minds to see how things had changed in that business. We were backstage and we saw kids with purple hair and jewelry in their nose. We said, 'Wow, things have really changed!'"

Sterban and the rest of the Oak Ridge Boys believe those changes can only help the spread of the country gospel sound. "Years ago, when we were trying to take gospel music to the mainstream, that was not permitted. Now, there is a place for young kids to express their talents, and I think it's great to see they are now accepting that in Christian circles."

From left to right, Tillman Franks and Johnny Horton.

TILLMAN FRANKS

Few people have participated in more flat-out country music history than Tillman Franks. A short list of his accomplishments includes introducing Hank Williams and Elvis Presley to the once-massive *Louisiana Hayride* radio audience, and managing Webb Pierce, Johnny Horton, Claude King, and David Houston. On top of that, he gave guitar lessons to a young man who grew up to be one of Nashville's most successful producers, Jerry Kennedy.

Most of Franks's exploits are covered in his 2000 autobiography *I Was There When It Happened*, including details of the car wreck that killed Johnny Horton and severely injured Tommy Tomlinson and himself. What you won't read about there is the residual sense of guilt he feels over playing music in places that sell liquor.

"I've changed my life around completely," Franks told me. "You know, I have a son that's a Baptist minister, and my brother is a Church of God minister. And I spent my prime time working honky-tonks and leading people the other direction. My son is a tremendous preacher, and yet I haven't done right in my lifetime, I know that."

The songwriter/bass player/manager also experiences deep conflicts about the near idol worship of his most famous associates, Hank Williams and Elvis Presley. "It's kind of a long story, but I was involved with all of it. I don't like to talk about Elvis and Hank, either one, because I was involved with 'em real personal when they was hungry, really. I tell you what, I had been real sick, and I fell out of the bed one time. I felt like there were angels who threw me on the floor to give me a wake-up notice, because they had already saved me in Johnny's wreck. I felt like I was floating. When that happened, I had a dream. I had died and I was at heaven's gate, and God said 'Tillman, what did you do down on earth?'

"I said, 'Well, I helped Elvis Presley and Hank Williams get started.'

"He said, 'Who are *they*?'

"Does that tell you something?"

5

THE ELVIS FACTOR

Elvis Presley was and will always be the King of Rock 'n' Roll, but he initially thought of himself as a country singer. While hawking his early Sun releases, he played venues that were vastly more country in nature than pop, sharing a bill with the likes of Hank Snow, Faron Young, Ernest Tubb, Johnnie & Jack, Johnny Horton, and George Jones.

Yet, despite fifty-four Top 40 entries on Billboard's country charts, country music was seldom the focus of Presley's recorded output. Indeed, most purists did not consider the Mississippi native's blues-based sound to be true country, but his immense popularity allowed program directors to rationalize his inclusion on their playlists. During the 1950s, country radio played Presley's records to keep from completely losing teenaged listeners. By the seventies, his string of southern-themed, adult contemporary comeback hits ("Kentucky Rain," "Don't Cry Daddy," etc.) made him country's answer to Neil Diamond; most of his attempts at true country sounded more like Mario Lanza than Eddy Arnold. Many of Presley's final hits ("Moody Blue," "T-R-O-U-B-L-E," "Way Down," etc.) clearly anticipated this era's ersatz-country movement.

But, aside from providing a standard of rags-to-riches fame for other performers to aspire to, Presley still changed nearly everything about country music, from how the labels marketed it to how the stars themselves created it. These changes did not go down easily. Some artists felt that the Hillbilly Cat all but destroyed the genre, but the smarter ones learned to adapt and capitalize on the fresh opportunities created in his wake.

The Jordanaires today (from left to right): Curtis Young, Gordon Stoker, Ray Walker, Louis Nunley.

GORDON STOKER
of the Jordanaires

"Well, we were working with Eddy Arnold and we went to the Ellis Auditorium in Memphis to do a show. Elvis came back behind the stage to meet us, not to meet Eddy. He said that he'd been hearing us sing on the *Grand Ole Opry* and he said, 'Man, let's sing some of those spirituals.' So we got to singing with him in the room. That's when he said, 'If I ever get a major recording contract, I want you guys to work with me.' He was on the

Sun label at that time. We didn't think anything about it; we had been told that by a lot of people. It didn't mean anything at all. But when RCA signed him in January of 1956, he asked for us."

That's how Gordon Stoker of the Jordanaires remembers his first meeting with Elvis Presley. Further, he's not shy about summing up the King's impact on the quartet. "When Elvis started using 'doo-wahs' in the background, then *everybody* wanted 'doo-wahs' in the background, and everybody would come in to Nashville and use either the Jordanaires or the Anita Kerr Singers. They were the only two groups doing it all."

The Jordanaires, formed in 1948, were well established in the country-gospel scene long before they ever met Presley. But their association with the Memphis Flash greatly enhanced both their fame and long-range commercial fortunes. In return, the quartet helped broaden country's crossover possibilities, and even changed how sessions were recorded.

Stoker joined the Jordanaires as a fifteen-year-old in 1950 when the quartet's regular pianist, Bob Money, was drafted. The lineup at that time consisted of Bob Hubbard and brothers Bill and Monty Matthews, but not long after, an unexpected personnel shift would change Stoker's life. "We were working at a supper club in Detroit; it was an eight-day run, and on the first night [first tenor singer] Bill Matthews suffered a complete nervous breakdown and was taken off the stage. He was the manager of the group and had a lot of pressures of family and a lot of pressures from showbiz. He just couldn't cope with it at all. They had the doctors take him away and put him in an institution."

With the remainder of the run at stake, Stoker was pressed into service as lead tenor, and he didn't feel ready. "Bill's brother Monty Matthews, who did all the arranging, said, 'You've got to sing Bill's part.' I said, 'I can't sing that high part.' He said, 'You've got to sing the part. We've got no choice. You've *got* to.' He was very firm and he had to be. I thought it was cruel at the time, but later on I realized that he did exactly the right thing."

Stoker's arrival ushered in more changes in the group's lineup. By 1954 the group consisted of Stoker, Hoyt Hawkins, Neal Matthews, and Hugh Jarrett and was featured prominently on Red Foley's portion of the *Grand Ole Opry*. Around that time, the Jordanaires also started supplementing their income by singing backup on recording sessions for Foley, Elton Britt, Jimmy Wakely, and Hank Snow.

One of television's early talent shows helped spread their appeal even further, as Stoker remembers. "We had won the *Arthur Godfrey's Talent Scout Show* by singing a black spiritual like 'Dig a Little Deeper God's Love.'" Their fondness for black gospel music was shared by Presley, and the group's impact on his RCA recordings should not be underestimated. Their smooth yet effervescent background work made Elvis's rawboned rockabilly palatable to both pop audiences and radio programmers. In addition, major smashes such as "Don't Be Cruel," "I Was the One," "Teddy Bear," "Too Much," and "Don't" exhibited the type of group interplay usually found in doo-wop, an effect Presley could not have achieved at Sun Records.

Presley was actually a frustrated group singer. He had auditioned unsuccessfully for the Blackwood Brothers affiliate, the Songfellows, and when I asked Stoker if Presley was disappointed over not making it into the gospel group, he responded, "Oh, he was *killed*." Stoker elaborates: "I finally ran into one of those guys and said, 'You mean Elvis auditioned for you guys?' He said, 'Yeah. Elvis sang good but once you gave him a part, before you knew it, Elvis was singing another part.' Of course, when you're singing in a group you can't do that. If you're given the second tenor part to sing, you've got to stick to the second tenor part. But, when Elvis would hear a pretty solo line, whether it was bass or whatever, he'd just start singing it. Well, you can't steal the bass singer's lines or the first tenor's, but the funny thing about Elvis was that he could sing all the parts and sing them pretty well."

On tour, the King's delirious, screaming fans made it difficult for the Jordanaires to hear the singer. As a result, Presley had the group stand very close to him on stage. "We could also tell by the movement of his head or the movement of his body where he was in the song," explained Stoker. "But, we would be as close to him as we could possibly be. He even wanted it that way in the studio. He always wanted us standing right behind him on those TV shows we did with him. Many times he'd step back on my toes."

At Presley's request, the Jordanaires received billing on all his releases, a sign of respect that he didn't accord guitarist Scotty Moore and bass player Bill Black. Unfortunately, the publicity windfall did not result in a rash of hit records for the vocal quartet. "We really wanted Capitol Records to push us. Lee Gillette, who was an official at Capitol Records, said, 'Gordon, let me tell you one thing. You guys are masters in the studio at doing background on recording sessions. If you were to get one or two hit records, you'll just fall by the way-side.' At the time he said it, we didn't want to hear it, but now we think back and he was so right."

Presley's astounding success caused an even greater demand for the Jordanaires as session singers. They began working with one of Presley's biggest competitors in the teen idol sweepstakes, Ricky Nelson, on a series of classic hits: "Lonesome Town," "Poor Little Fool," "Traveling Man," and "Hello Mary Lou."

"Elvis heard us with everybody else. You'd have thought he wouldn't want us with Ricky—because Ricky's records were very big—but he did. He loved Ricky. Everybody would've loved Ricky Nelson. He was too nice for his own good; everybody took advantage of him.

"I guess I'd rather listen to Rick Nelson with the Jordanaires than anything we have ever done," Stoker affectionately confesses. "He always had us up loud. He had us where Elvis wanted us and RCA would not allow that. We would get it where he wanted it in the studio, almost as loud as he was. That's the way he wanted it, but by the time New York got through with it, they brought us way down."

Ray Walker took over the bass spot from Hugh Jarrett in 1958, in time for the Jordanaires to begin working with Patsy Cline on such enduring hits as "I Fall to Pieces," "Crazy," and

"Sweet Dreams." At first distrustful of the group, she came to depend upon the Jordanaires to explain certain song lyrics to her. "Patsy didn't have much of an education and she'd walk over and say, 'Hey Hoss, what's this mean?'" Stoker chuckles fondly. "She called everybody 'Hoss,' and sometimes she'd make a funny remark about it. Sometimes she'd make a *suggestive* remark about it. She was a real character, but a lot of fun to be with."

Asked if the Jordanaires were given much creative direction from either artist or producer for their background harmonies, Stoker answers, "I'm sorry to say that 90 percent of the time they'd say, 'We're going to leave that to you.' So you really had to come up with something fast." (The group's arranger Neal Matthews supplied the catchy hooks that helped make hits of Jack Scott's "What in the World's Come Over You," Jim Reeves's "Four Walls," and Johnny Horton's "Battle of New Orleans.") "A good example of that is 'Big Bad John,' which was a huge hit for Jimmy Dean. Now, Jimmy Dean did not come up with one bit of that hook, 'Big John, Big John—Big Bad John.' The only thing he came up with was that story of a coal miner, which he had written on the plane coming down to Nashville. But he didn't contribute one thing nor did he have a suggestion for what we were supposed to do. Neal Matthews made that arrangement . . . and Jimmy Dean didn't even give us credit for that record. I can assure you that record would not have been a hit had we not had such a fantastic arrangement with the Jordanaires in the background.

"When Ralph Emery asked him to talk about the number, Jimmy said that he wrote it on the plane coming down from New York. Ralph Emery said, 'The Jordanaires had a very big part in that record.' He said, 'Yeah, they were on the session.' That's just the way he left it. Just that cold."

However, the group did collect something from Dean besides their session fee. "Well, he gave us two pounds of sausage each."

Whether making their own records or singing behind other performers, no one has recorded as prolifically as the Jordanaires. "We did two to four sessions a day for some twenty to twenty-five years," marvels Stoker. "A lot of people asked, 'How did your voice hold out?' Well, we would have substitutes, and the substitutes were always waiting at your fingertips on the telephone to run and do a two o'clock session or six o'clock session. The sessions ran 10:00 A.M., 2:00 P.M., 6:00 P.M., and 10:00 P.M. You'd go from this studio to that studio."

Out of necessity, Matthews developed the Nashville Number System, which uses numbers in place of the chord names. The system, still widely used today, allowed the group to follow the arrangement despite changes in the song's key. This innovation helped them log thousands of session hours with economy, speed, and taste.

The Jordanaires have done so many sessions that sometimes they've forgotten what they've done and for whom they've done it. "I think one of the funniest things that ever happened was when we were in Hollywood doing a movie with Elvis," says Stoker. "We were on our way to the studio and we heard this record on the radio and we said, 'Hey, that sounds like us.' We drove a little bit further down the road and said, 'Hey, that *does* sound like us. I believe that *is* us.' When it got through playing the announcer said, 'That's Conway Twitty with his new record "It's Only Make Believe."' Of course that was us, but we had done it six or seven months before that. It turned out to be one of the greatest records we ever did background on. It was his first hit record, and until his death he gave the Jordanaires credit for that."

Studio work proved to be so lucrative for them that when Elvis Presley returned to live performing in 1970, the group simply couldn't afford to take the cut in pay that lengthy Las Vegas gigs and tours would've represented. Their rendition of the Coca Cola jingle "It's the Real Thing" alone earned them more money than a whole year of live dates with Elvis would have.

Nonetheless, the Jordanaires had great sympathy for Presley and some of the obstacles he had to overcome in his career. "He faced problems from the people who booked him through the Colonel," Stoker recalls. "Of course he had a hard way to go with the Colonel. The Colonel had no love for him, that's what was bad. Elvis wanted to be loved. He wanted you to love him, and he wanted to love you. The Colonel was always about, 'You do your job and I'll do my job.' It was that type of thing. He just didn't have any love and respect for him, so Elvis had a hard way to go because of that. And he had a lot of obligations he had to meet. It always seemed like he was a day late and a dollar short. He died broke, which was an extremely sad thing to us. No reason at all for that. You read where the estate was worth ten million? That's because some Japanese outfit would've given ten million for Graceland. But Priscilla has turned that whole deal around and they've done well with it."

With great sadness, Stoker remembers the last time he saw Elvis Presley. "I had seen Elvis about a year before and I told my wife, 'If he's alive another year, it'll surprise me.' He had gone down too much since the last time I saw him. He put his arm around me and held me a second or two and there was just something in the meeting that really upset me. In fact, it upset me so much that I didn't sleep a wink that night."

After his death in 1977, the group began honoring their former boss by recording a series of tribute albums in both gospel and secular styles. Viewed by many as the last surviving links to Presley's best era, the Jordanaires found themselves in demand for nostalgia shows and began touring with Moore, Elvis's original drummer D. J. Fontana, and Presley sound-a-like Ronnie McDowell. By the late 1990s, they had augmented their own shows with tributes to Ricky Nelson and Patsy Cline.

Although death has claimed Hawkins and Matthews, the Jordanaires have stayed in business by hiring, among others, former substitutes Louis Nunley and Curtis Young. And while country music has changed rather drastically, requests for their in-studio services remains high. "Of course," he chuckles, "it is funny that every session we go to, among the first things they want us to do is get the four of us together for pictures."

During her days as the teenage queen of Sun Records.

BARBARA PITTMAN

Blues-belting Barbara Pittman's claim to fame rests on both the handful of singles she cut during the 1950s at the legendary Sun studios and her childhood friendship with Elvis Presley. A living witness to Memphis's musical history, she not only participated in the rise of rockabilly music, but also saw, firsthand, the biggest changes in Presley's life.

"I was born right here in Memphis," reports Pittman. "I was born in an attic on Easter Sunday. We were very poor. I have twelve brothers and sisters all together. My father tried to be the father of our country, I do believe. We were right in the city, in a, just a horrible poverty situation. But we overcame, and we all made it. I guess just because you're born in poverty doesn't mean that you have to turn out bad."

At the age of three she got her first taste of showbiz. "My uncle by marriage used to have a pawn shop on Beale Street, and that's where I grew up. There was a record out at that time, I forget who it was, but I liked it and started singing, 'He may be your man but he comes around to see me sometimes.' And everybody on Beale Street started gathering around me to hear this little half-pint sing those lyrics. I've been singing the blues ever since."

With a note of wistful nostalgia in her voice, Pittman explains her connection and relationship to Presley. "I grew up in the same neighborhood in north Memphis. It was *the* white poor neighborhood in Memphis. You had the poor Irish people and poor little Southern people. It was cheap living and cheap housing there. That was just where everybody ended up when they came to Memphis. Of course I was a few years younger than Elvis, but my brothers knew him at school; they all went to Humes. My older brother knew him from the teenage years.

"From that time on, I would see Elvis around town. My Uncle Abe and I would go to the movies uptown all the time, and he was an usher at one of the theaters. That was while he was still in high school. I was just a little girl and I was running around behind him and suddenly one day I grew up and he says, '*Hello* dere!'"

Pittman's mother also knew Mrs. Presley quite well. "They were both dietitians at St. Joseph Hospital here and that's how they met each other. They had Stanley parties, which were like Tupperware parties today, and they'd get together and sell these little brushes and combs and everything and play these little games. And my mom would go to their house or Mrs. Presley would come to ours.

"His mother used to tell us we looked like brother and sister; then we'd get in a fight! He'd look at me and say, 'I can't be that ugly, Mom.' So I wouldn't take that! I shot right back, 'Well, I certainly don't look like *you!*' I called him 'Bumphead' because he had little knots on his head. We were kids, you know. But he grew into his face and became gorgeous."

Many biographies have reported that the young Presley had hygiene problems and "green teeth." Pittman says that's just not true. "He had the prettiest teeth I've ever seen in my life. His mother made him take vitamins, brush his teeth, and I never smelled anything but good on him. He washed his hair every day. That's the softest, prettiest hair I'd ever seen."

Pittman not only shared Presley's love of the blues, she also had an itch to perform—an itch that got the teenager in a spot of trouble. "My first singing job where I got paid was with Elvis at the Eagle's Nest, and the juvenile court authorities found out I was there and made me quit. My stepfather turned me in. I couldn't even work in Memphis after that because I was too young."

She received another blow to her ego when she tried to latch on at Sun Records. "Well, Elvis had introduced me to Sam Phillips, and I went down and did an audition for him. He told me to go out and learn how to sing and then come back. Now Marion Keisker [Phillips's receptionist, the woman who discovered Presley], who didn't want any women in that studio at all, told me to go out and learn how to type or get married because I couldn't sing. I hadn't been singing very long. God, I was just a little kid."

Undaunted, Pittman secured work with movie cowboy Lash LaRue's traveling road show, where she was employed as a babysitter and part-time entertainer. She remembers the show well. "Well, you know he was 'King of the Bullwhip,' and he did the regular things like knocking ashes off of a cigarette, putting out fire, and doing a fight scene with a stunt man he had with him, and singing a song. He had a pretty good voice. And we ended the show doing a gospel song and that was our show.

"We had a little trio with us. I did things like 'I'll Never Let You Go' and I even sang some of his original material he had written. I didn't do that much. I'd go out and sing two or three songs but mostly he'd have me out front selling his picture.

"We traveled all over the country. He signed a contract with my mother that he would tutor me and everything. He took very good care of me until the tour was over and he

Pittman's debut with Clyde Leoppard and the Snearly Ranch Boys; Stan Kessler is on the left.

dropped me at a phone booth in Columbus, Ohio. Fortunately I had a cousin who lived there so I stayed with them for a while before I came back to Memphis."

Touring with Larue gave her voice some needed polish, and once she got home Pittman was ready to give Sun and Sam Phillips another try. "So, I went back and made a demo for Elvis called 'Playing for Keeps,' something Stanley Kesler had written. I went back with the demo, which we made at the Cotton Club in west Memphis, and Sam listened to it, and he didn't realize that I was that same girl that had auditioned a year earlier. He said, 'Hey, who is this? This sounds real good and I'd like to get her in here and do some things.'

"'Well, that's Barbara Pittman!'

"And Sam said, 'Well, I guess she did what I told her to.'"

Presley recorded her version of the pretty country ballad "Playing for Keeps" for RCA in 1957 and later copied her rendition of Hank Williams's "Cold Cold Heart." "Elvis said I was the only one he ever heard who could really sing that song," Pittman recalls today. "That really made me feel good."

A well-endowed, Elizabeth Taylor–style brunette, Pittman was generally treated like everyone's kid sister at Sun. "Well, I was so young and standoffish, I was scared of my own shadow," she laughs. "I was really a shy kid. I was shaking so hard that when I'd get around Elvis he'd call me his vibrator. 'Hey, my back hurts, lean up against me.' Mostly, I was kind of a loner, and I'd go right home. The band would take me home and pick me up, and [disc jockey] Dewey [Phillips] was real protective of me too. Jack Clement and I dated, we were pretty close, and Elvis and I were close friends, but we were never really what you'd call lovers. We dated and everything, but I just wasn't his type. But anyway, I didn't really have any problems."

Her relationship with Clement resulted in his writing "Ballad of a Teenage Queen," a major crossover hit for Johnny Cash. "That's true. She was a teenaged queen," affirms Clement. "Oh, was she beautiful—I was in love with her." He also produced her best rocker, the bold and lascivious "I Need a Man."

Hearing her daughter utter lines such as "I've got plenty of cash and a fine mink coat, but they can't give me what I need the most, I need a *man* to love me" provoked an immediate reaction from Pittman's mother. "She locked me in the closet for a week! She said, 'You can't go out. Just forget it.' Y'know, I looked so much older than my years because I was born with a training bra on. She was worried about me, but I was a good kid and she knew it, really."

One of the Sun label's biggest weaknesses was its inability to concentrate on more than one or two artists at a time. Sam Phillips routinely pulled all his resources from one record to put behind another. Such was the case with Billy Lee Riley's "Red Hot" and Pittman's recordings, which received solid airplay in Memphis, but never benefitted from a national push.

While Pittman's career floundered, her friend Elvis faced an even bigger crisis, the death of his mother. "We were up in his room, I stayed with him the last night he was home, because Elvis walked in his sleep and couldn't be left alone," Pittman reveals. "So, he couldn't be left alone, and he was still grieving over his mom. His mom had just died and he laid his head in my lap and cried, 'Why me? I know this is going to be the end of my career. My mom's gone and now my career is going to be gone.' And he was just very upset, and I comforted him. That's all there was to it. My brother was in the service but he wasn't giving up anything. As a matter of fact he was getting three good meals a day that he wasn't getting at home. But with Elvis, I could understand where he was coming from even then, and I was just a kid. He was mostly crying about his mom, he knew that everything was turning completely different from that point on in his life."

Pittman agrees that everything about Elvis and his world changed with the death of his beloved mother, but insists that Presley was neither a mama's boy nor painfully shy. "Well, he wasn't shy, and he wasn't the mama's boy they often make him out to be. He loved his mother like all Southern men do, y'know. I never seen one that didn't love their mother more than their father. He really did; he loved his mom—well, we all do. Southern people are very attached to their mothers. But Elvis was headstrong, hot tempered, and he knew what he wanted and went after it."

Plugging away at her own recording career, Pittman's last single for Sam Phillips, "Handsome Man," came out on Sun's Phillips International affiliate and was the most expensive recording attempted by the label—and expense was something Phillips just could not abide. "Well . . . that was the last record I recorded, and Charlie Rich wrote it and played piano on it," explains Pittman. "We had a vocal group there and all the strings and all the basic instruments plus guitars. Everything happened in that studio, nothing was overdubbed. They were all union musicians charging union scale, and it was going on all night long. Charlie Underwood, who wrote the other side of that record, "The Eleventh Commandment," was engineering, and he was the one who put this thing together. Sam was at home in bed with pneumonia. When somebody called him and told him what was going on, he got out of bed and came down during a blizzard to find out what in the heck was going on."

Asked about working with the young Charlie Rich, Pittman shares a memory from the session. "Charlie, y'know, kinda tilted the bottle a little. Well, a lot actually, and he was pretty well gone. We were just singing away and the vocal group was doing their 'ooh-wahs' and the violins were going. Suddenly we missed the piano and Charlie. There was a hole in everything and we looked at the piano for Charlie and he was under it! He was *out*, sitting there with his head resting against the piano bench. We got him awake and we went on with the session."

The recording scene in Memphis ground to a halt during the early 1960s, so Pittman decided to try her luck in Hollywood, where she would see Elvis for the last time. It was then she realized that her old friend was in the process of some profound emotional changes. "I never made any real money in Memphis," says Pittman. "So, I went out to L.A. in '62, and I saw Elvis a few times out there when he was renting [Rudolph] Valentino's house. I wanted to see it, so I went over. But when he met Priscilla, he was talking about her even then, and he was saying that she looked like a female Valentino. He had this worship—he believed he was the reincarnation of Valentino. At times he would actually talk like he had dreamed he was [Valentino] at one time or another. Anyway, after that, when she came on the scene, I didn't go around him anymore."

Fortunately, two other former neighbors from north Memphis were able to give Pittman a helping hand, Johnny and Dorsey Burnette. "They were trying to get me on labels and everything. Then Johnny got killed and everything just stopped. That was the saddest day of my life. [Johnny Burnette died in a boating mishap in 1964.] But they were real good friends, Dorsey was very helpful to me. He got me going when I got out there."

Pittman rattled around Hollywood for several years, appearing in clubs, singing on Sammy Master's television show and on a project spearheaded by Mike Curb. She also did some movie soundtrack work, played bit parts in the biker exploitation films *Wild on Wheels* and *The Hell's Angels*, and recorded "Making Love is Fun" for the dubiously titled *Dr. Goldfoot and the Girl Bomb*. A true showbiz foot soldier, she never really made the big time. She was nearly forgotten until the death of Elvis Presley caused a renewed interest in his fifties contemporaries, especially among European fanatics.

"Suddenly I was discovered," Pittman crows. "It took me forty years before people started saying 'What about this one female artist on Sun?' I've been to Europe a few times and just had a ball! They treat you like royalty over there."

That said, those European tours haven't been lucrative enough to completely support her year-round. Times have often been desperate for Pittman: she lost her home and went through a bankruptcy; a proposed recording deal fell through; and stateside bookings are thin. Yet she still loves to sing: "It beats any food you could put in your mouth." Moreover, she is grateful for her memories of her late friends.

"Sometimes I think that Elvis Presley and Dewey Phillips were the only people who ever really believed in me. Just the thought of that keeps me going a lot of times."

Just two young lovers.

WANDA JACKSON

"I began working with Elvis in '55 after I graduated from high school," remembers Wanda Jackson. "I worked with him for two years until he went to Hollywood and started his movie career. Elvis liked my voice. Well, we liked each other. We dated while we were on tour; he gave me his ring and I wore it around my neck. We were boyfriend and girlfriend."

Jackson had two major influences in her musical career. The first was Hank Thompson, who hired her to sing with his band, the Brazos Valley Boys, while she was still a teenager. The second was Elvis Presley, and his effect on her was more than just romantic.

"Anyway," continues Jackson. "He thought I should start doing this new music, because he was just starting to really get big. I was with him when he did the Dorsey Brothers show—you know, the one where they wouldn't show him from the waist down—all this stuff going on. I said, 'I don't think I can do that because I'm just a country singer.'

"He said, 'Well, I am too basically, but I think you're gonna need to do this because it's going to be the next really big music.'

"Well, how right he was.

"So, we'd go to his house and play records. Then he'd get out his guitar and say, 'Now just take this song . . .' and then he would just put his style to it. It was through his encouragement that I got into rock 'n' roll music and Daddy agreed with him thoroughly. He said, 'You can do it and I think you should.' My producer Ken Nelson didn't have feelings one way or another about it—it didn't matter to him so long as I sold records."

Jackson had already had some exposure to the blues from her father, who loved Jimmie Rodgers and some of the old-time blues singers. "To me, that was what Elvis was doing; it was kind of that style, only a little faster," says Jackson today. "So it didn't seem all that foreign to me, but I just didn't think I could sing it. But in 1958, I recorded 'Fujiyama Mama.' I had heard the song on a jukebox and said, 'I've gotta sing that thing.' I went out and found the record, and I was already doing that growlin'. 'Hot Dog! That Made Him Mad' had a growl thing in there so I could do it, I just didn't have the material."

This lack of material forced Jackson to record one of Presley's songs at an album session. It proved to be her breakthrough hit. "'Let's Have a Party' came along at the tail end of the session where I did my first album at Capitol. I needed one more song and I didn't have one, and I had my band there, so I said, 'Let's lay this "Let's Have a Party" down and see what Ken [Nelson] thinks of it. It was from Elvis's movie *Loving You* and I had been singing it for a while and people really liked it. So Ken said, 'Well, I like that, that'll be cute, we'll just put it on the end of the album.' Two years later, that song came out of that album, which was almost totally unheard of in those days, because you always put a single out and if it was a hit then you put out the album around it. So this was very different."

Jackson, who has been married to her manager, Wendell Goodman, for over four decades, still has the ring Elvis Presley gave her.

In 2003, after a long absence from the recording studio, Jackson recorded a new disc of tunes titled *Heart Trouble*. One of the songs featured a duet with a different Elvis—Elvis Costello. "It was a real thrill to cut 'Crying Time' with Wanda," marveled Costello. "It was done live and spontaneously, just the way all her best records sound. She's certainly got the spark."

No doubt, the other Elvis would agree.

Dressed like his first benefactor, T. Texas Tyler. (The note is addressed to steel guitar player Neil Livingstone, who played on the original "Hot Rod Lincoln.")

GARY BRYANT

Here's something you won't find in either history or trivia books: the phrase "Elvis has left the building" was coined to help quiet a screaming, Presley-crazed crowd so a young country singer named Gary Bryant could take the stage.

It didn't help. The girls kept screaming for Presley.

"I thought I was going to get lynched," remembered Bryant. "I never heard so much booing and hissing in my life. This scared the hell out of me. Well, you knew they didn't want to see you and you couldn't hear anything. There was just this high, keening wail. They all wanted Elvis."

Bryant was one of the many country artists whose career fortunes were caught in the crosshairs of rock 'n' roll. The mortifying, momentum-stopping incident typified the misfortune he suffered throughout his career. Indeed, Bryant told me with a rueful chuckle, "I've turned lousy luck and bad timing into a high art form."

Born in Spokane, Washington, on May 11, 1936, Bryant first heard country music through two uncles, vaudevillians billed as the Purple Sage Riders, who often rehearsed in his grandmother's kitchen. But Bryant knew he wanted to be a country singer too the day when "Purina Mills opened a new feed mill here, and to open the thing they had a big-time country music show. The first time I ever saw one. They had Eddy Arnold, Minnie Pearl, Blackie Crawford. Anyway, they did it on a loading dock. Arlie Duff had on this royal blue cowboy suit and I remember saying, 'I'm going to get me one of those.'"

Bryant took up the guitar at age fourteen and began "writing songs like mad"—he even got fired from a job because he would often pitch songs to visiting artists rather than run his assigned elevator. The following year, he had his own fifteen-minute radio program on KSPO before moving to a daily half-hour slot on KGA. Bryant's favorite recording artists included Webb Pierce, Faron Young, and Hank Snow. He also particularly liked Carl Smith and would perform his songs at grange dances. Encouraged by the locals' response, the restless young singer would often hitchhike out to Nashville or Los Angeles, angling for a break. During one of these trips, he was picked up by T. Texas Tyler. Upon learning the seventeen-year-old was a performer, Tyler—known as the "Man with a Million Friends"—gave Bryant his first break with a spot on his show as a "featured singer."

"There are three master showmen I had an opportunity to work with, and they've been a big influence on me," stated Bryant. "One was T. Texas Tyler; he was a master. Ferlin Husky, he was a master, and Little Jimmy Dickens. Dickens and I would talk about Tyler and how we both stole stuff from him, his mannerisms, ways to use a hat, spinning the guitar, all kinds of little showbizzy type things."

Landing in Nashville again, Bryant lucked into accommodations with Ferlin Husky through a Washington State University graduate named Bob Ferguson. Besides being "a wonderful guy" and "one of the greatest entertainers who ever lived," Husky also provided Bryant a few musical opportunities. "He got me on those *Grand Ole Opry* films you'll see sometimes," Bryant informed me. "I was on thirteen of them, sitting on a bale of hay clapping my hands. When I was living at Ferlin's house, he did 'I'll Babysit with You,' [#14, 1955] and I'm part of the vocal background. I'm one of the guys singing 'be my baby.' This was the first time I had ever recorded anything."

Bryant tried to capitalize on his situation by pitching songs to everyone in sight, and by his own count had contracts from twenty-eight different publishers, though only a few of his songs were ever cut. He hung out with up-and-coming songwriters such as Roger Miller—who, by Bryant's account, was "squirrelly." But he and Donny Young, later known as Johnny Paycheck, were genuinely close for a time.

"When I first met the guy, we were so broke," Bryant recalls grimly. "We only had enough money for three of those Krystal Burgers, and we split one. I think they were a dime apiece, something like that. I did the starvation thing in Nashville, there's no getting around that."

Broke and hungry, Bryant returned home to Spokane before heading to Shreveport, Louisiana, to try out for the *Louisiana Hayride*. Dubbed the "Cradle of the Stars," the *Hayride* was beamed across the southern United States over two 50,000-watt clear channel networks, played on V-discs over Armed Forces Radio, and picked up for an hour each week by the CBS radio network. The weekly broadcasts provided valuable exposure for such up-and-coming country stars as Hank Williams, Webb Pierce, Faron Young, Johnny Horton, Johnny Cash, and Elvis Presley, to name but a few. It seemed to be the perfect jumping-off point for Bryant; however *Hayride* boss and host Horace Logan proved hard to impress.

"Good old Horace Logan asked, 'Sonny, you got a hit record?'

"I said, 'No sir.'

"He said, 'Well, come back when you've got one. This is where you wind up, not where you start!'"

Smartened up by his experience in Nashville, the determined Bryant befriended "a friend of someone who knew someone who knew Buddy Attaway," a *Hayride* artist who sometimes scouted talent. "I had to sing through all these people until they finally introduced me to Buddy Attaway," laughed Bryant. "Then Buddy took me to the *Hayride* and stashed me in the dressing room. Well, Johnny Horton and Tillman Franks were in there, and I was pitching songs to 'em like crazy! I never shut up. [*Hayride* announcer] Frank Page would stick his head in the door every once in a while. Finally he ducked his head in and asked, 'You want to do a song on the show?' One of the acts had left early. I said 'Sure.' So I did and I encored and I encored and I encored. The next week, Buddy brought me back and I did the same thing. I did identically the same thing the next week, encored again, and so the third time I came off stage, there was Horace Logan. [Laughs.] Y'know, I had been trying to dodge that man. But there he stood with a check. So from that point on, I was a member of the cast. Then Tillman Franks decided to become my manager."

Franks booked shows, scouted talent, ran the Artist's Service Bureau, acted as *Hayride* producer at various times, nurtured acts, and cowrote songs, all while playing bass with Johnny Horton. He testified about his young protégé: "Gary was one of the best entertainers that was on the *Louisiana Hayride* and he toured lots with Johnny Horton on some real big dates. I could always depend on a good show from him. He was real popular on the *Hayride*. He had a tremendous personality and he sung good and had some good records out on Decca."

When I asked him what made Bryant special, Franks replied with conviction: "His personality, his charisma. That's what makes a star—personality and charisma—and Gary had it. He could do anything Carl Smith and the rest of 'em could do. He had all the ingredients. He was in line to get a hit record because they liked him so much, and he come pretty close to really having some monsters. Owen Bradley and them liked him—I had got him on Decca."

"I was on the *Hayride* a week before Decca signed me," remembered Bryant proudly. "I think I was the first person they ever put on there without a major recording contract or who hadn't had a record out. But I needed a record. Tillman Franks and Johnny Horton had to go up to the *Ozark Jubilee* in Springfield. While they were up there, they ran into Paul Cohen and they pitched me to him. When he came back to Shreveport, I was at the drugstore across the street and Tillman hollered out the window of the radio station, 'Gary, Paul Cohen's on the phone!' I didn't know who in the hell Paul Cohen was. Then Tillman said, 'Paul Cohen—head of A&R for Decca wants to talk to you.' So I auditioned for him over the telephone . . . and then he told me, 'Contract's in the mail.'"

At his first Decca session, Bryant was thrilled to find he'd be working with the late Hank Williams's old band, the Drifting Cowboys, and guitarist Hank "Sugarfoot" Garland. His recordings of the self-penned "I'm Just Wild About You" backed with "Summer Love Affair" sounded like the work of a much younger Carl Smith: good hillbilly music with a beat.

Childhood friend Bobby Wayne, the first northwest rockabilly, recalls that his local music shop sold out of its five hundred copies of Bryant's debut singles and speculates: "If Elvis hadn't come along and changed the whole course of music, I sincerely believe Gary Bryant would've been another Carl Smith or Faron Young. He really had a unique style and wrote great songs."

But Elvis Presley did come along, and he changed *everything*, though at first Bryant's career was unaffected. According to Tillman Franks, "[Bryant] was on a good many shows with Elvis. Did real good. His personality was tremendous, really. He toured with Johnny Horton lots of times and on this tour, when Elvis was on it, Gary held his own."

For his part, Bryant and several other *Hayride* regulars just didn't "get" Elvis. When I asked him about the Presley phenomenon, he sounded as though he was still puzzled. "The main thing is, none of us could understand why or how. We'd watch him go, and we'd all say 'Well . . . what is it?' Y'know, when Elvis left the *Hayride*, he wasn't the polished performer he was when he came back for that final show. He was awful rough. He'd stand there and scratch his butt, wipe his nose on his sleeve . . . and they'd scream! He triggered this mass hysteria that began with somebody screaming, then somebody else would pick it up, and the next thing you knew it was pandemonium! It was a very peculiar situation that fed off itself like an amoeba. Elvis just changed the total complexion of everything. You either had to beat him or join him, and there wasn't no beating him. I was just in the wrong place at the wrong time. He just flat took over after a while."

The straight country crowd had another reason to be bitter. "Back in the Decca days, all the majors put everything towards the old established artists trying to keep them alive when rock 'n' roll came in. So the newer [country] artists suffered. That was another thing which didn't endear Elvis to us."

As part of the buyout of Presley's contract, Colonel Tom Parker agreed to have the rock 'n' roll sensation perform on one final *Hayride* show, with the proceeds going to charity. With his emergence on RCA, Presley had been transformed from a hot regional artist into a national phenomenon. "For that last appearance he made on the *Hayride*, when he left and came back months later, no one wanted to follow him," Bryant laughed. "They took the show out to the fairgrounds and none of the other acts wanted to face his fans after he left. So, I said, 'I'll do it.'"

It was a mistake. Even today it's hard to understand why they just didn't end the show with Presley's appearance. On several compilations of Presley's *Louisiana Hayride* broadcasts, you can hear Horace Logan struggle to regain order so Bryant could take his spot at the microphone. In the process, he created a historic phrase used countless times since. "Well," Logan explained, "I was out there trying to help [Bryant], and eventually we got 'em calmed down. In fact that was where the phrase 'Elvis has left the building' originated."

Despite Logan's efforts, Bryant faced a hostile crowd in a rapidly emptying coliseum. Out of desperation he closed with his rendition of "Blue Suede Shoes," but the crowd's reaction just got uglier. The debacle completely knocked the wind out of Bryant's sails, supplying him excuses to drink more, which in turn made him undependable.

Other circumstances out of the singer's control worked against him as well. As more and more young fans tuned in to hear Elvis on pop radio stations, the *Hayride's* popularity crumbled, along with Bryant's once promising career. Like any country singer worth his salt, Bryant could rock a bit, but in the *Hayride's* find-another-Elvis sweepstakes, he got passed over for the likes of Tommy Sands and Bob Luman. This situation was exacerbated by the fact that Bryant had recorded for two strong labels, Decca and Starday, yet had been unable to score a national hit.

Tillman Franks tends to blame himself as much as fate: "It's just the breaks sometimes. Back then, he had good distribution, a good record, and good exposure. But at that particular time, I was so wrapped up in Johnny Horton. I was just promotin' Johnny even though I was running the *Hayride*, so [Gary] didn't get that extra promotion that it took."

"I was always sucking hind tit to Horton, y'know," Bryant chuckles, then speaks solemnly about the only example of good timing he ever benefited from. "Y'know, I left Horton a few months before he got killed [in a car wreck]. It's probably a good thing I did, because in all the time we traveled together the seating arrangements had been the same. Tillman never drove. Horton would be driving and I'd be sitting in the middle. In those days we used an acoustic bass and it rode inside the car with us. There were four of us in that car living around that bass fiddle, and I'd have been in the middle, so I know I would've bought the farm too."

Never into the big dollars—the *Hayride* paid only eighteen to twenty-one dollars per show—Bryant had a tendency to attach himself to whoever could help him or keep the party going. Briefly, that someone was George Jones. "Well, we hit it off, and we always drew the same room together on the road. I was kind of an orangutan back in those days, you have to understand this," explained Bryant. "I was kind of a matched set with Jones, you know, with his reputation. So a lot of his escapades were mine and vice versa.

"There was one deal, after he left the *Hayride* and went to the *Opry*. They canned him and I went up there on a leave of absence with Carl Belew. We were just knocking around town and we ran into Jones who was tipping a few. He said, 'My uncle's got this place in Houston. He wants to call it George Jones's Country Corner. Why don't you come down and run the band for me?'

"Well, I was sick of Nashville and I didn't want to go back to Shreveport just yet, so I went down there. And the place he was talking about was on the waterfront, on McCartney there in Houston. It was just a big tavern and the homicide squad would just check in there on a regular basis, because all these foreign seamen would come in there. His jukebox had nothing but George Jones and Gary Bryant records on it.

"That lasted about six weeks. Then he took off on one of his escapades, and I got tired of waiting around, and so everybody just split up. It just didn't work. Y'know, you can get by with two or three days without the star, but you go any further than that, and boy you're dead in the water. They want to see the star."

With the *Hayride* on its last legs, Bryant shuttled out to California for a semiregular gig with the Tex Williams western swing band on KCOP-TV. He worked one tour with old friends Johnny Cash and Rose Maddox and appeared on the television program *Town Hall Party*, but this exposure never translated into stardom or much-needed dollars. California was bursting at the seams with country singers vying for every job and Bryant just didn't have the clout behind him to succeed. Destitute, he simply wanted to go home, but his impatience and intemperance caused him to blow another opportunity.

"Well, there was this song Merle Kilgore and I had written called 'I Can't Dance.' I was in L.A., and I was starving and I wanted out of town, but I wasn't going to let anybody know it really. So I had been to *Town Hall Party* and pitched this song to Rick Nelson, and he liked it, but didn't commit himself. Horace Logan had moved out to California at that time, and he told me, 'Rick Nelson wants you to meet him at the studio because he wants you to run this material by his dad.'

"Well, the night before, I had been with Faron Young and his manager Hubert Long, and they got me a little corked and waved a little bit of money in front of my nose. Well, I wanted out of town and I'm half snockered. So I sold them my half of the song *and* Merle's half.

"So, the next day I went to pitch some stuff to Ozzie Nelson and he said 'No, no! We want that other song, that

"I Can't Dance" thing.' And I didn't own it anymore! I could've had Rick Nelson's next release and I sold it to Faron! Then he recorded it and it was one of the worst things he ever did."

Once home, a fresh opportunity opened up at the Seattle-based Jerden Records, where Bryant was to do his finest work. Label founder and producer Jerry Dennon recalls, "Bobby Wayne introduced Gary to us, and we always thought he had the ingredients of being a star, but perhaps because we were in Seattle and the country world centered on Nashville, it never happened. I always felt Gary was a great songwriter and a good singer. He deserved to hit the big time."

By the early 1960s, Bryant's voice had deepened, enabling him to vent more pure emotion. Singles such as "Just a Nobody" and "Open House" allowed him to embrace the rockabilly beat with style and verve, yet it was the ballad "She Was You Again" that emerged as both his masterpiece and most successful single. "That was '64 when we did that. I got a bull's-eye in *Cashbox* on it. I'll tell you the funny thing about 'She Was You Again.' We did a basic rhythm track at Kearney Barton's studio in Seattle and I needed a bass player. I hired my brother-in-law to play guitar for me, and went down to the public market and there was this guy called 'Barefoot John.' He had an acoustic bass standing there and I said, "You wanna work on a record?' We came back and did the rhythm track and the next time I heard that thing, Aldon Laurie . . . put the strings and voices and all that behind it. That record was the only thing I was ever really proud of." "She Was You Again" topped the Seattle charts for six weeks and received pockets of airplay in other small markets such as Rhode Island and Washington, D.C., though it never broke nationally. There was something bigger than Elvis Presley keeping him off the charts this time: Beatlemania.

He kept at it, but the hardscrabble, hand-to-mouth existence of a honky-tonk singer had taken an awful toll on him and his family life. Subsequently, Bryant forged a fairly steady career in local broadcasting, first as a switcher for KMED-TV in Medford, Oregon, then running audio for KXLY in Spokane, where he ended up hosting their *Dialing for Dollars* program. Bryant returned to radio during the early 1970s and began to augment his income with weekend music gigs—he finally seemed to have found his niche. However, yet another emerging trend finally drove a disgusted Bryant away from mainstream country music.

"You remember when 'Lady' by Kenny Rogers came out?" asks Bryant. "I was PD [program director] and music director of this little country station in Yakima. We were a recording station for the trades. So I get the call from the label. This guy asked, 'Where do you have Kenny charted this week?'

"I said, 'Charted? I don't even have him on the playlist.' At this time that record was #2 in the nation.

"He said, 'All the other stations are playing it.'

"I said, 'Well, I'm trying to preserve a country identity for our station and there's no way that song is country.'

"He said, 'Do you like our *service?*'

"He was implying, 'You either chart him or you get no more of our product or product from any labels we're affiliated with.' So that's the way they got their foot in the door."

Bryant moved into radio sales for a while, worked various odd jobs, trained to be a cabinetmaker, and recorded for a handful of small labels such as Billy Boy, MRM, and Northern.

By the late 1990s, changing tastes appeared to finally be working in his favor. The neo-twang and alt-country movements were struggling to recreate the very sounds Bryant effortlessly achieved every time he stepped to the mic. For the first time in years, he planned to record an LP of his type of country music and tour with his new band, the Sharecroppers. Tillman Franks even called him about coming down for a proposed *Louisiana Hayride* revival.

It never happened.

During the course of his conversation with me, Bryant was cogent and expressive. Singing pieces of his old songs in a voice warm and melodic, he betrayed no sign of the illness that had been plaguing him for so long.

I observed, "Despite all the hardships and near misses, you've pretty much stuck to it," then asked, "What keeps musicians bucking such impossible odds?" Bryant's answer provided his ultimate epitaph.

"Because it's an ingrained thing that has struck a chord somewhere in your psyche that says 'This is what I do. This is who I am. This is a part of me. I can't help it.' You get away from it, but then something comes up and before you know it, you're back on the road. It's good to you. It'll build you up, and then it'll drop you like a hot potato. You can't stay away from it. You go do something else and there will be a lure there that keeps you coming back. So you've just got to follow it, to what ends you just don't know, but you've got to follow it. It'll stick with you until they close the box on you."

Gary Bryant died from complications of a brain tumor on November 19, 1999.

6
COUNTRY COMEDY

From the baggy pants and blacked-out teeth of Rod Brasfield to the relatively sophisticated redneck monologues of Jeff Foxworthy, humor has occupied a special niche in country music history. Indeed, Minnie Pearl's pun-laden letters from home were often the most eagerly anticipated aspect of the Grand Ole Opry *radio broadcasts, and parodies from Homer & Jethro and Ben Colder (aka Sheb Wooley), among others, have allowed country music to laugh at itself before anyone else could.*

Case in point? Cledus T. Judd. The Clown Prince of Country Parody has continued this tradition by singing most of his songs in the voice of his hyperactive, helium-voiced character. When he sang in his real voice for his parody of Toby Keith's 2001 hit "How Do You Like Me Now," he got the drop on casual fans who thought the manic twang used on his early records was what he really sounded like.

Of course, this gear switching isn't exactly new. The Statler Brothers invented a whole group of musical caricatures, Lester "Roadhog" Moran & the Cadillac Cowboys, and prior to that, Ferlin Husky created Simon Crum to handle all the comedy chores. As Crum, he recorded two Top 10 country hits—"Cuzz

Yore So Sweet" and "Country Music Is Here to Stay"—and became country's first comedy alter ego.

Long before performance-art comic Andy Kaufman came on the scene, Husky demanded that his comedy character be treated like a real person. He would even buy tickets for two airplane seats every time he flew—one for him and the other for Simon Crum. Once, Little Jimmy Dickens couldn't get a seat on a flight and asked if he could have Husky's extra ticket. Husky said no before asking his dear friend, very seriously, "Where would Simon sit?"

Personal manager Richard Davis told me that Crum is often easier to deal with than Husky, and swears that sometimes, when a disagreement with his friend and client would get too intense, he'd tell the singer, "Ferlin, I can't talk to you right now . . . put Simon on the phone." Such situations reminded Davis of similar dealings with a renowned puppeteer: "Steve Hall could be a real jerk, but Shotgun Red and I got along pretty well."

Contemporary comics—Bill Engval is a prime example—choose to be closely associated with the music and often record a song and a music video with a big-name country performer to aid their chances of getting airplay. It's a pretty sophisticated marketing idea: drive-time disc jockeys play a parody or comedy routine set to music, then fans seek out the song and purchase a mostly monologue-laden CD.

As with the music, country comedy is no longer just concerned with rural matters. But the down-home, Southern perspective it espouses often reflects a country background all too rarely exhibited by today's musicians.

America's Bubba.

T. BUBBA BECHTOL

As a teenager, T. Bubba Bechtol's life was profoundly affected by the two summers he worked as a driver for country comedy legend Brother Dave Gardner. (Though forgotten by comedy aficionados today, Gardner's albums *Rejoice Dear Hearts!* and *Kick Thy Own Self* hit #5 on the pop charts during the early 1960s.) "Brother Dave gave us permission to be Southern. My favorite quote of his was 'You can't go through life with two catchers mitts on—every now and then you've got to throw something back.' When I was a kid I just tuned into that totally."

Since then, James Terrance Bechtol IV has entertained in every country venue from Jaycee halls to the stage of the *Grand Ole Opry*, and enjoys a well-earned reputation as one of this era's brightest observational comedians. Often compared to another great country monologuist, Jerry Clower, Bechtol has redefined "Bubba" to mean "king of Southern comedy." But his joviality masks the underlying hunger and ambition generated by his humble beginnings.

"Well, I was born in Mississippi and grew up on the Gulf Coast—a little ol' town called Fountainbleu outside of Ocean Springs. I lived in Mississippi until I was twenty-two. I know that's a long time to live in Mississippi, but I didn't know I was free to leave!

"I come from a culture where I didn't have a television as a child. I didn't have electricity until junior high school. My mother worked in a garment factory and supported four boys on that. We didn't have a car. She rode the school bus into town to work and got a ride home in the afternoons. For comfort we just sat around and made up stories."

Bechtol's grandfather and four uncles were Baptist ministers, and he was expected to follow in their footsteps. Like the late hard-rock comedian Sam Kinison, young Bubba Bechtol worked in tent revivals at age ten. However, secular desires dissuaded him from a career in theology. "When I got to college and found out about Jack Daniels and cheerleaders, I discovered that the Lord done called me to a whole different life! I'm still a deeply religious person, but I have a lot of fun with it. I tell people that I am a Southern Baptist. Baptists are a unique group in themselves. They don't believe in premarital sex only because they believe it will lead to dancing. We don't even believe in synchronized swimming. Which is one of the reasons I kept my comedy clean."

It's with no small amount of pride that Bubba mentions his scholastic accomplishments, and the advice that led to his first fortune. "I was a President's List student, I made straight As. I was playing football in college, got my junior college degree, and went on to Southern Mississippi—University of—and after my first year there, they sat me down and said, 'It's time for you to choose a major.'

"Professor Higgins said, 'Bubba, what do you want to be?'

"I said, 'Rich!'

"He said, 'I guess I'm not making myself clear. What do you want to become?'

"I said, 'Hell, I want to become wealthy! Preferably at something legal.'

"He leaned back in his chair and I never will forget what he said. 'Well, you don't need to be in college. Because the biggest failure the university system has in this country is that we teach people to work for companies; we don't teach people to own companies. If you want to make money and that's all that's important to you, go find something you believe in that everybody wants to buy and sell it.' That made more sense to me than anything in the world, and I left college the next day and went to work selling."

A natural closer who employed a lot of funny patter, Bechtol had a knack for predicting and selling consumer fads. During the 1970s, he scored big by importing Wolf Tanning Bed systems from Germany and became a millionaire before the age of thirty.

Bechtol also thrived as a member of the Jaycees, and eventually was elected their national president in 1979. As his term ended, a fellow Jaycee—Ronald Reagan—asked him to run a presidential campaign program called "Commitment '80." When he was voted into the White House, Reagan took Bubba with him as a member of the speech-writing team.

"Reagan was a pretty funny person," discloses Bechtol. "He just had a lot of fun with contrasts. He loved to tell people the difference in things. Actually what I did on the team was not funny. Occasionally I would give him an idea about what I thought was funny or strange. But my job on the team was to research which service organization he was talking to and make sure he knew what he was talking about if he didn't already know 'em. But Reagan wrote most of his own humor."

Did Bechtol ever edit or punch up Reagan's speeches?

"No, he did that with one person, usually Lyn Nofiger. But he'd sit there and fine-tune it all himself, though. We'd send a speech in and it'd come back just redder than hell. He'd just take what he wanted out of it and get out there and plain talk it. He knew what he wanted to say."

At the president's urging, Bubba ran for a congressional seat in 1982. "I won the primary and lost the general election. I ran against a guy who voted for a pay raise and then came home and told everybody he didn't. I just thought I could knock him out. He got elected saying one thing, then he went up there and sold his soul to Tip O'Neill and I just exposed him for what he was. I didn't beat him, but the RNC paid for my campaign because I did so well against him. So it was fun, but there were serious moments. You can't get too funny in politics."

Bechtol's congressional defeat stirred requests for his services as a patriotic speaker. His speech "What's Right with America" twice earned him the George Washington Freedom Foundation award. Gradually, his natural sense of humor leaked out, until he was booked solid as a professional after-dinner speaker, where his Southern accent was a plus, and he was often compared to another great country funnyman. "The comparisons with Jerry Clower are inevitable because we're both from Mississippi, we're both large, and we're both loud. But that's where it stops," explains Bechtol. "Our comedy is nothing alike. Jerry was the last of the great storytellers, but today on radio and television you can't take ten minutes to tell a story. So I learned to do it quick, and my comedy is observational."

The analytical Bechtol believes his twenty-year career as a certified professional speaker provided him with better training than he would've gotten working comedy clubs. "You see the problem with kids that come out of comedy clubs is that they've got a straight twenty-five or thirty minutes, and if it's wrong for the crowd, they're dead. But I've got about ten hours of material, and I'm going to find something that will fit 'em. I can honestly tell you I haven't had a bad show in twelve years."

Would T. Bubba ever play a comedy club? "I would today, but most of 'em can't afford me," he laughs. "So, given the opportunity, I would, if they had me in there with the right person. If they put me in between two guys who are saying 'f— this and f— that,' then I come on being superclean— well, people just can't shift gears that fast."

The chunky comic's clean, intelligent humor and Southern zeal made him an able substitute when his friend, author Lewis Grizzard, had to bow out of speaking engagements due to failing health. TNN's *Crook & Chase* spotted him at one of those engagements and immediately booked him for their program *Music City Tonight*. His thirty appearances on the program helped establish him as a favorite with country audiences.

Eventually Bechtol was accorded the ultimate honor for a country comedian, a regular invitation from the *Grand Ole Opry*, though he realizes that humor has changed since the *Opry*'s salad days. "It has become very sophisticated. It used to be you could go down to Nashville and hoke it up and then go to Iowa and tell old stories and away with it. But them farmers in Ames, Iowa, and Boise, Idaho, are sitting there with satellite television. They've been getting the same sophisticated entertainment that New York and L.A. has been getting for the last twenty years. You better be good enough to do Leno and Letterman if you're gonna go after the country audience now. If you're not, they're going to turn you off. I've been lucky. They like me."

Bechtol predated Jeff Foxworthy, but credits him with opening a lot of doors for Southern comedy. "Jeff was so good. He proved that you can find Bubbas and rednecks everywhere. Up north they just call him Biff, but he's the same guy."

So what is the difference between Foxworthy and Bechtol's approach?

"I worked hard to show that Bubba is not a redneck," Bechtol answers. "He's a descendent of rednecks, but he's not a redneck. He done gone to junior college three or four years, got him a little degree and he might be president of a bank now. But he still hunts and fishes on weekends, and he will cook if there's danger involved. Bubba is a lifestyle, not a look. It's like being Jewish. It's both a culture and a religion."

This point of view resonated with appreciative audiences nationwide, yet Bubba was frustrated that the albums he made for Bill Lowery's Southern Tracks label—*Bill Ain't No Bubba* and *Unclogged*—sold poorly. But the move to MCA and release of his 2002 album *I'm Confused* changed all that. "My albums are in every record store in the country right now," he reports. "In fact they can't keep 'em in there."

Still a Jaycee at heart, Bechtol has used his remarkable success to do some good. Currently the president and CEO of the thirty-five-thousand member "Bubbas of America," he donates all moneys from their product sales to scholarship funds. Moreover, at Christmastime, he takes on the persona of his favorite alter ego, Bubba Claus. "He's Santa Claus's third cousin twice removed. He dresses in green, lives at the South Pole, drives a magic jeep because he don't want to clean out reindeer stalls, and takes care of kids that ain't been all that good."

Yet T. Bubba Bechtol feels his greatest accomplishment resides in how he changed the preconceptions of his nick-name. "My name and the phrase 'he's a Bubba' has come to denote a big ol' lovable galoot with a good heart."

"Hey, Dementoids and Dementites!"

DR. DEMENTO

"Country music has been a meaningful part of my life since 1952, when I realized at age eleven that I liked Hank Williams's version of 'Jambalaya' better than Jo Stafford's," says Barrett Hansen, better known to radio listeners as Dr. Demento. "Since then I've collected and enjoyed thousands of country records from Eck Robertson to Vince Gill."

Easily the best-known comedy music host in broadcasting history, Hansen has been showcasing zany recordings from all genres of music since he started his *Dr. Demento* program in 1970. On any given night his syndicated show may feature artists as diverse as Barnes & Barnes, Harry "The Hipster" Gibson, Cledus T. Judd, and his discovery, "Weird" Al Yankovic.

A noted archivist, Hansen has researched and compiled dozens of collections issued by Rhino, Specialty, and Time-Life Records, and has written authoritative pieces about early R&B for various publications. His knowledge of pre–World War II blues and country secured him regular airtime on the public broadcasting outlet KPFK.

Hansen credits the early L.A. club scene for expanding his country horizons. "I met several all-time-great country performers while working at the Ash Grove in Los Angeles, Southern California's top club for traditional music in the 1960s. Bill Monroe, the Stoneman family, the Kentucky Colonels with Roland and Clarence White, to name a few. Another time, I met Tex Ritter. All of these [artists] made me respect and love country music more."

During the days when the Sunset Strip dominated California's music scene, Hansen was often alone among his peers in his appreciation of classic country. "When Bob Wills appeared at the Palomino in North Hollywood circa 1965, I couldn't get anyone I knew to go along with me, and the crowd there hassled me some because of my hippie-ish looks.

But it wasn't all that bad, and I'm sure glad I got to see Bob and his band."

Although he feels far from isolated, Hansen's love of country continues to be a solitary pursuit. "My wife doesn't like country music very much. Neither did my parents. But I can deal with that. It's not a major issue. We each have our own stereo."

Asked what his favorite nonparody country recordings are, the famed disc jockey answers, "Hank Williams's 'Jambalaya,' 'Settin' the Woods On Fire,' Buck Owens's 'Love's Gonna Live Here Again,' the Carter Family's 'Keep on the Sunny Side,' and lots of joyous string band music from the 1920s. Leake County Revelers' 'Johnson Gal,' Eck Robertson's 'Sallie Gooden,' etcetera."

As you might have guessed, vintage country appeals to Hansen more than the genre's contemporary sounds. "To me, most country songs of the past forty years are just clever concoctions built around a catchphrase, enlivened by heartfelt singing (sometimes) and fancy pickin'. Enjoyable enough, but not something to guide the course of my life. The earlier country music that I love makes me tap my feet and dance around the room, and/or appreciate the depth of its feeling, but that doesn't rule my life either. For serious emotional issues, blues works a lot better for me . . . more truly uplifting."

Then, with tongue in cheek, he adds, "country songs have often encouraged me to have another beer. I'll readily admit to that."

Hansen began adopting the on-air persona of Dr. Demento for the free-form Los Angeles rock station KPPC.

When it moved to KMET in 1972, the show proved popular enough to syndicate in 1974. Since then, Dementians and Dementites have been tuning in to hear the hilarious and twisted sounds of "Fish Heads," "Dead Puppies Aren't Much Fun," and "Christmas at Ground Zero."

When it comes to his area of expertise, the knowledgeable record spinner has some definite advice for those looking to start a country humor collection. "Homer & Jethro wrote the book on country parody, but Ray Stevens took it to the top of the charts, and Pinkard & Bowden were real good while they lasted. 'Mississippi Squirrel Revival' and 'The Streak' by Ray Stevens have probably gotten more requests over the years than any other genuinely country recordings that I've played. I still love Ray's work, but he was better in the 1960s when he did character voices that livened up his music. He hasn't put as much effort into his records since he began working the country music field instead of pop music."

How has country music changed his life? The man called Dr. Demento answers quite sincerely. "I think it's helped me get more in tune with how working class Americans feel and express themselves, and made me a little bit more of a mensch than I would have been had I only been exposed to the fine art culture my parents loved."

Living the life Buffett writes about.

BRENT BURNS

S inger-songwriter Brent Burns recalls with delight how legendary radio host Paul Harvey turned his satirical ditty "Cheaper Crude or No More Food" into a national hit. "That thing was released in 1979, but I actually wrote it in '76," explains Burns. "I shelved it, and a buddy of mine from San Diego called me one day and said, 'You remember that song "Cheaper Crude or No More Food"? If I get something going with that thing, could I get a little piece of the publishing?'

"I said, 'Well, sure, Ray.' He had produced my first rock 'n' roll records, and we were buddies, and I trusted him. So a few days later he called and said, 'Paul Harvey wants a release on it.'

"I said, 'What for?'

"Ray said, 'I don't know, maybe he's going to quote from it.'

"[Harvey] didn't play music, so I said, 'Well, what have we got to lose?' So, I signed a release for Paul Harvey, and then I forgot about it. Well, his people called my people, as they say, and said, 'Be listening to our Wednesday broadcast.' Now remember, this is a tape in the can, we don't have a record or anything. So, Paul Harvey, who at the time *owned* radio, played 'Cheaper Crude or No More Food.'

"Our phone lit up! Within days we were on the front page of the *Arizona Republic*, I was being interviewed by the BBC, and I had a record company fly in from Nashville to sign us up and get some vinyl out as quickly as possible. They had product on the street within seven days. Then, Paul played it again on Friday because he had such a reaction to it. Then he played it *again* on his Saturday show, because his phones were just lighting up all over the United States. It just exploded on the scene."

The surprise backdoor hit not only gave vent to Burns's sometimes controversial humor, but also boosted a career that provides a textbook example of how an artist can actually thrive outside of country's mainstream.

Born in Seminole, Oklahoma, and transplanted to Maryvale, Arizona, in 1958 when he was nine years old, Burns first learned how to play the guitar from his dad. Although some of his earliest influences were such Arizona-based performers as Waylon Jennings and Marty Robbins, the youngster's first taste of regional fame came with the 1960s rock group the Grapes of Wrath. "We recorded a lot back in the sixties and early seventies," says Burns. "I left the group in '68, but we recorded from '65 until after I left the band for a couple of years. We had a couple of singles that did well regionally. I even get a royalty check every once in a while."

When Burns was drafted into the U.S. Army in 1968, his rock 'n' roll career came to an end, but he began to finally appreciate country music. "My father told me, 'You need to get into country music; that's where the money is for you.'

"I'd just say, 'Yeah, right, Dad. I'm not listening to the *Grand Ole Opry* for nothin'.'

"But in the service, you'd run into these guys from the South who like country music, and they're cranking their stereos up and stuff, and I really started to grow fond of it."

During a tour of duty in Vietnam, Burns was "shot pretty severely in the chest and leg" and awarded the Purple Heart. But neither injury nor recurring, life-threatening infections could keep him from making music. "I was actually picking music before I got out of the hospital. I got transferred to the VA hospital in Phoenix and had a family, one kid, and I wasn't making that much of a pension.

"I was an inpatient at the VA hospital and I was hooked up to a needle. Every six hours they were giving me intravenous injections of antibiotics because of this infection I couldn't get rid of. I would leave the hospital to go and play a gig with this needle tucked under my long-sleeved shirt, come back, crawl back in bed, and they'd hook me back up. It was a weird thing. I'd do my gigs three nights a week, and the rest of the time I was an inpatient at the VA hospital."

Once fully healed, Burns vacillated between rock and country until he scored with his breakthrough hit, "Cheaper Crude or No More Food," a pointed response to the skyrocketing gas prices of the mid- to late seventies. Soon after, Burns began appearing on shows headlined by Merle Haggard and Hoyt Axton.

The song not only touched a nerve with a fed up American public, it also drew a surprising amount of controversy in political circles. As an example, "Nippon TV came over from Japan, and they were doing a special called *Food as a Weapon*," remembers Burns. "They came to Gulf Shores, where I was playing at the time, and interviewed me. We got to talking, and there were about eight of them in the film crew, and one of them spoke English. Well, they mentioned that they had been in Washington, D.C., filming, and the undersecretary of agriculture would not give them an interview because he knew they were also coming to interview me. The song had caused such a fervor and became such a popular chant that he would not grant them the interview."

The success of his initial hit convinced the singer that he should move to Nashville and hone his songwriting skills.

"Then, I went and did something that wasn't good for my songwriting career," confesses Burns. "I went through about a ten-year-long songwriting block. Oh, it was terrible. Literally, for ten years, I hardly wrote at all, and I tried a lot. I was living in Nashville, and I would try to write with guys, and I wasn't cutting it. I don't know what happened. A song-writer's block of ten years is near death for a writer. I just thought, 'I'm just not going to do this anymore. God just took it away.'"

Once he moved away from the pressures of Nashville to Gulf Shores, Alabama, Burns began writing again and started to unpack all the funny ideas that had built up inside him over the years. In 1998, he formed his own label, Sand Spur, and began recording and marketing his own discs.

The key to the singer-songwriter's renewed popularity? He writes from an everyman angle about things his regional audience relates to. "A song I wrote is a hit in the South and some warm places; it's called, 'If It's Snowbird Season, Why Can't We Shoot 'Em?' It's one of those deals that goes on the edge of bad taste and just doesn't quite fall off," Burns laughs.

A constant presence on local morning radio, Burns finds that his mix of country, Jimmy Buffett, and rock confuses some fans. "People who are country don't consider me real country. They say, 'You kind of do that rock 'n' roll stuff.' I say, 'No, not really.' By contrast, the rock 'n' roll people think I'm real country. I don't know what I am, and I don't try to put a name on it. It depends on what song it is. If a song is a real story song like 'FTF' or 'I'm Going Ugly Early Tonight,' how many great story or novelty songs are done in rock 'n' roll? Country music is the best vehicle for those songs because you're telling a story."

In early 2003, with the war versus Iraq looming and the French government declining support to the United States, Burns wrote the incendiary "FTF (Forget the French)." The record has been his biggest mainstream success since "Cheaper Crude or No More Food," and like his earlier hit, has benefited from airplay on talk radio and word of mouth. "'Cheaper Crude' and the 'FTF' songs are very similar in that they speak in a different venue than just newspaper print, and they tell what people are feeling," explains Burns. "That's why, when I do 'FTF' live, I can't get through it for all the people yelling, 'Yeah, man! Damn right!' But they're also laughing. And that's the trick, to make them say 'Yeah! Damn right,' but still make them laugh."

The main thing Burns has learned from his experience is to just relax, be himself, and get creative with his marketing strategy. "One of the greatest things for independent artists of all genres right now is the Internet. It's fabulous. Internet radio stations are playing my stuff. It used to be, for a small artist like myself, you might get some airplay in Laramie, Wyoming or Kingman, Arizona, and there were no record stores that would carry my product because they only carried the Top 40 as listed in *Billboard* magazine. But now, if you get airplay in Laramie, Wyoming; Kingman, Arizona; or Foley, Alabama, once they type in 'Brent Burns,' my Web site automatically pops up, and they can buy my product."

With writer's block a thing of the past, and a solid following in clubs, Burns is genuinely pleased with how country music has changed his life. "I live less than a quarter mile from the beach," he crows. "I realize that not living in Nashville anymore is hurting my career a little bit, but I have a lot of friends here. I have three wonderful kids, I'm doing what I love, and I'm actually making really good money. As my buddy at BMI said, 'You're probably making a lot more money than artists on major labels right now because nothing is selling.' Life is pretty good and I'm happy. Yeah, it'd be great to sell a million records—and I might— but if I don't, I'm having a ball writing those songs."

"May the bird of paradise fly up your nose!"

LITTLE JIMMY DICKENS

From Johnny Carson to Minnie Pearl, Little Jimmy Dickens has gotten a lot of his best material from other stars. But in the case of Hank Williams, it's the story, not the song, that stayed with Little Jimmy.

"I traveled quite a bit with Hank Williams in concert," remembers Dickens with a chuckle. "We just became good buddies and shared the same dressing room and so forth. Well, we were flying one time to Wichita with Minnie Pearl and her husband in Minnie's airplane. [Hank] said, 'Tater, you need a hit.'

"I said, 'OK, everybody needs a hit.'

"He said, 'Let me just write you one. Get a piece of paper and a pencil.'

"And I did. Minnie Pearl got into the glove box and gave me a scrap of paper and a pen, and he started quoting lines. Just off the top of his head: 'Hey Good Lookin'.' He wrote that song in a half an hour, and he said, 'Now you record that and it'll make you a hit.'

"I said, 'I'll do it the next time I'm in a studio.'

"I saw him about a week later up in the hallway at the *Grand Ole Opry* building, and he said, 'Tater, I recorded your song today.'

"I said, 'What song?'

"He said, 'Hey Good Lookin'.'

"I said, 'You *didn't*!'

"He said, 'Yeah I did, yeah I did.'

"Those are things that you don't forget."

As for Minnie Pearl, she helped him develop the comedy portion of his song-and-monologue act. "When I first came here, we worked concerts together with Red Foley, Ernest Tubb, and Roy Acuff on package things from here to California and back. She knew I was new on the *Opry*, and she took a liking to me. I'd go on the stage and do some little gag, and she'd watch me while I worked. When I'd come off she'd say, 'Do you want me to show you how to get a better laugh out of that joke?' Then she'd take the time to show me what to do, the timing on it. The timing on being funny is the most important thing, and she taught me all that."

Asked why the "Gal from Grinder's Switch" was so popular, Dickens had a ready answer. "A lot of people related to what [Minnie Pearl] was saying because they knew people just like who she was talking about. The 'rural route people' knew what she was talking about anyway."

Jimmy was one of those "rural route people" himself. "We were raised up in the coal fields of West Virginia," he reminisces. One of thirteen children, he was raised primarily by his grandmother. There was always a guitar around the house that either his mother or uncle would play, and he learned the basics from them and forged his style during family sing-alongs. "I knew from childhood that I wanted to be an entertainer," remembers Dickens. "That was my one wish in life, to be on stage as an entertainer."

Radio proved to be the only way Dickens could realize his dream and escape the hardships of the local mines: WJLS in Beckley, West Virginia, with the Bailes Brothers and Molly O'Day; WMNN in Fairmont, West Virginia; WIBC in Indianapolis, with T. Texas Tyler; WLW in Cincinnati; WIBW in Topeka, Kansas.

And along the way, he got help from his fellow stars. "Texas Tyler taught me more about stage presence and the dos and the don'ts of it than anybody in the world. He was a man with words," says Dickens, impressed by Tyler's mere memory. "He knew the right thing to say at the right time, and he was a great salesperson. During the early days of radio, when we sold products over the air, he was the biggest mail puller I've ever seen. It was nothing for us to get four or five thousand letters a week during World War II. He was just a natural born salesperson, and he would sell himself to the people first through his humbleness. When we worked together as a duet, he just considered me his little boy and people just loved that."

Another star who helped Dickens become one himself was the man they once called the "King of Country Music," Roy Acuff. "I met Mr. Acuff when I was at WLW," says Dickens respectfully. "I met him at his concert and talked with him. He had me do a number on his show and liked what I did. We corresponded for two or three years, and then he came to Saginaw, Michigan, where I was working. I opened the show for him that day; I had a little band, and he said that he might make arrangements for me to come down to the *Grand Ole Opry*, and he did that. I came down for two guest appearances on the Red Foley portion of the show, and the third time I came back he told me to just bring my belongings because he thought he could arrange for me to stay here.

"I never did funny songs until the *Grand Ole Opry*," Dickens states. "Of course my first recording [in 1949] was a novelty song, 'Take an Old Cold Tater and Wait.' So I had to follow that with others songs in that line, like 'Sleepin' at the Foot of the Bed,' 'Plain Old Country Boy,' 'Out Behind the Barn,' and those things. I just got branded as a novelty singer. But when we shipped the records out I always had a ballad on the back; the DJs just wouldn't play 'em because to their way of thinking that wasn't Jimmy Dickens."

Because of "Take an Old Cold Tater and Wait," his first Top 10 country hit, Dickens acquired the nickname "Tater," which his friends call him even today. Of course not all of his hits were novelty records; his renditions of "My Heart's Bouquet," "We Could," and "I've Just Got to See You Once More" were pure country romance. That said, live audiences seemed to respond better to funny songs such as "I'm Little but I'm Loud" and "It May Be Silly (But Ain't It Fun)."

As for the *Opry*, as Dickens says, "I've been here since 1948!" And he remains there today, one of the last *Grand Ole Opry* members of yore who can still really entertain his audience with his unflagging energy and folksy humor. Standing just four feet, eleven inches tall, Little Jimmy is one of country music's most beloved figures because he sincerely relates to an audience as if they're his friends.

How ironic, then, that his most lasting claim to fame was the classic put-down song "May the Bird of Paradise Fly Up Your Nose" (originally one of Johnny Carson's favorite catchphrases). Dickens remembers the session well: "I was in the studio finishing up an album for Columbia and my friend Pat Wilson walked in; he was with Central Songs in California, but he lived here. He's the guy that had brought me 'Sleepin' at the Foot of the Bed.' So he brought this new record in and said, 'I think I've got a hit for you if you've got time to listen to it.' It was the middle of a session, but I took a five-minute break to listen to it. I knew when I heard it that it would be a great piece of material for me, if nothing more than an addition to my show because of Johnny Carson kicking that phrase around. So I went ahead and did it and, you know, we ran it down one time with the band, and on the first actual take, that was it. We got it on one take!"

At the peak of the song's success, Dickens appeared on *The Tonight Show* and played it for Johnny Carson himself. "He loved it," chuckled Dickens fondly. "He thought it was great."

Was he disappointed that he never had another hit the size of "May the Bird of Paradise Fly Up Your Nose"?

"That's a once-in-a-lifetime occurrence," states Dickens philosophically. "It's hard to follow a song like that. Novelty songs are here today and gone tomorrow. For the time being they're hot when they're hot and not when they're not."

But Dickens's most lasting impact on American popular music may well be on the fashion front, where he also got a little help from western wear's greatest designer. "Well, I was the first one on the *Grand Ole Opry* to wear rhinestones," confesses Dickens. "Mr. Nudie had made some suits for me during the early fifties without rhinestones, and one day I was in his office there in north Hollywood, and he said, 'I'm doing some things in rhinestones now if you'd be interested in it.' Then he showed me some of his work that he had done, and I said, 'That's for me!' So I started wearing the rhinestones—and the rest is history. Everybody wore them from there on."

What was the audience reaction like the first time the spotlights hit those rhinestones?

"Oohs and ahs! That plays a big part in my act," he chuckles. "I've tried it both ways. I've gone out in a western-cut suit and then gone out with the rhinestones, and I could tell the difference in the audience reaction."

In return for the help given him, Dickens has always been helpful to younger performers. He first brought super-picker Thumbs Carlisle to Nashville and also had a hand in bringing Marty Robbins to national prominence. "I had a little input on that," says Dickens modestly. "I can't say that I discovered him, but we were in Phoenix with the *Grand Ole Opry* show, and they asked me to go by his television show and plug our performance for the night. I heard him sing, and when I got to Los Angeles I told [Columbia A&R chief] Mr. Satherley about him, that there's this boy down in Phoenix that should be listened to. The next thing I knew he was on Columbia Records. He had more control and more quality to his voice than anybody I've ever heard."

Dickens's personal manager, Richard Davis, confirms his client's generosity. When I asked him if Dickens likes the new breed of country singer, he said, "Absolutely—and they love him right back. Not too long ago, the *Opry* featured a performance by Martina McBride on an anniversary program. Well, her performance ran a little long, so they didn't have time to wheel out the cake or something. So backstage, some of the old hens at the *Opry* gave her a real hard time about it. Well, Tater wouldn't stand for that, and he came to her defense. Apparently that meant a lot to Martina, because on her next album she recorded Little Jimmy's song "I'm Little but I'm Loud." Now with all the songwriters pitching her material all the time, she didn't need to go digging that one up, but she did it out of appreciation for Tater. Needless to say, his royalty statements took a big jump."

A modest man, Dickens would never tell a story like that himself. For him it's all about getting on stage and entertaining the people, which he still does at the age of eighty-three. Asked how country music changed his life, the singer of funny songs speaks with humble gratitude. "Well, from a little guy running up and down the hills and hollows of West Virginia, not knowing what direction I was going in, working my way up to where I am today. I've made a lot of friends all through the years, and I hope that we're all still friends."

7

BIG STARS AND
AN ICON

It's one thing to have a hit record, but quite another to build a career. Although the genre has had plenty of one-hit wonders, country music is perhaps best defined by its artists who have been in it for the long haul. To these people, the music hasn't changed their lives, it is their lives. During interviews for this project, the most common answer to the question "how has country music changed your life?" was "it gave me a job doing something I love." So the questions that remained were, how did you get this job, and how did you hold on to it?

Today.

BOBBY BARE

A true country music giant, Bobby Bare scored nearly sixty Top 40 hits between 1962 and 1983. With a laconic vocal style that embraces both wry wit and poignant storytelling, the Ironton, Ohio, native has a literate, cross-cultural appeal that has earned him the sobriquet the "Springsteen of country."

As he will attest, Bare's early life wasn't exactly easy. "Well, my mother died when I was five," he states plainly. "That was in early '41. I had two sisters, one was seven, one was two. My dad couldn't take care of all us. So my younger sister was adopted to some people who lived down the road. Then, my other sister stayed with my grandparents and different relatives. When I was seven my dad remarried. I was very bright in school. As a matter of fact, I was in eighth grade when I was eleven. Then, when I was sixteen, I left home. I couldn't get along with my stepmother. So, I left home and stayed with my grandmother, my aunts and my uncles, and put a little band together."

He regularly listened to the *Grand Ole Opry*, but Bare also enjoyed the big bands of the forties, the southern-fried, fast-talking humor of Phil Harris's "That's What I Like about the South," and even the salacious R&B of the Dominoes singing "Sixty Minute Man." "And then, of course, there came Hank Williams, Carl Smith, Webb Pierce, Hank Thompson, and Little Jimmy Dickens," remembers Bare warmly. "I loved all of that, still do. The first country music show I ever went to was with Little Jimmy Dickens. The first song I ever sang in public was Little Jimmy Dickens's 'Sleepin' at the Foot of the Bed.'"

After forming his first band, the sixteen-year-old Bare lucked into an early morning radio show. "You just go and audition, talk to 'em, and tell them you're willing to do it early in the morning for nothing, and that's it," he jokes. That experience led to an even better radio slot, four hours every Saturday in Wilston, Ohio, where he and his band would attract an unusually large drive-up audience.

"Looking back, I was really hot," observes Bare. "We were broadcasting live from a radio station which was a farmhouse out in the middle of a field. This was before TV completely took over in about '52 or '53. On Saturday afternoons, it wasn't unusual to look out the window of the radio station while we were broadcasting and see a hundred cars parked in that field watching the farm house. Weird, if you think about it. It was just jammed on Saturday night."

While playing in Portsmouth, Ohio, the devil-may-care young singer accepted an offer that eventually put his career in motion. "Some old boy came in from California; he had a Palomino Club bumper sticker on his Dodge convertible with the window out in the back, and he had a Nudie suit," reminisces Bare. "First one I ever saw in my life. Anyway, he said, 'Boys, you guys could get work out there in California.' It was December and colder than hell, and I could see that I had done everything around there that I could do. We were having big crowds because they were building that atomic plant outside of Portsmouth. There were construction workers in these beer joints and people were fighting every night. I realized that just wasn't what I wanted to do with my life. Anyway, this guy said he knew some of the big time musicians that I had heard of in California, Jimmy Bryant and Speedy West and all that. So he said, 'Why don't you go with me to California?'

"I said, 'Hell, I'll go.'

"My steel player said, 'I'll go.'

"But our bass player had a wife and kids, so he couldn't go. So, we took off."

Lest you think the stranger with the Dodge convertible was motivated solely by Bare's talent, think again. "The reason he wanted us to go was because he didn't have any money, and he needed someone to pay for gas," Bare drolly reports. "I only had forty or fifty bucks, and my steel player, every time he paid his bar bill he didn't have any money. I didn't know that the forty or fifty bucks I had was the only money we had among us." When they started to run out of money in the southwest, Bare and crew played bars for tips and a piece of the door until they got to California, which is where Bare would call home for the next ten years.

"It turns out this old boy we were riding with really did know Jimmy Bryant and Speedy West," says Bare. "He introduced me to Speedy West, the steel guitar player for Cliffie Stone. He had played on a lot of hits like 'Shotgun Boogie' and all them. Speedy loved my singing and started taking me around. I wrote songs for his publishing company, met Cliffie Stone, and I'd do his radio show. Then I got a job at a big showroom in Long Beach, the Sailor Club, and I was there. Speedy was the one who got me a record deal with Capitol." Another Capitol artist, Wynn Stewart, befriended Bare and allowed the younger singer to stay at his home while he established himself as a recording artist.

"The very first side I cut, Ken Nelson produced it," recalls Bare. "He played me a record on Pep Records by Buck

Owens called 'Down on the Corner of Love.' I had already heard the record. I told Ken, 'I love Buck's singing.'

"He told me, 'Well, Buck's a good guitar player, but he can't sing.'" (Ken Nelson later ended up producing most of Buck Owens's massive string of Capitol hits.)

"So, I cut two sessions for Capitol. Buck played rhythm guitar on 'em and Merrill Moore played piano. Actually, on the demos I cut in Garrison Studios in Long Beach, I used Wynn Stewart's band. It cost thirty-five dollars; the band played for nothing. I hocked everything I had to get that thirty-five bucks."

When nothing came of the first single, Nelson, who also produced rockabilly greats Gene Vincent and Wanda Jackson, hoped to record Bare in the style of Elvis Presley. "I did one thing called 'The Living End,' and 'I Beg Her,'" says Bare of his lone rockabilly outing. "They weren't very good records. Then I told Ken, 'I've got some ideas of where we could do something fresh and different and new.' He made some kind of a spiel about how Wrigley's doesn't change the flavor of their gum. Anyway, I told Speedy that I needed to get away from Capitol.

"At that time, the friends I had worked with in Long Beach were called the Champs, and they were on Challenge Records and had a big hit called 'Tequila.' The fact is, I used some of those guys on the last session I cut with Capitol. But, I knew I could get a record deal with Challenge, which I did."

None of the Challenge sides were successful either, and Bare's first appearance on the charts would come under someone else's name. "Along about that time, I was working a club in Riverside and doing real good there," explains Bare. "There was an old woman who was an alcoholic owned the club. The guy she was leasing from didn't want to deal with her anymore because she was too old, too crazy, and too drunk. She was losing her lease, so I just took the place over, and she let me have all the stuff. We're doing real good there until I got drafted in '58. I went down to L.A. and took my physical, passed it, and then I had to go back to Ohio to go into the army. So, I just dumped the club, went back to Ohio.

"The month before I went in, a buddy of mine who used to be my bass player just got out of the army, Bill Parsons. He kind of sang like Carl Smith, and he was wanting to try to get a record deal. Well, I knew that what you had to do was cut some demos. So, we got some musicians off the streets of Dayton, Ohio—I was staying there with my sister—and got this old boy who bought the club I used to work in—his name was Cherokee—and he wanted to be in the record business. So, he was paying for the studio time and the musicians.

"We went to King Records in Cincinnati and did some demos, spent most of the three hours working on a thing called 'Rubber Dolly,' with Bill singing it. In the meantime, I was making up this talking blues song about going into the army. We had fifteen minutes left and I said, 'Let me put this down real quick so I don't forget it.' So, I did. We put it down in about four or five cuts. That was 'The All-American Boy.'

"Cherokee, who was paying for all of it, wanted to get a copy made but Syd Nathan was revamping his studio then and had all of his equipment tore down, his copy machines and everything. So, he suggested that maybe Harry Carlson of Fraternity Records in Cincinnati could make a copy off that tape. Bill and I went back up to Dayton to a bar we used to hang out in and Cherokee went down to the record company to get an acetate made, and they heard it and wanted to put it out. While he was there, he called us at the club and said that they had offered him five hundred bucks. I said, 'Hell, take it. Just don't put my name on it,' because I think I was still under contract to Challenge.

"Anyway, Cherokee got five hundred bucks for it, and he came by the club and gave me fifty dollars and Parsons fifty dollars, and he took the other four hundred and used it to pay for the rubber check that he wrote to finance the session. That was the end of that; I forgot about it."

"The All-American Boy," issued under Bill Parsons's name, was really about Bare, but record-buying audiences responded to its allusions to Elvis Presley's rapid rise and abrupt army induction, which made it a massive pop hit. Bare was engaged in basic training at Fort Knox when he learned of the record's success. "I forgot about it until I heard it on the radio one night during basic training," remembers Bare. "[Disc jockey] John R. was playing it on WLAC and this was in November. A month later, I went home for Christmas, and it was the hottest record in America. It was scary. Bill [Parsons] was scared to death. He said, 'What in the hell am I going to do? They want me to do the Dick Clark show, and I don't even know that song! Let alone lip-synch it.'

"I said, 'Take the money and run. I'll be in the army for two years, and it's only rock 'n' roll; it'll be forgotten in three weeks.'"

Parsons did the promotional tours, but at least one prominent person wasn't fooled into believing he was the actual singer of "The All-American Boy." "He went to New York, Philadelphia, and the fact is he was on that tour when the Big Bopper and all them guys got killed. The show had to go on, so he was one of the ones they called in to finish out that tour. That's when he met Waylon [Jennings, who was playing bass for Buddy Holly] and that's the first time Waylon had ever heard my name. He went up to Bill and said, 'That ain't you doing that record.' Bill said, 'No, that's Bobby Bare, a GI from California.' I think Bill did one more tour, playing bass for the Everly Brothers, and that was about it for him."

Bare never received a royalty check from the hit and claims not to care that Parsons' name was listed on the label. "Fact is, it was really good that my name wasn't on that record. Because then I probably wouldn't have had any serious hits like 'Detroit City,' I would've been pegged as a novelty type guy."

During his army stint, Bare entered an all-army talent contest, and won first place with an instrumental group called the Latin Five. Part of the honor of winning included an appearance on the *Ed Sullivan Show* in New York, the memory of which remains clear in Bare's mind. "We all loaded up on the bus and went to New York, my first trip there. By then Fraternity Records had figured out that it was me doing that record, so I had agreed to do a record for them. It was supposed to be reviewed that week in *Billboard*. So, when we pulled up in front of the Shelton Towers, I saw a little newsstand right over from there. The little lady running it looked like my grandmother.

"I hopped off the bus, ran over and asked her, 'Do you have a *Billboard* magazine?'

"She looked at me and said, 'You fucking jerk!'

"I said, 'Wh-what?'

"'I said you're a fucking jerk!'

"'What do you mean?'

"'You know I don't have a *Billboard* magazine. You ask me that every week.'

"I said, "No, I just got here."

"She said, 'You're a fucking jerk!' and she was getting louder every minute and I'm backing up. She scared me.

"The other boys asked, 'What did you say to that old lady, Bobby?'

"'I just asked her for a magazine and she went off on me.'

"That was my introduction to New York."

Did Ed Sullivan know Bare was the singer of the current smash "The All-American Boy"?

"No," laughs Bare. "He didn't even know who was on the damn show. He was never there. That's why he was so bad MCing and mispronouncing names: he'd just come down for the show. He looked over the names just before he went on, but really, he had no idea what was going on."

Post-army recordings for Fraternity didn't fare too well, although Bare did appear on *American Bandstand* to plug his single "The Book of Love" and wrote some songs for the 1962 drive-in flick, *Teenage Millionaire*. Luckily, he had friends who believed in him as a country artist.

"I made records for about a year or so for Fraternity," say Bare. "By then all my friends that I started out with in California—Harlan Howard, Hank Cochran, and all them people—had moved back here by then and became really successful. So, I would come to Nashville, stay at Harlan's house, and record sometimes. But, they all ganged up and told Chet [Atkins] how great I was, and he wanted to meet me. So I met Chet who said, 'Come back in a week and we'll have you a contract and look for songs, cut you a record.'"

Signed to RCA, Bare's career broke wide open with a series of crossover hits that were as much folk as they were country. The singer attributes much of his success to producer Chet Atkins's willingness to listen to his ideas, and Bill Justis's arrangement skills. "I told Chet right up front that I didn't want to use any of the regulars, I wanted new pickers. I got Jerry Reed, Joe South, Charlie McCoy, and Ray Stevens. We got some fresh stuff," Bare modestly admits. "Bill Justis is a great arranger. I went in with this idea for a horn sound on 'Shame on Me' and he took that and ran with it. Then, 'Detroit City,' he took that and ran with it and did the strings. The strings in Nashville back then were real screechy, bad players; they didn't have a symphony here yet. But Justis, he was able to write 'em where they wouldn't hurt your teeth."

Even though he was now a star on his own terms, that didn't mean he couldn't be embarrassed. "'Shame On Me' was a big pop song," states Bare. "The record company had me do a record hop with Marc Avery. The first thing I did was I went down there on Santa Monica Boulevard to one of those cheap places and bought one of those shiny, tight-legged suits. I was doing record hops for Marc up there in Detroit and the stage was just high enough—about three or four feet high—and I thought, 'Should I leap on the stage or should I walk around?' I decided to leap on the stage like a rock 'n' roll star. Just as I leaped, the whole ass of my pants said, 'Rip!' Cheap material. It ripped sideways and my ass was sticking out. It turned out good, though, a bunch of them girls there fixed me up with some safety pins."

Avoiding the dreaded sophomore slump, Bare hit even bigger with his Grammy-winning rendition of "Detroit City." "I heard Billy Grammer's record of 'Detroit City' while I was driving down the street one day and I damn near wrecked my car. I thought it was the greatest song I ever heard in my life. As soon as I got back to Nashville, we recorded it. Chet loved that song too. I think he had already done it on Porter Wagoner for an album or something."

Boasting a keen ear for a song, Bare adapted another major smash from a vintage folk melody. "I wrote '500 Miles Away From Home'; that's an old folk song," he explains. "Me and Don Bowman were driving back home from San Diego one night when I lived in California, and I heard Peter, Paul, and Mary sing that, and I said, 'Goddamn, that's great!' I remembered that title.

"Well, Glen Campbell lived right down the street from me at the time, and he had just done a bluegrass album or something with that in it and brought it to me. As soon as I got it home, I played it, but it was an instrumental version of it. So, I just wrote a new set of lyrics and recorded it. I still don't know the original lyrics."

When asked what his working relationship with the late Chet Atkins was like, Bare responds with amazement. "Pretty uncanny. I was living in California and coming back here to record, and I'd bundle up a whole bunch of songs that were my favorites, that I really thought I'd like to record, like 'Miller's Cave,' 'Detroit City,' and all those. Well, I'd come back and Chet would have the same songs. We were close on that. His instincts were the best I've ever seen on what would be a hit and what wouldn't. Very seldom fooled. If he thought a song was going to be a hit, it would be."

The singer's crossover streak ended after "Miller's Cave," but he continued to rack up Top 40 country hits well into the 1980s. The key to his longevity has been his ability to find great material such as Tom T. Hall's "Margie's at the Lincoln Park Inn" and "How I Got to Memphis." Many of his best-remembered songs were written by the late Shel Silverstein, who can be heard doing the voodoo scream on Bare's 1974 #1 hit "Marie Laveau."

Credited with recording the first country concept album, 1967's *Bird Named Yesterday*, the artist recalls how 1973's far more popular *Bobby Bare Sings Lullabys, Legends and Lies* was conceived. Was Silverstein always his first choice to write it?

"No, I was trying to get Hank [Cochran], Red Lane, Don Cook, Harlan [Howard], and all those guys to write me an album. Number one, it would keep me from having to go around and dig up songs. Number two, if you get a great, brilliant, successful writer to write you twelve new songs, the odds are very good that a couple of them are going to be hits. So, I approached all of them and they were all geared for single records. They didn't think albums; they could come up with two or three songs they thought would be hit singles, but for twelve sides that would make sense and tie together, they didn't have it.

"Then, I approached Shel at Harlan's house. He had a big party every year; Kris [Kristofferson], everybody was there. Anyway, I got to talking to Shel and told him what I was looking for. This was on Saturday night. Well, by Monday morning he called from Chicago and he said, 'I've got you an album.' So he hopped on a plane, came down to my office there, and sang me some of those songs. One of them was 'The Winner,' and I had to make him stop halfway through because I was laughing so hard. On that first album alone was 'Daddy What If,' 'Marie Laveau,' and 'The Winner.'"

The last project Bare and Silverstein worked on together was 1998's *Old Dogs* album with Waylon Jennings, Jerry Reed, and Mel Tillis. "We spent about a year in the studio working on that," Bare recollects. "We had a ton of fun. That's the last thing Shel ever did. I was just devastated when he died. I was here at home with a couple of my fishing buddies, and I got a call from Herb Gardner, the playwright from New York. He and Shel had been friends; they started out together. Herb called me. 'It ain't good, Bobby.'

"I said, 'What?'

"He told me that Shel had died the night before. It just floored me because he was the last one I expected to go. He was the only one of all my friends who took care of himself. He ate right, he exercised, and everything. That was a real shocker. With most of my other friends, you could see it coming. With Chet, I could see that coming for two or three years at least. With Cliffie Stone, I could see that coming. I could check on Cliffie at least once a week and see how he was doing. And, Harlan, I didn't expect him to last as long as he did because he drank so hard there at the end. Waylon, we knew that was coming. But with Shel, we weren't ready for that; we were blindsided. But, I loved Shel with all my heart. I'm not over him dying yet. I'll probably never get over it."

The early twenty-first century finds Bobby Bare *Jr.* recording acclaimed rock-country for the Bloodshot label. Although obviously proud, Bare claims he hasn't advised his son on his career. "It's a brand new ballgame, what he's doing," he quips. "My phrase to him was, 'Son, I can't help you with this.'"

Asked how country has changed his life, Bare, whose career has spanned five decades answers, "Well, I've never had to get a real job."

When I express my belief that he does indeed work for a living, Bare responds with great sincerity. "No, I said a *real* job. I had a dream when I was a teenager and I was able to fulfill it. I was very lucky, and I got to know some really talented people. I've never had to deal with anybody I didn't like. I never had to deal with any assholes. All of the people I've dealt with I loved dearly and still do. I've never been disappointed."

"Ride the bull at your own risk!"

MICKEY GILLEY

"Well, I grew up in a little old small town called Ferriday, Louisiana, with my two famous cousins, Jerry Lee Lewis and Reverend [Jimmy Lee] Swaggert," says Mickey Gilley. "The style of piano we play was created by Jerry Lee, who began playing when he was about eight years old. I didn't start playing piano until I was thirteen. I first started out playing guitar, but piano really intrigued me."

In interviews, Gilley always takes the bull by the horns and mentions his two famous cousins, knowing that writers will bring them up anyway. After all, they are more famous and definitely more notorious. Yet being known as the "normal one" has its perks, and Gilley is easily the most successful of the three today. He has not publicly disgraced his faith or reputation, commands higher concert fees, and has his very own theater and restaurant in Branson, Missouri.

Unlike Lewis, Gilley is pleasant and off-the-cuff, loves to poke fun at himself, and is professional enough to muster enthusiasm for questions he must have been asked thousands of times. In this way, he is a greater ambassador for Jerry Lee's music than the Killer is himself.

Asked if Lewis ever taught him runs on the piano as a traditional teacher would, Gilley answers no, and then explains: "Jerry was a lot more advanced at the keyboards than I was. I had to struggle because Jerry Lee wasn't a great teacher. I'd watch him play, and I picked up a lot of things from him by listening to what he was doing. His first record was 'Crazy Arms,' and I started listening to that and fooling with the piano more seriously. I was about eighteen or nineteen years old. So, it was very easy for me to visualize what he was doing. I had never dreamed of going into the music industry as a profession, but I quit school in the tenth grade, and I thought I knew everything there was to know."

Gilley grew up with the same musical influences that Lewis and Swaggert did. He listened to the *Louisiana Hayride* and the *Grand Ole Opry*, hung out at the infamous blues dive Haney's Big House, and enjoyed early rock 'n' roll, especially Fats Domino, Little Richard, and Chuck Berry. He is also quick to give credit to Lewis's chief influence when analyzing his cousin's style.

"Moon Mullican," states Gilley. "If you listen to the early style of Jerry Lee you hear Moon Mullican's right hand, and you listen to the early hits of some of those rhythm and blues people you'll hear the left hand. I worked quite a bit to establish myself as far as playing the left hand goes. I've always said that Jerry Lee played a sharp piano."

Asked what that means, Gilley does his best to explain Lewis's keyboard attack. "What I'm trying to tell you is, he's on and off the keys so quick, that it's a sharp note instead of just"—and he sings some ordinary notes. "You listen to his early records like 'Whole Lotta Shakin'' and 'Great Balls of Fire,' you'll hear him playing real sharp. Somebody else might play 'Great Balls of Fire' and it would go like this: bum-bum-bum-bum. A flat sound. But Jerry's on and off the notes so fast with his fingers on the piano, and that's the one thing gave me a problem as far as playing 'You Win Again' and some of his earlier songs. For example, I did a version of 'Break Up' that I thought was pretty good, but the ride [the solo piano break] drove me up the wall. Because it was a real on and off sort of thing to play, and I had a lot of trouble with it at first."

The wages Gilley earned as a mechanic and in construction were a pittance compared to what Lewis was commanding at the crest of his rock 'n' roll fame. Knowing he could pump the piano in the same fashion, Gilley became an entertainer. "Although I didn't know that much about the music industry, once I got into it, I found that I liked it," he says today. Yet at the start of his career, there seemed to be room for only one Ferriday piano man.

Gilley's audition demos for Sun Records are available on several different boxed sets released during the late 1990s. Though these auditions were apparently set up by Lewis, if the Killer did anything else to help or encourage his cousin, it has gone undocumented. Indeed, in a Lewis fan club newsletter from the mid-seventies, Gilley himself mentions that Jerry Lee didn't invite him up on stage to play until after he began scoring hit records.

Sun Records didn't hire him. They had plenty of other Lewis sound-a-likes in Carl Mann, Charlie Rich, house pianist Jimmy Wilson, and another of Lewis's cousins, Carl McVoy. So Gilley signed up with Dot in 1958 and cut one single. From there he tried his luck with other deep south companies such as Crazy Cajun, Goldband, Paula, and his own Astro label.

On these early, cheaply produced recordings, Gilley offers pale imitations of some of Jerry Lee's big hits such as "Down the Line" and "Breathless" and remakes "Whole Lotta Shakin'" as "Whole Lotta Twistin' Goin' On." He fares better with his redrafting of Gene Vincent's rocker "Lotta

Lotta Lovin'" and the pleasingly melancholy "World of My Own," which hints at what he would later accomplish.

Collectors and overseas rockabilly afficionados prize his early work, but Gilley cringes comically when he speaks of it. "People ask me sometimes, 'Is there anything you would change if you could do it over again?' I say, 'Absolutely. I wouldn't make all those bad records I made back in the beginning.' That was a learning stage. I had recordings out there that were so bad, but to me at the time they were great. They were the best I could do at that time, and I listen to them now and I think, 'God, how did I ever make it in the music business? How did I ever get as far as I got?' But if you want to make it in music, you've got to have determination and the tenacity to stick with it regardless of all your downfalls. You have to say, 'I know I can do it. I know if I do this I'm going to get a little bit better.' You have to continue on, be yourself, and don't try to be something that you're not. Eventually, something will happen for you, and you'll see things start to change. That's what happened for me. Once I relaxed and became what I was really all about, things started happening for me."

What did happen for Gilley was that with little more than a regional hit record, he became an extremely popular club attraction in Houston, Texas. It was part of his career conundrum. "I tried to change my style over and over and over because everybody accused me of trying to copy my cousin Jerry Lee Lewis," admits Gilley. "I admired him and I was very close to the fact that I loved to play Jerry Lee's style of piano, and I could sing the songs. I was successful in the

With cousin Jerry Lee Lewis at Gilley's.

clubs because I could do his music. People would come listen to me, they'd come in from out of town and people would tell them, 'You've got to go out and hear this guy; he sounds just like Jerry Lee Lewis.'"

A regular sit-down gig at the Nesadel Club in Houston made him a local star. Then, in 1970, Sherwood Cryer approached Gilley about becoming the featured performer at a Pasadena, Texas, dance hall. Rechristened "Gilley's," the club was well publicized as the "world's biggest honky-tonk," and the performer's regional star shone even brighter. The last thing on his mind was a hit record.

"When I recorded 'Room Full of Roses' [a hit for George Morgan in 1949], I really went in to record 'She Called Me Baby.' I didn't need to have a hit record; I had a local TV show, and I had the club going. The club was doing great, and

I was still basically a young man at that time. But I recorded 'She Called Me Baby' for the lady who ran the jukebox in Gilley's. She wanted three hundred copies and I couldn't find Harlan Howard's version of it, so I agreed to go in and record that song for her. For the flip side, I recorded 'Room Full of Roses,' and when the record came out, the radio station flipped it over and played that side because it was different. Basically, it was what I grew up singing with Jimmy and Jerry."

Hugh Hefner's Playboy Records label picked up the single, and it became one of the biggest country hits of 1974. By this time there were some clear-cut differences between the two piano-playing cousins. Gilley's right hand was more melodic than Lewis's, and he could incorporate elements of Floyd Cramer's slip-note style into ballads. Vocally and instrumentally, Gilley was less concerned with intensity and personal hubris than with exploiting all the potential of a heartfelt song with a great hook.

Gilley's career exploded at the exact same time his cousin's started to falter. Aided by Eddie Kilroy, who masterminded Lewis's country comeback hit "Another Place, Another Time," Gilley recorded the type of classy honkytonk revival music the Killer had stopped dishing out when he returned to rock in 1973. As a result, after fifteen years in the shadows, Gilley emerged as a full-blown hitmaker in his own right.

For Gilley, his emergence as a national star was the most exciting thing in his life, and he gathered some valuable counsel on his first tour with Conway Twitty. "I have never enjoyed anything more in my life than I did sitting and talking with Conway Twitty," says Gilley. "When I first went on tour with him, he never said anything to me. I finally went to the guy that plays bass guitar for him, Big Joe Lewis: 'I don't think that Conway likes me.' Joe said, 'Yeah he does, he's just shy. He don't have much to say.' That was a fact—that's why Joe would do all the talking onstage. He said, 'You go up and talk to him.' So one night I went up and said, 'Conway, I want to talk to you about putting a group together, and I just want to get your input on the thing.' He did more for me as far as helping me make the right decisions . . . he was such a great guy. If you wanted to know something about business you would ask Conway Twitty."

More of a crooner than a blues shouter, Gilley was able to do something Lewis couldn't do—sell remakes of R&B songs such as Sam Cooke's "Bring It on Home," Lloyd Price's "Lawdy Miss Clawdy," and Big Joe Turner's "Chains of Love" to country radio. Not to mention that, one of Gilley's true classics, "Don't the Girls All Get Prettier at Closing Time," was better than anything his more famous cousin could muster at the time.

"I kept telling everybody, 'If I could just get my foot in the door, I think I can make it,'" remembers Gilley. "When 'Room Full of Roses' hit, I felt like I got my foot in the door, but now, can I keep the door open? Then, when I cut 'I Overlooked an Orchid,' I was little bit reluctant to say that 'this is going to be a hit.' Then I cut 'City Lights' and 'Window up Above,' and they hit.

"When I felt like I really started making it was when 'Don't the Girls All Get Prettier at Closing Time' hit in

1976. Then I went to the Academy of Country Music Awards and they gave me five awards that night. I was kind of embarrassed because I didn't feel like I really deserved everything they were giving me. I always admired Merle Haggard, and I always had admired Conway Twitty and these other people who were so big in the music industry, and here they were giving *me* all these different awards, and I'm saying, 'Gee, do I really deserve all this?' But, I was thankful at that time that I had won those. That's one thing they can't take away from you. They can get a lot of things away from you, but once they give you something like that, it's yours to keep forever."

Gilley was able to do something special with his new-found fortune. "Well, I was able to buy my mother and father a home. They had rented this house, and when I finally made it in the music business, I bought the house they had lived in all those years and gave it to them."

Already a country music sensation, Gilley became a hot mainstream act when an *Esquire* magazine article about his Pasadena nightclub resulted in the movie *Urban Cowboy*. Asked if he felt the movie was good for country music, Gilley is adamant. "There's no question in my mind! I told everybody that and when I hear somebody putting the *Urban Cowboy* craze down, it irritates the hell out of me. John Travolta came and danced on the old nightclub floor at Gilley's and introduced country music to a lot of young people who wouldn't ordinarily listen to it. He broke the ice. He just came off of *Saturday Night Fever*, and I don't mind telling you that *Urban Cowboy*, all it was was *Country Night Fever*, anyway you look at it. It just irritates me when I hear somebody say something bad about the *Urban Cowboy*, not because I was a part of it, but because it did so much for the music industry."

The singer has particularly fond memories of the film's star. "I think the times I enjoyed the most came when I was working with John Travolta, talking to him, and I even got to fly with them. I got to go out to the airport when he went through his training, and it just thrills me right now to see he's flying a 747. You know, he treated my son and the other kids around there really well, and he's just a helluva nice guy. I cannot say enough good things about him."

Urban Cowboy signaled a stylistic departure for Gilley as well. Epic Records producer Jim Ed Norman convinced him that he didn't need a piano to make hit records, and soon his versions of Ben E. King's "Stand By Me," Little Willie John's "Talk to Me," and Ray Charles's cover of "You Don't Know Me" were getting nearly as much adult contemporary airplay as country.

In all, Gilley registered with forty-two Top 40 country hits, seventeen of which hit #1. He seemed to be everywhere, talking about his namesake establishment being in the *Guinness Book of World Records* as the world's largest honky-tonk, his friendship with Sherwood Cryer, and those damned mechanical bulls. Yet dissension was brewing beneath the surface of this seemingly ideal business arrangement.

Gilley began to hear complaints from his fans about the nightclub. The trouble started when he relayed these concerns to Cryer. "He didn't take kindly to it. I asked him if he would take my name off the club and that really upset him. So, my last resort was to sue and have my name removed from the club, and that's what I did because I felt like he was degrading what I stood for. I didn't mind the decor, but it was the way he ran the club.

"To give you an example, Loretta Lynn was booked at Gilley's. I came in off the road and I saw her name on the board. I heard in Nashville that she wasn't going to make any more of her dates because she was in the hospital. I went all the way to his office and said, 'Sherwood, you need to take Loretta Lynn's name off that board out there, because she's not going to be here this Saturday.'

"He said, 'Who says?'

"I said, 'She's ill.'

"He says, 'I've got a contract on her.'

"I said, 'I don't care what you've got on her, she's ill and she's not going to be here this Saturday.'

"'Well, we'll see.'

"He kept advertising her and when it came time for her to appear that night, at 6:00 he put a little sign up. 'Due to illness Loretta Lynn will not be here tonight. C'mon in and have a good time at Gilley's.'

"Now to me, that's what was degrading to the name Gilley's as a club, because he knew that she wasn't going to be there, and I knew she wasn't going to be there. But he advertised her all the way up to that point. Somebody drove all the way across town, about thirty-five or forty miles, and he even had the people when they answered the phone say, 'Yeah, Loretta's going to be here tonight,' right up to 6:00

that night. That's not right, I didn't condone it, and that's the reason why we parted company. I hated that it happened like that. He blames me on the demise of Gilley's, but I was not the demise of Gilley's."

Despite the bitter court battle, Gilley feels the dissolution of his partnership with Cryer was one of the biggest disappointments in his career. "That was the sad part about it. We were so close it was like a father-son situation. I felt so bad about the fact that we had split up, and he'd been such a big part of my life."

The nightclub burnt down in 1989, around the same time that Gilley's run of hits ended.

A canny businessman with a string of products bearing his name, Gilley gradually backed away from the record-industry rat race. He built his theater in Branson, where he appears from March through December, and is very happy there, thank you very much.

Onstage, he tells his audience just how country music changed his life. "I now do a medley of songs that were #1 for me, like 'Room Full of Roses,' 'I Overlooked an Orchid,' and 'Window up Above.' When I talk to the people at the show, I tell them, 'I want to thank all you ladies out there for making these flower songs number one. Let me tell you what you did for me, you got me out of that old nightclub, and I don't have to deal with those drunks anymore.'"

Hank the Hired Hand, circa 1946.

HANK THOMPSON

I f it hadn't been for country music, Hank Thompson might have pursued a career as an electrical engineer.

"I was a radio technician in the navy. After I got out of the service I was going to go to college and get a degree in electrical engineering. When I went to Princeton and then SMU in Texas, that's what I was studying to do."

Fortunately for the music industry, Thompson was talked out of that idea and brought his electrical know-how with him to help craft a musical legacy that encompasses several decades and sixty hit records.

The first stirrings of his vast commercial promise came in 1942. "Well, I did this radio show for WACO [billed as "Hank, the Hired Hand"] while I was still in high school," recalls the Texas native. "There was a song out at that time called 'There's a Star Spangled Banner Waving Somewhere.' I used that as my theme song."

Regional radio was vital for performers trying to build a following, especially in the spacious Southwest. "Everybody listened to the radio and you didn't have all that many stations," remembers Thompson. "WACO was a thousand-watt station. It covered that central Texas area real well. That was kind of a springboard for me and really the kickoff to my professional career."

The navy also offered valuable showbiz experience for the young singer. "I took my guitar along with me when I was in the navy," explains Thompson. "I guess that's really where I honed my skills. I was able to perform a lot. I'd pick and sing a lot for my fellow service people and I really got a lot of mileage out of those things. Then I started writing songs because I was not able to get new ones."

After World War II, Thompson saw a real working man's future in electrical engineering, but musical opportunities sidetracked his studies. "When I went back home to Waco, I got a program on KWTX. It was an instant success. Back then, people wrote a lot of fan mail, and man, I'd come up there every day and there'd be a box of mail. It was amazing. I was just on a local radio station, we weren't on a network. We were on one station in central Texas and we'd get all this mail. People requesting songs, people wanting you to do dedications, all that sort of stuff. That was in the spring and I was going to go back and get my degree in the fall at SMU. I had already enrolled through the GI Bill and all that stuff."

The efforts of two men provided the deciding factor for the course of Thompson's career. "Hal Horton, who had the *Hillbilly Hit Parade* on KRLD in Dallas, he played my first record of 'Whoa Sailor' and 'Swing Wide Your Gate of Love,' and both sides of that went to #1 on his program. Then Tex Ritter came through there on a tour and Hal Horton told Tex Ritter about me. When Tex appeared in Waco, Tex had me on his show and brought me to the attention of Capitol Records, and that was really the big giant step. The early influences were one thing, but the direct assistance came from Hal Horton and Tex Ritter.

"But I had made that record in August, and there was a program director where I was, at KWTX in Waco, and he said, 'You know, you ought to give that a second thought. I've got a college degree and it's an asset, there's no question about it, but really it's what you can do that is important rather than having some college degree or some training that you'll never even use. You have a talent and people like what you're doing. You might be able to launch a real successful career doing what you're doing. If it doesn't work out, you're still awfully young. You can still go back to college and get a degree.' That was in the fall of 1946. From that point forward, I've never done anything else but pick the guitar and sing."

However, Thompson's technical expertise helped him devise a better stage setup for his live shows, a setup that revolutionized the business. "It was always my theory that unless people can see you and hear you, it doesn't make a difference how good you are," states Thompson. "All that electronic experience came in very handy because after the war, the equipment we had to work with was very meager. But, I was able to take existing equipment on the market and update it and improve it. Also, I could redesign and build my own sound system, a lot of it through components. So, I put all this stuff together and physically made the cabinets according to the manufacturer's specifications and I put together something similar to what was in the recording studios and made a portable unit out of these things.

"So, not only did I have the sound system where I could be heard, I had a place in Hollywood, California, make me a portable lighting system that I designed. When we set up we set our own lights, our own sound system, and we had the very best equipment available. There was no other act on the road that had anything like it. Most of 'em had to play on these little old tin-can PA systems. You had a couple of deals of speakers folded up, you put the amplifier in the bottom of the speaker deal, and you had your mic and mic stand in your other hand, and you walked in and that was your PA set. Needless to say, quite inadequate. You get a bunch of noisy people in an old dance hall and it was useless. I realized right then that we had something to offer, but we had to be able to project it to be successful with it."

Versatile, innovative, and tight, various incarnations of Hank Thompson and the Brazos Valley Boys were voted the top country and western band fourteen years in a row by *Billboard* magazine. Besides acting as "den mother," Thompson challenged his boys not to follow quite so closely in the footsteps of another Texas legend.

"One of the hardest things I ever had to do was break 'em from playing Bob Wills's music," explains Thompson. "I said, 'Look, there's already a Bob Wills. He's very popular and I'm a big fan of his too, but the public doesn't need another Bob Wills band. We're going to play *Hank Thompson* music and we're going to play it with a different sound. We'll devise our own endings, our own type of intros, our own riffs. We're not going to be imitators, we're going to be trendsetters.'"

Spelling out the difference between his style of swing and Wills's, Thompson explains, "With Bob Wills, the band was prominent and the vocalist was incidental. With me, I was the prominent thing and the band was incidental. So I would put me out front with the songs and I was the focal point and not the bandleader."

Thompson's career was groundbreaking in other aspects as well. In 1952, his live Oklahoma City–based television show was the nation's first to simulcast in color. "We were the logical thing [for television]," laughs Thompson. "I had the #1 band in the country and, man, we had all those fancy, colorful Nudie suits."

The savvy bandleader also anticipated the arrival of rock 'n' roll when he discovered future rockabilly queen Wanda Jackson. A fellow member of the Oklahoma Music Hall of Fame, Jackson reminisces, "I was only fourteen and I was doing a local fifteen-minute daily radio show. Well, he called me one day after my show and invited me down to sing with the Brazos Valley Boys. Of course he was my very favorite singer; I did all of his songs. This was one of the biggest thrills of my life, though I remember telling him, 'Hank, I would love to but I'll have to ask my mother first.'"

Thompson made the teenager part of his troupe, taking her father along as a chaperone, and though he recorded for Capitol, was instrumental in getting Jackson a recording contract with Decca. Her first hit, "You Can't Have My Love," featured the Brazos Valley Boys with Billy Gray at the helm. Two years later she would join her mentor's label and transform herself into a hot, growling rockabilly.

Jackson remembers Thompson as an understanding employer. "When he started doing television, he invited me to be a regular and he put up with some really bad stuff," she admits. "I was scared to death because I started forgetting my words. The first week, that can happen to anybody. The second week, I forgot 'em again and it was kind of funny. About the third and fourth week, I was getting so scared and nervous, and Hank would just laugh and laugh. He just thought that was so funny. One time, I had written all the key words to a song on the inside of my hands, and he caught me. I'd swing my hands up, take a look, and try to sing. But all he ever did was just hug me, kiss me on the forehead, and say, 'That's OK, you're gonna make it.'"

Another far-sighted venture was the Hank Thompson School of Country Music at Claremore College in Oklahoma. A fully accredited two-year program, the curriculum included courses on radio, television, engineering, songwriting, booking, and publishing. Although a rash of tax cuts terminated the venture during the early 1980s, in its time the school attracted students from as far away as Japan and Australia. One of its more prominent alumni is guitar wizard Junior Brown.

Part of Thompson's longevity stems from his accessibility. The gregarious veteran firmly believes in getting out and mixing with the fans. "We would play these ballrooms and in between sets I would walk around the place and stop at tables and shake hands with everybody, thank 'em for being there, ask 'em, 'How are you enjoying the music?' Signing autographs for anybody who wanted it, just to let them know that we were all part of the same thing. We were all there to have fun."

It was during just such an expedition into the audience that Thompson met his second wife. "I had moved from Fort Worth to Lubbock," explains Ann Thompson. "In Fort Worth I thought I was a hepcat. Back then it was called rhythm and blues, it wasn't even called rock 'n' roll yet. And then I moved to Lubbock and the only thing they had out there was country music at that time. I really wasn't that familiar with it. A bunch of us went out to Reese Air Force Base, Hank and his band were performing out there. Of course, we were all really impressed, they were all cute guys.

Hank today.

They dressed so good with all the rhinestones and the white hats. Hank is real good about coming out in the audience and visiting with people. So he came out and asked me if I was having a good time and I said, 'Not particularly.' He said, 'Why?' I said that I didn't really like hillbilly music. Well, he informed me in a hurry that he did not play hillbilly music, and that he played western swing and there was a big differ-ence. Needless to say, our romance did not start that night.

"In the meantime, I had moved to Midland and learned to like country music because that's a country music area out there. He was playing over in Odessa and I remembered how cute he was. So I gathered up a bunch of girlfriends and we went over, but I was thinking, 'There's no way he's going to remember that I'm that smart mouth from Lubbock.' When I got up to the head of the line he said, 'Well, have you learned to like country music?' But I had on skintight, gold lamé western britches, and so I think that overcame my smart mouth. Then we started getting a little interested in each other."

Traveling with Hank, Ann Thompson has seen the world and "every town in America." It can be a rough life, but she feels the fans make things a bit easier. "We don't understand the new young artists that won't have anything to do with their fans, because the fans are wonderful," she says. "There's some of them who are kooks, but if it wasn't for the fans we really wouldn't enjoy the road. Hank has a really big fan club and everywhere we go we have people that we already know and they say, 'Hey, we're going to be there, what can we do to help?' They all help on the sales table and they help Hank if he needs something. Many of them have become our dear friends. I joke about it. I say, 'Dear Lord, we couldn't be on the road without these friends.' And it's true. Two people can't do everything."

Did she ever learn to like country music?

"Seriously, that's the only form of music I can stand to listen to now."

Hank Thompson and the Brazos Valley Boys made other converts with such enduring hit records as "The Wild Side of Life," "Green Light," "Rub-A-Dub-Dub," "Wildwood Flower," "Wake Up Irene," and "A Six Pack to Go," many of which were penned by Thompson himself. The financial burdens of carrying a nine-piece band around the country began to wear on Thompson during the sixties. As a result, he began whittling down the size of the group until the Brazos Valley Boys were completely disbanded by the end of the decade. Although the band is sorely missed, this stream-lining has allowed the singer greater flexibility in his book-ings and has eliminated the need to take filler dates "just to pay the band."

"When it comes right down to it, I never really made a lot of money in the band business. But what I was able to do was perpetuate and improve the thing that I was doing and make a good living. I never amassed any big sums of money by any means. It just wasn't there. My gosh, some of these guys today go out and make more money on one job than I made in a whole year."

Label-hopping from the late 1960s through the early '80s, he scored chart successes of various sizes at Warner, Dot, and MCA. After the hits dried up, Thompson valiantly plugged away, recording for smaller labels and playing gigs all around the world. In recent years, the western swing revival has brought renewed interest to his early work, resulting in several fine reissues and as many live bookings as he can handle.

Proud of the role he played in helping shape country music as a business and an art form, the still vibrant and cocksure member of the Country Music Hall of Fame doesn't plan on completely retiring anytime soon. When I ask him how country music changed his life, the sharp-witted Thompson replies, "That's like saying, 'How did beans and cornbread change your life?' That's what I was raised on and I never knew anything else. So, it never changed anything. It was always there. I never knew there was any other kind of music."

Today.

JOHNNY WRIGHT

As one half of the innovative team Johnnie & Jack, Johnny Wright injected the "rumba beat" and R&B cover songs into country music and racked up hits from the 1940s through the '60s. When you add to that the fact that he is married to and helped plan the career of the one and only Kitty Wells, you have a pivotal figure in country music history. But he and partner Jack Anglin would never have gotten their career rolling if they hadn't started out masquerading as another, more popular duo. "Nobody had television back then," Wright chuckles today. "That's how we got by with it."

Indeed, Wright's earliest memories predate both mass-market radio and country music as a mainstream business. "I was raised on a farm fifteen miles east of Nashville, Tennessee," Wright begins. "A little town called Mount Juliet, Tennessee, Route 1. I've got two brothers: my oldest one was called Delbert Wright and the second boy was Thomas Wright. I was the next to the last, born on May 13th, 1914. My daddy was a farmer and I had to walk about a mile to school back in those days. But we had plenty to eat. We raised hogs, chickens, and once a week they had a market wagon as we called them. It was a covered wagon and they'd come around once a week and blow the horn, the same type of trumpet they use in the service, and they'd come to all the people that lived on Mount Juliet, Route 1 up to Crittendon's Bend."

When asked about his early influences, Wright's memory goes back to country's infancy. "Where I was raised up, there wasn't a whole lot to listen to. The Carter Family, they started making records, and a guy named Old Dad Pickard and the Pickard Family. They weren't doing any solos back then at all. If they were, we didn't hear them. But we had these little crystal sets where you put on the headphones and there was a needle on this little piece of metal and you worked that needle around until you could pick up the *Grand Ole Opry*. It would crack and pop and buzz, but we listened to it.

"We sang everybody's songs that had a record out. We'd get a record and play it and I'd try to sing it myself. That went on until we moved out to Mt. Juliet—that's where I went to school. That's where we went from the radio with the headsets to the radio with a battery. You put it on to an automobile battery for power. We got electricity out of Mt. Juliet. I forget the year but I think it was 1925, so we could pick up the *Grand Ole Opry* better but it would still crack and pop and squeal."

After moving to Nashville, Wright took a job as a cabinetmaker, and during the Depression years he was glad to have the work. "It was a pretty good money. I guess nobody back then was making really big money. I would get the cabinets ready for the finishing and when I was done with them I would drop them on a chute and they'd go to the finishing room. From there they would sell to the stores down in Nashville. Everything was so cheap back then. We worked a week and maybe'd make about thirteen dollars for half a week. When I finally got a raise it was seventeen or eighteen dollars a week. It was real cheap to live and I went through two Depressions in my lifetime."

Wright didn't think much about making a regular living in the music business until circumstances threw him together with his future partner Jack Anglin. "My sister and my brother Tom got a job at the Phillips and Burdoff Manufacturing Company where they made iron stoves and stuff like that. He worked there and my sister got a job in the cotton mill. We did that for a long time. When we moved in to Nashville, we moved four or five doors away from Jack Anglin and his family. Jack and his brother Jim, and Red, they called him—Jack, Jim, and Red. They had a little group together, a trio called the Anglin Brothers."

Wright played a bit with the Anglin Brothers until they disbanded. When Anglin and Wright decided they weren't willing to give up, the two young men got their feet in the local club scene by impersonating one of country's classic brother teams.

"There was a group called the Delmore Brothers, they were one of the most popular duets around," laughs Wright in recollection. "So Jack and I started imitating the Delmore Brothers. Jack and myself would drive around to these little nightclubs around Nashville and I had a fellow who worked with me back then and his name was Odel Hart. Jack, Odel Hart, and myself would go around to these little joints where they sold sandwiches and other things.

"Odel Hart, he'd go in and say, 'Y'all ever heard of the Delmore Brothers?'

"'Oh yeah, yeah! I really like 'em. They're good.'

"Well, Jack and I could sing just like 'em. So Odel Hart said, 'Well, I've got 'em right out here in the car.'

"They'd say, 'Well, go out and get 'em!'

"He'd go out and get us and then we go in there and pick the guitar and sang and everybody thought we were the Delmores. We'd sing 'Nashville Blues,' 'Downstairs Blues,' and all that. Jack could play around on guitar just like Alton did on the Delmore Brothers hits. We'd go in there and they'd give us some money, fifteen cents, sometimes we'd get a quarter.

"This is a true story, really. Those people would come up and say, 'We listen to you every Saturday night.'"

Money wasn't an issue for Wright and Anglin because there wasn't much to be had, but that didn't curtail their ambitions. Still working full-time jobs, the team caught its first big break on local radio, although nervousness almost caused them to blow it. "There was a show called *The Old Country Store* that they'd have on Saturday afternoons," explains Wright. "Everybody would gather around and anybody who wanted to sing could sing on the air. Anyway, *The Old Country Store* on WSIX was similar to the *Grand Ole Opry*. One time we went up there after they had a flood up in Nashville, and Jack and I went to help raise money for people who had to move out of their homes. Joe Calloway was the program director and he said, 'If you want to sing, go up and sing.' We just stood there.

"So Joe said, 'So, Johnnie and Jack, want to sing?'

"I told him, 'Yeah, we'd be glad to.'

"So we went in and started singing. That was my first time to be on the air. I was scared to death, really, because we didn't know what we were going to do for all those people listening all across the country. So Jack and I went up there and we started doing 'What Would You Give in Exchange for Your Soul.' I started out with the lead part, 'What would you give,' and Jack hollered out 'in exchange!'

"Then I started singing 'What would you give' and he hollered 'in exchange' again. When we got to the third time,

I was out of breath, scared to death, and barely whispering. We finally got through that. But that was the first time ever on the radio, during that flood. We started singing on *The Old Country Store* on Saturdays."

The WSIX program was also where Wright would meet his future wife. "She and her cousin was singing up there, they called them 'Muriel and Bessie—The Deason Sisters.' When I met Kitty, she was working in Nashville too, at a garment factory." Eventually Wright would marry Muriel and Anglin would marry his partner's sister Louise.

Asked how his wife came to be known as "Kitty Wells," Wright tells the story. "We left Nashville in 1937 and went to North Carolina. We went over to WNOX. The way she got that name was, we were in Knoxville, Tennessee, during World War II, and Lowell Blanchard was a sports announcer and did the news at WNOX. Well, Kitty was singing under her real name, Muriel Deason. She sang for a week or two like that and then Lowell Blanchard came over to me one day there and said to me, 'Johnnie, that wife of yours is a good singer, but I don't like the name Muriel Deason. I don't think anybody will ever remember that.' This was before she ever recorded. He said, 'You get a good name for her and she could go to the top.'

"I said, 'Well, we'll talk it over tonight.'

"So Kitty and I were living at an apartment there, all the band was too, and we used to sing an old song about an old darkie that died and this fella was down by the grave kneeling and praying over 'Sweet Kitty Wells.' [Sings.] 'You ask what makes this darkie weep/what makes the tears roll down his cheek . . ." and it goes on and on and says 'weeping over the grave of Sweet Kitty Wells.' We used to sing that song, so we just thought of Kitty Wells.

"I said to her, 'What do you think about "Kitty Wells"?'

"She said, 'It's all right with me if you want to change it.'

"So, the next day we went to do the *Mid-Day Merry-Go-Round* in Knoxville and Lowell Blanchard asked, 'Well, have you come up with a name yet?'

"I said, 'Yeah. We've got one but I don't know whether you'll like it or not. What do you think about Kitty Wells?'

"He said, 'That's it! That's it! She's got a name now.'

"We just took it from there and it was a success. A lot of the older people remembered that song, so it went from there and she's sold more records than I ever thought about."

Johnnie & Jack broke first on records, recording for Apollo and King before signing with RCA in 1951. Wright credits Tillman Franks with giving their career the boost it needed.

"Well, we went to the *Louisiana Hayride* and the boy down there booked us, he also wrote songs, his name was Tillman Franks. He was a songwriter and played bass fiddle and he wrote a song for Kitty that she recorded and made a hit with. He's the cause of Jack and I doing 'Oh Baby (I Get So Lonely),' and 'Poison Love,' that was our first hit. I think Tillman had a hand in writing that and we started the calypso beat, or the 'rhumba beat,' as we called it.

"Tillman said, 'You and Jack sound good but you need something to make the music a little different from everybody else's.' So, that's when we came up with the calypso beat and we were able to come to Nashville and record it. It had a different sound and when it came out it just automatically went right up [the charts]. I'm not sure if it went #1 or not, but if it didn't it scared it to death. We did a lot of the rhythm and blues songs and put the calypso beat to them. We did the 'Banana Boat Song,' 'Ashes of Love,' 'Down South in New Orleans.' We had a lot of hits. Jack's brother wrote a lot of those songs we did. His name was Jim Anglin."

Johnnie & Jack's covers of R&B songs, particularly the Spaniels' "Goodnight Sweetheart" in 1954, predated Elvis Presley's country and blues hybrids at Sun Records. According to Wright, he was the one who picked the songs. "We'd hear 'em on the radio and I'd go get a copy of the record, then I'd get somebody to type it up for us. Owen Bradley, he was our A&R man, and Chet Atkins played on 'em. That's what was selling back then, they wanted us to do 'em, so we did 'em. It all turned out real good, but my favorites were when I was singing the real sad songs like 'I'm Dying a Sinner's Death' and all those. I like something that hits everybody at one time. 'Lonely Mountain of Clay' and things like that."

Guitar virtuoso Chet Atkins was a prominent member of the Johnnie & Jack band for a time. Asked if he took any pride in Atkins's success, Wright answers with a mix of gratitude and humor. "I don't try to take any pride in it because he was such a good person and I helped him a lot and he helped me. He helped me start at WNOX and then we left and worked at different radio stations, but we always worked good together. Chet kind of copied Merle Travis. Chet was a good person and he loved Merle Travis. As a matter of fact, I think they married sisters. But he could pick anything. He could get hot on the guitar or play just as corny as anybody, but he loved it. Chet was one of my best buddies. I always say, 'He's one of the best people who ever worked for me.'

"When he came to Nashville, Steve Sholes, the A&R man for RCA-Victor had died, so Chet took over as the man, and it didn't change him a bit. He stayed the same Chet Atkins right on up until he passed away."

Another great friend is Ray Price, with whom Wright once competed over a song. "Jack and I were the first ones, besides [Skeets McDonald], who wrote it, to cut 'Don't Let the Stars Get in Your Eyes.' So we recorded it and Ray Price recorded it just after we did and we were on tour together. So, Jack and I would open the show and sing 'Don't Let the Stars Get in Your Eyes' and then Ray would come on after us and he'd have to go through with it. We did that for about two or three weeks working theaters. Ray came to me one day and said, 'John? My God, let *me* sing it every once in a while, I've got that out too.' [Laughs.] So we just rotated it. We let Ray sing it first and then we'd do it the next time. He's a good person, Ray Price is. One of the best singers ever, countrywise or anywise."

Johnnie & Jack were nowhere near as successful on record as Kitty Wells, so Wright made a bold, revolutionary move. "My wife was doing real good, so I brought her into the show and I called it the *Kitty Wells Family Show*. I billed her first because of 'It Wasn't God Who Made Honky-Tonk Angels.' Everything she was putting out would run right on up there. So I asked her what she thought about it saying 'Kitty Wells, Johnnie Wright, Jack Anglin,' and like that. Everybody said it was the wrong thing to do. Roy Acuff told me, 'You never can headline a show with a woman.'

"I said, 'I don't see why. This woman can sing and she has big hit records. Why couldn't she?' There were a lot of women like Kate Smith who were out front singing, so I said, 'I'm just going to try it and see how it works.' So we tried it as 'Kitty Wells, Johnnie Wright, Jack Anglin, and the Tennessee Mountain Boys,' and it worked."

The duo recorded with varying degrees of success for RCA and Decca until Anglin's untimely death on March 7, 1963. "Jack had an automobile wreck on the way to Patsy Cline's funeral," remembers Wright soberly. "I was at the funeral home and he came around the curve a little too fast and his car left the road and killed him instantly.

"To tell you the truth, I didn't know what I was going to do when that happened. Jack and I had a good run of hit records and then I started recording after Jack passed away. I started headlining the show as 'Kitty Wells and Johnny Wright.'" (After his partner's death, Wright changed the spelling of his first name from "Johnnie" to "Johnny.")

A moderately successful solo act, Wright scored a major hit with one of Tom T. Hall's first Nashville offerings, "Hello Vietnam." The singer remembered where he was when he heard the record hit #1. "We went over to the St. Lucien Islands and played over there, Stonewall Jackson, Kitty, and myself. We went to the desk to check in and the guy at the desk said, 'We'll get your luggage in your room and if you'll come back down here, we'll do a little interview.' He was also a DJ on the radio station there. I went down and did the interview and everything and I got tickled because I'm pretty easy to get to laugh. But then I couldn't stop. When we went on the stage that night, the MC came out and said, 'Johnny Wright has a #1 record. It's #1 all over the country.'

"Well, I started singing 'Goodbye darlin', hello Vietnam,' and I was so ashamed of myself. There's a recitation in it and they all just gathered around watching me. But when I got to the recitation I couldn't help but laugh. I'm that type of person. I was doing the recitation and they were all just looking at me. So, I just started laughing and I had to leave the stage. We put another song in and then I came back and finished it. I made an excuse but really I was ashamed of myself. But it was a big hit for me. I love to sing it. I still do it."

Wright's children, grandchildren, and great-grandchildren all live within four miles of Johnny and Kitty. "They all come over, sit and talk to us, swim, we just carry on like ordinary people," chuckles Wright. The son and daughters have been moderately successful as country singers. Carol Sue can be heard on "How Far Is Heaven," although she never pursued a singing career as an adult. Rita was part of the popular trio Nita, Rita, and Ruby. Under her own name, she took a page out of her mother's book and recorded "Dern Ya," a response to Roger Miller's "Dang Me."

"Ruby got out of the business," says her dad. "She had a good job. Ruby can type and all this stuff, so she just got out of the business."

Son Bobby Wright is best known to inveterate television viewers as Willy on *McHale's Navy*, but he's been a show-business professional since he made his first records at the age of eight. These days, the younger Wright takes Anglin's place in the family stage shows. "He sings the tenor part," explains Wright the elder. "We have a complete band, we have some *Grand Ole Opry* people that go out with us. We get the same sound out on personal appearances that we used to on records. I try to stick with that, tell a few jokes, and try to be funny."

Grateful to still have an audience, Wright is proud of his wife's legacy and what he and Jack Anglin accomplished.

"We helped change country music and make it what it is today. But I'm the same person that I was back then," he jokes, "only I'm a lot older."

Today.

KITTY WELLS

Let's just get this part out of the way right now. Kitty Wells is the single most significant female performer in country music history. Without her there would be no Loretta Lynn, no Tammy Wynette, no Brenda Lee, no Dolly Parton, no Tanya Tucker, no Faith Hill, and no Shania

Twain. Oh sure, they might have been born and lived to a ripe old age, but the opportunity to make it big in country music probably wouldn't have existed if Wells hadn't paved the way.

There were other female singers before her, but none whose recordings resonated with fans on such a wide scale. Her series of "answer songs"—starting with "It Wasn't God Who Made Honky-Tonk Angels"—popularized the female perspective, and gave her the wherewithal to establish her own distinctive style and become country's first woman headliner.

Yet for all that, the former Muriel Deason sounds a bit amused when you tell her she was country's pioneer feminist. "Yes, it sounds like that, but I never even thought about it," she tells me. "Just singing the songs was the main thing that I thought about."

For Kitty Wells, country music was a job, a way to get out of the garment factory and help give her family a better life than she had. Her early childhood is vintage Americana. "I was raised right here in Nashville, Tennessee, and my daddy was a brakeman on the Tennessee Central railroad. I attended school here in south Nashville where I was born, and I attended Lipscomb School. I had three brothers and two sisters. We lived here until we moved towards Memphis in the country on my granddaddy and his brother's farm. We lived there about four years and I started school in the country. We had to walk two and a half miles across the hill and three miles on the regular road. It was a pretty good distance to go to school. I finished the first grade there and I was starting the second when we moved back to Nashville. I had the rest of my schooling in Nashville, Tennessee.

"My dad worked on the railroads, he ran from here to Monterey, Tennessee, to Hawkinsville, Kentucky—that's the route he had. We lived kind of close to the railroad and when he'd go out on the road, we knew what time the train was coming by, we kids would go out and wave at him as the train came by.

"When the Depression hit, they laid him off for a good long while. That was really a rough time for everybody, I think."

Wells credits her father with getting her interested in music. "Well, my dad played the guitar and sang those old-time folk songs. I used to sit on the floor and listen to him play and sing. Then I had a boyfriend, he showed me my first chords on the guitar—G, C, D, and A. So I started learning how to play the chords on the guitar." Wells sounds particularly moved as she adds, "When my dad found out I was learning to play the guitar, he brought his guitar in and gave it to me."

Much of Wells's story is intertwined with her husband Johnny Wright's, who is the chattier of the two. (If you call their home, she identifies herself as "Mrs. Wright" and defers decisions concerning interviews to him.) But she does remember her first experience on radio with her cousin Bessie, and it was no less embarrassing to them than it was to Johnnie & Jack.

"When I got a little older, my cousin and I sang on that program on WSIX called *The Old Country Store* on Saturday afternoons at three o'clock. Anybody who wanted to play on it could go up there and play and sing. But the first time we sang on *The Old Country Store*, they cut us off the radio. Well, they got so many calls about it that they started letting us sing.

"So she and I got our own program on WSIX at six o'clock in the morning for about fifteen minutes. We'd sing 'May I Sleep in Your Barn Tonight, Mister,' all the old-time songs like that. Of course, they didn't write any songs for girls until I hit with 'It Wasn't God Who Made Honky-Tonk Angels.' Then they started writing songs for girls."

Wells also sang as part of a trio known as the Harmony Girls, but the association was relatively short-lived. "Well, Bessie married and we didn't sing together after Johnny and I got married. We didn't sing together for a long time after that. She was one of the Harmony Girls, and Louise, Johnny's sister, was the other. Eventually they quit singing. Of course I didn't sing a whole lot after Johnnie & Jack first left Nashville and started singing."

In country music then as now, an artist had to chase the opportunities, which often meant repeatedly uprooting one's family, as Wells explains.

"When Jack [Anglin] went in the army, Eddie Hill and Johnnie joined up together and we went to Knoxville, Tennessee. That's where I first started with the name of Kitty Wells. Then, after we left Knoxville and came back to Nashville, Jack got out of the service and they went to North Carolina for a while. Our youngest daughter was a baby at the time and I didn't work for a long time. Then we came back to

Nashville and went to Shreveport from there. That's where I started singing quite a bit with the *Hayride* down there.

"So, I recorded for RCA while I was down there, same time Johnnie & Jack was recording, and of course the songs didn't do very good. They were mostly religious and semireligious songs. I grew up singing gospel songs and I used to sing and play around at prayer meetings and places like that when I was growing up."

It was a final move to Nashville that provided the opportunity that made her a star, even though she still thought of music as a sideline. "I wasn't really serious about it," Wells admits. "When we left Shreveport and went back to Nashville and Johnnie & Jack went to work on the *Grand Ole Opry*, I had just decided that I was going to quit and stay at home with the children because the records I had recorded didn't get played very much, and they weren't in the record shops.

"We had sent Paul Cohen [Decca Records' A&R representative] a record to listen to while we were in Shreveport and we hadn't heard anything from him. So, while Johnnie & Jack were playing at the *Ernest Tubb Record Program* on Saturday night, Paul Cohen happened to come by there. He had a record that he just heard and he asked Johnnie, 'Do you think Kitty would be interested in recording this song?'

"He said, 'Well, I don't know. We'll take it home and listen to it and if she likes it, we'll record it.'

"So he brought the song home and it was an answer to Hank Thompson's 'Wild Side of Life,' 'It Wasn't God Who Made Honky-Tonk Angels.'

"So, I listened to it and I told Johnnie, 'Well, if you want me to, I'll record it. At least we'll get the union scale out of it.' I thought it'd be like the others I had recorded on RCA. Well, I recorded it and they released it."

Hank Williams's ex-wife was the first to notify Wells that "It Wasn't God Who Made Honky-Tonk Angels" was a fast-rising hit. "I was home one day and Audrey Williams, she had been down to Montgomery and she called me when she got back home saying, 'Girl, you've got a hit on your hands! Every station I switched to while I was coming home from Montgomery was playing that song!' That really was a surprise to me. So, I had to go back to work. I had a very short retirement."

Cohen, who knew a good thing when he heard it, quickly brought Wells back into the studio to do more answer songs, including "Paying for that Back Street Affair" (answering Webb Pierce's "Back Street Affair") and "Hey Joe" (a response to Carl Smith's hit).

Was Wells speaking out on behalf of oppressed womankind?

"No," she chuckles, "I never even thought of that."

The folk element in Wells's music is what makes her plaintive sound so appealing today. It seems like all of Appalachia runs through her vulnerable utterances, and when she sings a tearjerker, it cuts right to the heart. When told that she seems to have recorded more sad songs than anything else, Wells is quick to respond. "I know it. It seems like that's what the people like to hear me sing, sad songs. Country songs are mostly written about something that hap-

pened in somebody's life, might've been the person who
wrote the song. It might've happened to him or a friend, and
the song just tells a story. That's the type of song they like to
hear. 'How Far Is Heaven,' that's a song Tillman Franks
wrote that I recorded and it's about a little girl who wants to
know how far it is to heaven because her daddy's passed away
and she wants to know when she can go see him. It's a sad
song. I can sing that song and I can see people in the audience, tears coming in their eyes. They'll be wiping their eyes
and after the show they'll tell me that maybe their father had
passed away or something. They always love that song.
That's one of the most requested songs that I do."

One of country music's staples is the duet between two
popular performers, and Wells had a chance to record with
one of the biggest stars of the era, labelmate Red Foley. "He
was very popular at the time and had out a lot of big records,"
says Wells, sounding awed still. "I had a song that I wanted
Red to do on record because he was good at doing recita-
tions, a song Pee Wee King and Redd Stewart sent to me,
'I'm a Stranger in My Home.' 'One By One' was the back
side of that, we thought 'Stranger in My Home' was going to
be the hit. So Paul Cohen said, 'He might do it. Let's ask
him.' Well, Red said, 'She don't need me.' He said, 'Yeah,
she needs you to do that recitation.' So he agreed to do it and
we did the song and then we said, 'We've got to have a song
to go on the back of that.'

"Johnnie had a little songbook in his guitar case that had
the words to 'One by One,' so we got the little book out and
he'd sing a line and I'd sing a line, then join up on the cho-

rus. You know what? That turned out to be the #1 side on that record. It stayed on the charts almost a year."

Besides popular duets with Foley, Webb Pierce, and Roy Acuff, Wells recorded some solo classics such as "Makin' Believe," "Release Me," "Searching (For Someone Like You)," "Mommy for a Day," and "Heartbreak U.S.A." By the end of 1968, she had placed sixty-four songs in the country Top 40 and had several bestselling LPs.

Wells credits her long string of hits to her husband's keen ear for a song. "Johnnie usually went out, sometimes I went with him, but he did pick out most of the songs. Before we'd have our sessions, he'd go around to the different publishing companies. Sometimes they would bring 'em over to the house. We never had any trouble with [Decca producer] Owen [Bradley] on songs. He said, 'Let's hear what you've got.' We'd show him and then he'd say, 'Well, let's record.'"

Of course, being the first major female country star meant that Wells had to juggle a family and a career. Fortunately, she had some help. "Well, by the time we moved back here to Nashville with the children, Sue was about seven years old and the others were older, Ruby about eleven, Bobby about eight or nine. My mother lived here in Nashville, this was our home, and she stayed with the children when we were out on the road. So I knew they were taken good care of. Other than missing out on things, school and things like that, sometimes one of 'em would get sick, that was kind of rough being out on the road when something like that happened."

Another hurdle she faced? Showbiz was not deemed a proper vocation for a young woman. "Especially if you traveled around with a band and a group of men," Wells laughs today. "I was fortunate enough that I always traveled with my husband and his partner or I wouldn't have been out there on the road singing."

Did Decca Records treat her any differently because of her gender?

"I never had one thought about that," Wells plainly states. "I was the first one to sign a lifetime contract with them. As a matter of fact, after that I think Ernest Tubb signed a lifetime recording contract with them and I don't know if anybody else did or not."

The longevity of Wells's career has been nothing short of amazing. She hit the singles charts up until 1979. She has traveled the world singing her brand of country music and is surprised when people in foreign lands crowd the stage and mouth the words with her. When asked how she feels about the singers who have credited Kitty Wells with opening the doors to country music, she is characteristically modest. "Well, I appreciate them saying that. I think that I was just fortunate enough that I got that answer song. I think anybody else could've taken the same song and made a hit out of it. But I really appreciate the compliments they give me."

However, Wells does view her 1976 induction into the Country Music Hall of Fame and her 1991 Grammy Lifetime Achievement Award with some quiet pride. She has also received a Native American Music Award. When asked if she does indeed have much Indian blood in her, Wells happily replies. "Yes, Cherokee blood. It's real funny, we were working a casino up in the northern area of Minnesota. A lot of the Indians came out to the show and one of them came up to me one night and said, 'What tribe are *you* from?' I guess it's my high cheekbones. But there are a lot of Cherokees running around Tennessee and North Carolina."

Wells still plays casino dates with her husband and son, but has no plans to record again anytime soon. "Because it's kind of hard for real country artists like we are to get your records played anymore."

That said, she's not complaining. Other country singers have made more money and benefited from greater acclaim in the contemporary era, but if life is about growing old together, enjoying good health, and being surrounded by family, Kitty Wells has got them all beat.

"Well, you know I think that I've had a very good life," she says with customary understatement. "I was fortunate enough to get a good man to help me get the life that I have. We have three children, eight grandchildren, and eleven great-grandchildren. We've got a pretty nice family, and I've enjoyed the work that we've done, and the music business has been a good life for us. I don't know what else we could have done and there's not anything that I would change that I know of."

8

REDEMPTION

For a few select performers with troubled pasts, country music has offered both respectable postincarceration employment and a way to publicly redeem themselves.

Perhaps the best-known example is Merle Haggard, whose teen arrest record is clearly on display in his 1981 autobiography Sing Me Back Home: My Life. *Although they certainly caused his family distress, most of the Hag's early crimes seem laughable today: driving stolen cars and repeatedly escaping from the California Youth Authority. He finally crossed the line in 1958 when a drunken burglary resulted in his residence in San Quentin as prisoner A-45200.*

Placed in solitary confinement for brewing beer in his cell, Haggard chatted through the air vents with the execution-bound Caryl Chessman and got scared straight. A prison concert given by Johnny Cash renewed the future superstar's desire to make music for a living. Earning early parole, the singer-songwriter began to fashion a body of work that resonated with both rock and country fans alike. Memorable hits such as "Mama Tried" and "Working Man Blues," along with the liberal-baiting anthems "Okie From Muskogee" and "The Fightin' Side of Me," made him a fan favorite. In 1972, Haggard's country music achievements earned him a full pardon from California governor Ronald Reagan.

Audiences, when presented with an exceptional talent and a great background story such as Haggard's, tend to be forgiving of an artist's past indiscretions. In an earlier age, fans seemed to realize that circumstances could have turned on them just as easily as they had on their musical heroes. When the age of the movie antihero hit during the late 1960s, followed by the outlaw movement of the seventies, country fans perceived an added measure of credibility and iconic rebellion in their favorite artists.

Johnny Paycheck in the mid-seventies; his biggest hits can be found on the compilation *The Soul and the Edge: The Best of Johnny Paycheck.*

MARTY MARTEL
on Johnny Paycheck

As contrary and combative as he was talented, Johnny Paycheck was the quintessential hard-ass. Born Donald Lytle, his first taste of major trouble came in the navy, when he received a court martial and brig time for fighting with a superior officer. After years as a noted Nashville session singer and songwriter, Lytle changed his name to Johnny Paycheck, after a "bum-of-the-month" heavyweight knocked out in the second round by Joe Louis. During the mid-sixties, he saw some chart success on Andrew Mayhew's Little Darlin' label, but was left in the lurch when the company went belly up.

Broke and running wild, Paycheck ended up nearly drinking and drugging himself to death in Los Angeles. When he finally sobered up, Billy Sherrill at Epic Records resurrected the singer's career with a string of seventies hits including "She's All I've Got," "Mr. Lovemaker," "I'm the Only Hell (Mama Ever Raised)," and his signature smash "Take This Job and Shove It."

Success seemed to only exacerbate Paycheck's problems. Lawsuits and bad check charges dogged him during the best of times, and when the hits ran dry, things got ugly fast. In 1985, Paycheck shot a man during a barroom brawl, and after exhausting the appeal process, the fallen superstar was convicted of aggravated assault and served the better part of two years in Ohio's Chillicothe Correctional Institute. Governor Richard Celeste paroled him in 1991 with the provision that he stay clean and sober. He returned to recording for small labels and playing some live shows, but his was a life badly in need of redemption.

That's when Marty Martel entered the picture.

Martel currently books shows for the legends of country music through his company, Midnight Sun Productions. A passionate believer in true country music, he was also

Johnny Paycheck's friend, manager, and champion during the last years of the singer's life. To Martel, Paycheck wasn't just a classic artist, he was also a great teacher. "My experiences with him gave me a better understanding of what it takes to manage an artist, especially legendary artists. It made my company a little easier to manage and he taught me, in his own way, the tricks of the trade, so to speak, of management and booking."

More than anyone else in the business, Martel can vouch for Paycheck's turnaround, both professionally and personally. "I spent eight years with him—until his death—and I know how he felt," says Martel. "Although he did a lot of drugs and booze and got in a lot of trouble, he was basically a shy person. That bandstand made him the real Paycheck."

Martel didn't tiptoe around the singer, but he quickly learned what not to do. "He just didn't want anyone to back him against the wall and tell him that it had to be done this way. He felt like, 'I can take an explanation, but I don't want you force it on me, because if I think the explanation is wrong, why should I have to do it?' But it cost him. Every grain of wood he went against cost him, but it never diminished his skills."

The beginning of Martel's professional association with the singer exemplified Paycheck's in-for-a-penny-in-for-a-pound personality. "He just threw [his career] in my lap. I talked to him two or three months before that at a show I had him on, and I just said, 'People are not booking you right.' So, two, three months later he called me one night and said, 'You got it, pal.'

"I said, 'I got what?'

"He said, 'You got it all. I just walked away from every agency in town. They were all angry with me.'

"But I didn't call him, he called me, and he was never signed to anybody in the later years. He signed with me. I didn't find him hard to get along with because I could argue with him face-to-face, eyeball-to-eyeball."

Realizing that Paycheck's talent was intact and his effect on live audiences was as great as ever, Martel made a pitch to get his client a regular spot on the *Grand Ole Opry*. As he recalls, the idea was not an easy sell to *Opry* manager Bob Whittaker.

"Bob took me into his office and said, 'OK, here's what I'm going to do. Against the wishes of a lot of people, I'm going to bring him into this fold, because I believe in him. You say he's been free and clear of everything, that he doesn't do junk anymore.'

"I said, 'Let me tell you something, Bob, let's get this straight right here and now. Since the day Johnny Paycheck got out of prison, and even while he was in prison—he has never touched tobacco, booze, or any hard stuff. He's been clean as a whistle for many years.'

"He said, 'That's good enough for me, Marty.' Then Bud Wendell came in and he talked to Bud and he asked, 'Is this the truth?' I said, 'It's the God's truth.' So, he joined 'em.

"When he came to *Opry*, he knew that there was talk that several of the artists didn't want him there because of his past. They were unforgiving people. The same people embraced him after he joined and he showed them that's what he wanted to do."

According to Martel, Paycheck was "strong, drawing crowds, and young people were coming to see him." The renewed attention led to plans for a big comeback album on Sony Records. "Three years after he comes to town, he joins the *Opry*, and Jim Zwickel, his attorney, got him a contract that was as good as anybody's in this business. People like Blake Chancey at Sony saw the vision in Paycheck. He brought him in the office; they talked for five minutes. The attorney was there; I was there; Paycheck was there. Blake didn't ask none of us any questions. He talked to John and the basic line was, 'When can we get started?' They had it signed in about a week's time, and it was a major contract. It was as good as Garth Brooks would've got. That's how strong it was. If he had gotten a record out, they would have marketed it worldwide and he was singing so good.

"The one thing Blake Chancey said after Paycheck's death was, 'I pulled a boner, didn't I?' I said, "I know what you're talking about, but you didn't pull a boner because there was nothing we could do.'

"He said, 'We never cut no sides. We got the material but we never got the material cut because he really got sick.' That was the sad reality of his life. You're not going to see a lot of crap come out of the can, because there's not a lot in there."

Martel witnessed firsthand his client being progressively ravaged by emphysema. He also saw Paycheck's unflinching loyalty to his friends. "The emphysema and asthma stopped him from staying out in the summer months. A lot of people would call him names when he wouldn't do a complete show. They didn't realize that he did shows right here in Nashville where he had no business being up on a stage. For example, the Tim McGraw New Year's Eve bash? Johnny came out of a hospital bed, took an I.V. out of his arm in Atlanta and drove up here. Tim hollered at *me* because he thought I made him come. He could've dropped dead. But he went out there and got a standing ovation from 15,000 people. Tim McGraw was his great friend and Johnny believed in him. He wouldn't let Tim down."

The embattled singer also had faith in Daryl Singletary. Together they remade Paycheck's 1986 hit "Old Violin." "Johnny's recitation for 'Old Violin' was done in a hospital bed. He fought the devil until the bitter end. The devil didn't beat him. When we did 'Old Violin' and he was sick as a dog? He wanted to hear the mix. We brought it to the conference room where he was staying and shut the door. There was Nick Hunter from Audium Records, Chuck Rhodes, Daryl Singletary, myself, and Ray Waddell from *Billboard*, Peter Cooper from the *Tennessean*, and one other. He said, 'Geez, Daryl, is it any good?' 'Why don't we just play it, John?'

"So they played it and he looked up at Daryl when he did the recitation, and you could tell he was sick on the recitation, and said, 'Daryl, you did one hell of a job, son. Best I've ever heard.'

"At that time, the ball cap was put down over Daryl Singletary's eyes and he was crying. We all were crying. We got to talking about that later. 'Shit, he's half-dead and he's worried about the *mix?*' He didn't want Daryl to have a bad record."

In early 2002, after several heartening rallies and torturous near-death moments, Paycheck passed away. Newspaper obituaries played up the outlaw angle and extensively cited his troubled past. Martel feels the press just doesn't know the whole story. "A lot of new writers in this town, all they can talk about is his past. There were a lot of things that nobody will ever know about, just between me and him and the band. Just stuff that happened. Good stuff, funny stuff, stuff when he would get mad. But he did redeem himself in a lot of ways.

"Let me tell you what, Johnny Paycheck made my life easier. There are doors that I can get into that the regular person in this town can't get in. It was through the name Johnny Paycheck that made Midnight Special Productions what it is today. I have people talk to me and say, 'Weren't you Paycheck's manager?' I say, 'That's right.' When everyone in town found out that Paycheck was with me and was going to stay with me, they would call for interviews, or to have him sing a song on their CD. When everyone saw that he was really working with me, then they wanted to talk about Johnny Paycheck and other artists that I was booking at the time. It was easier for me to call a record company, other agents, etc., and with them knowing that I was his manager and booking agent, things were good for John and myself. It took a long time, but I appreciate what he done for me.

"A lot of people said he died broke, owing everybody. That's not really true. He didn't owe me nothin'. I owe him my business. I owe him my business sense, and I owe him visions of what I want to do because he taught me that visions can come true if you believe in them, work for them, and fight for them. I owed him and everybody owes him for the great years he gave them and the great talent. I think John Paycheck is owed. He was a pioneer and visionary."

Mr. Easy Lovin'.

FREDDIE HART

Soft-spoken and oozing gratitude for all he has been able to achieve, Freddie Hart is certainly no antihero. In fact, his ability to persevere through hard times is the stuff of country music myth. Born Fred Segrest in Loachapoka, Alabama, he was one of fifteen children of poor sharecroppers. As a youngster he entered the Conservation Corps so he would have enough to eat. More than a bit wild, when he was fifteen years old his parents helped him lie about his age so he could join the marines. He learned jujitsu and judo and eventually saw action in Guam during his three-year, five-month stint.

The young soldier's lifelong yearning to be a country music singer sustained him during the grizzliest moments of combat. His earliest memories are of standing on a tree stump and pretending to perform on the *Grand Ole Opry*. Yet, just a few short months into his new civilian life, he nearly had that dream beaten out of him in a jail cell.

The artist has asked that names be removed, but the story is as Hart himself told it.

"I was working in Longview, Texas. I was working stocking Cokes and beers after I got out of the service. I was still underage at that time. I wasn't allowed to drink. They had a little trailer where I slept in the back; it was a little bitty thing. It sort of looked like a ducktail. But that was where I lived, in back of the club there. Once in a while they'd have me come out and sing a song. They had a speaker outside so people could listen, and there was a girl, about fourteen years of age, who would sit and listen to me sing. After the show, the little girl would come out with me and my girlfriend. If we went to a restaurant, we'd take her with us.

"One night, I was waiting out there and a few police came out. I went by the name Fred Waynard at that time, and one of the policemen asked me, 'Are you Fred Waynard?' I said, 'Yes sir.' That's when one of the police hit me on the side of the head with a slapjack. When I came to, I had handcuffs on."

(According to former tourmates Bobby Wayne and Gary Bryant, Hart was always demonstrating judo on his friends. Once, after Bryant's off-tempo rhythm guitar playing adversely affected Hart's show, Hart allegedly walked over to him and said in his sweetest preacher's voice, "Look at this hand, Gary. You see it? If I wanted to, I could stick my hand right through your body and shake hands with someone on the other side. Don't ever mess up my show again." In addition, Sonny Burgess says that Hart used to chase his bass player, Johnny Ray Hubbard—who was scared silly—around an Arkansas radio station trying to practice karate on him. Could these public displays of martial arts be the reason the police chief slapjacked him from behind?)

"They got me in the car and began to drive and I asked, 'What are you doing this for?' I didn't know what was going on. They called me every name in the book. They took me in to the police chief; he's dead now, died of cancer, I heard. I had no shorts on so they gave me a pair of his shorts, and he was a big man. The shorts wrapped around me about three times. So I put on the shorts, and then they handcuffed me to this chair there. They slapped me around for a real long time. Man, I could hardly see nothing. And this police chief would get drunk and he'd beat on me. They had a loop on the floor of the cell that they hooked the chain onto and they had me chained there. He'd come in and reach out and hit me.

"I was there for three days before they told me what was going on. By then I could hardly see; my eyes were all swollen from the beatings. Now this is kind of distasteful, but sometimes when he came in, I'd turn my back on him, and he'd go to the bathroom on me.

"Boy, I called him everything in the book. I said, 'Get these chains off me! You can get a knife or whatever you want to.' But he wouldn't do it. Eventually, they told me that I had been accused of raping this little girl. But it wasn't in the papers or nothing. So I wondered about that. Why didn't they put it in the papers so people would know what was going on?

"Well, I know why now, it's because they didn't have anything on me. Because there was a place across from us called the Red Ball Transfer Company, and the man came over and I gave him some sandwiches at the time this was supposedly happening. So they knew where I was. My girl-friend knew I was there that night. I was with her that night up to a certain point, and I was supposed to take her home because the little girl had borrowed my girlfriend's car to drive herself home. She lived about forty or fifty miles away.

"On the way down—I found this out later—she picked up three boys. They got to drinking and one of them got behind the wheel. They took her in the back of a car and raped her and everything. Well, they got in a wreck, hit the side of a bridge. The little girl got her throat badly cut up and they set her behind the car. One of the boys had one of his legs cut off in the wreck. They took a piece of wire and wrapped it around the leg to cut the circulation off. Then they took off in every different direction. They buried the leg out in the field. Someone close by must have heard the racket, because they came and got her and took her to a doctor. They fixed her up but she still couldn't talk because her throat was cut in a certain way. Later on, I was still in jail at the time, they saw some buzzards circling above and they found where that leg was buried. So they figured it out.

"They had a hearing for me, and I couldn't hardly talk or breathe, and my eyes were still nearly closed shut from the beatings. I remember, though, they had a guy there who warned the police chief, 'If you touch that man one more time I'm going to have your job.' He meant it, too. He was the only one there was nice to me. They had this hearing and the mother took the stand with the daughter, and she told the jury that I was just a friend and everything. But we never could find my girlfriend, which was weird. But the mother told the jury how good we had treated her little girl, how we'd go out to eat and everything, one time we bought her a little dress, and that I had never mistreated her in any way—ever. Then, she told them about the boys. They found one of the boys, the one with the leg cut off, in a ditch covered up with leaves and bushes. He died. They found the other boy not too long after.

"The judge told me that a great injustice was done to me. He said, 'Is there anything I can do?'

"I said, 'I'd like to go out to get drunk.'

"He said, 'Well, anything you want, hotels and cafés, they're all open to you, all free if you want a drink. But I don't think you ought to. We can give you some money if you need some.'

"I said, 'No, I don't need any. There's one thing I would like to do, judge. It's personal.' I said, 'There's a guy here, the chief of police.'

"Then I told the judge what that police chief had done to me. The judge said, 'Well, sometimes he can get a little crazy, but he's a good policeman otherwise.'

"You know, there's bad ones in every crowd. Maybe he was good man. You don't get to be a police chief without knowing something. He was just a bad man when he drank.

"I said, 'I can't sleep and I can't live with myself, I've got to have some kind of satisfaction. I promise I won't kill him, I won't break nothing, but I've got to have some satisfaction.'

"The judge said, 'Well, you go right ahead, and if he calls in, I'll fix it up. But you come back to me when you're sober.'

"I said I would.

"The police chief lived right outside of town, and I walked out there, and I just tore the door down and walked right in the house. He was in the bed with his wife. I sat down on the side of the bed there. He tried to reach for his gun.

"I said, 'Hey, you go right ahead. I'd just love to see you try it. You want me to hand it to you?' He shook his head no. I told his wife what he'd done to me. I said to him, 'You go outside in the field and wait for me.'

"He said, 'I'm going to call in, you know.'

"I told him that the judge said if he called in, he wouldn't get through to anybody. Then I said, 'Now you go out there, don't try and run off because there ain't no place you can go. I'll have your own police force round you up if you run away from me.'

"I went out there and I knocked him out and then brang him to, knocked him out, brang him to, knocked him out, brang him to. He was a big guy. One time I got carried away, and I began smothering his face with dirt. I caught myself and I uncovered him. I would have killed him, you know. I'm not proud of any of this, my friend. I'm not proud at all. I'm ashamed of it really, but it's just something I'd done.

"Then I said, 'You can go back and tell the judge whatever you want to.' I didn't break nothing on him, I'm thankful to say.

"So I walked the eight miles back to town, went to the judge and told him. After that, for a while there, I'd get drunk and lay down on the streets there and the police would just step right over me. After a while, they set me outside of town, gave me some money and let me go, so I took off.

"Well, you don't forget something like that. But I had my satisfaction, and he was the only one, really, who mistreated me.

"Well, you know you give up hope a lot of times in cases like that. You don't know where you're going or what's going to happen. You know, I've worked just about every job you could name. I was a cook, worked in the oil fields, I worked in timber, hay fields. But I always kept my dreams going."

Ironically, among the many jobs the struggling singer held was a judo instructor for the Los Angeles Police Academy. "I just taught self-defense and disarmament. I worked on temperament with a lot of 'em. I'd walk by and slap one across the face just to see his reaction. Temperament is important to a policeman. You've got drunks and all kinds of things you've got to tolerate. After a while I'd give them a gun or knife and tell them to come after me. A lot of 'em won't do that. It shows that they've got feelings, and hey, we need good law. I wish we had a billion good policeman and they were paid what they were really worth. The fire department and the police department, we need them so very badly, and they do things above and beyond the call of duty. I think they deserve the best of everything. But as far as my training, I didn't have time to teach them enough, just enough so where they wouldn't get hurt. It takes a long time to learn it all. [Judo] is a wonderful thing for the mind and body."

Eventually Fred Waynard changed his name to Freddie Hart at the behest of his manager Steve Stebbins (Hart was Stebbins's wife's maiden name), and things slowly began to happen for him. A prolific songwriter, Hart wrote hits for the likes of George Morgan, Carl Smith, Porter Wagoner, Billy Walker, Buck Owens, and Rose Maddox. He learned the ins and outs of the business touring with Lefty Frizzell and even scored a few modest hits for Columbia Records, including oft-copied versions of Harlan Howard's "The Key's in the Mailbox" and the eerie prison-themed "The Wall."

"Well, it was real to me because I had been there," Hart said of "The Wall." "I haven't been in prison, but I've sung there. I've been in a lot of jails growing up. That's just part of growing up, my friend. I'm thankful for all those times because it's taught me an awful lot."

It wasn't until 1971 that he scored his breakthrough hit. Speaking from his Burbank, California, home, Hart recalls,

"Well, I wrote my dream song in 1970, 'Easy Lovin'.' People often ask me, 'What did you have in mind when you wrote that song?' Well, I always tell 'em that I wanted to write something that every man would like to say and every woman would like to hear. I didn't know that it was going to come out that way, but it did.

"It was the first song to have 'sex' in it ["Easy lovin'/so sexy looking"]. It kind of scares you when you first hear something like that, and I was going to take it out. I'm glad I didn't. Oh, I had 'Christmas' and all kinds of things in that song, but when I finished it, it was how you hear it now. But everybody on the session didn't seem to care one way or the other about the song, because two months later I was fired from Capitol Records.

"They had the song on an album called *California Grapevine*, which they put back on the shelf when they fired me. A couple of months later the song burst wide open. It sold a million copies right there in Atlanta, Georgia. WPLO was the one that really broke it. Right after that, they booked me in there. What a blessing that was.

"They had over 22,000 people, and I sung 'Easy Lovin'' eleven times! They wouldn't let me off. They wouldn't let me go. The people out there were jumping up and down on their cars, the police had their sirens going just to be playful. All shapes, sizes, and ages were looking up at me on stage and singing along. I got so carried away that I just couldn't take it no more. I went and hung my legs off the stage and just cried. I knew 'Easy Lovin'' was a hit, but I had no idea how big until that moment, and people were crying right along with me.

A country superstar arrives.

"You know, a lot of artists won't go out and meet the people, but I do, and that day I spent close to five hours just signing autographs. I'd rest a while, and they'd stay out there, then I'd come out and sign some more."

"Easy Lovin'" won Hart multiple awards and was the first of six straight #1 singles and twenty-nine country Top 40 hits. Although the singer lost much of his fortune in an ill-fated trucking venture, the Hart Line, he remains active, still writes songs, and is profoundly grateful for his country music career. "Well, it made my dream come true. It has given me a chance to help my brothers and sisters, gave me a chance to show my kinfolk to people and help them meet people they'd never met before. To have a family and give them what they want and need. It gave me a chance to do what God wants me to do. To do some good in the world. I get a chance to record gospel songs and sing in the churches. Meet people and treat people right. My goodness, how much of a reward do you want? I could fill my house with awards. I've got four walls full of 'em, but those were gifts that people gave to me, and you can only be thankful for those rewards. Country music has given me everything in the world, everything I could ever dream of."

INDEX

Numbers in italic denote photographs.